THE PSYCHOLOGIST'S COMPANION
A Guide to Professional Success for Stu
and Researchers
Sixth Edition

The Psychologist's Companion (sixth edition) is written for students, young professionals, and even mid-career scholars. It is the most comprehensive guide available to both written and oral communication processes for academic psychologists. It covers the topics necessary for career success, including planning papers, writing papers, presenting data, evaluating one's papers, writing grant proposals, giving talks, finding a book publisher, doing job interviews, and doing media interviews. Because the book is in its sixth edition, it is market tested for success in reaching and engaging its readers. Three special (new) pedagogical features are "Experience is the best teacher," which draws on the authors' personal experiences to help make the book more personalized and exciting to readers, "What's wrong here?," which gives readers an opportunity for active learning while they read the book, and "Give it some more thought," which encourages readers to reflect further on what they have read. The authors have written the book in a personable and often humorous style that will keep readers engaged.

Robert J. Sternberg is Professor of Human Development at Cornell University. Formerly, he was IBM Professor of Psychology and Education at Yale University. He is a former president of the American Psychological Association and Federation of Associations in Behavioral and Brain Sciences. His PhD is from Stanford and he holds 13 honorary doctorates. He is a member of the National Academy of Education and the American Academy of Arts and Sciences as well as a fellow of the APA, APS, AAAS, and AERA. Sternberg has written over 1,600 books and articles and has been cited in the professional literature roughly 115,000 times.

Karin Sternberg is Research Associate in the Department of Human Development at Cornell University. She has a PhD in psychology from the University of Heidelberg, Germany, and an MBA from the University of Cooperative Education, Karlsruhe, Germany. She has studied at Yale University and did her postdoctoral work in social psychology at the University of Connecticut. Sternberg worked as a research associate at Harvard University's Kennedy School of Government and School of Public Health. She held a grant from the National Institute of Aging on developing cognitive skills in older individuals. She is the author of *Psychology of Love 101* (2013).

The Psychologist's Companion

A Guide to Professional Success for Students, Teachers, and Researchers

Sixth Edition

Robert J. Sternberg
Cornell University

Karin Sternberg
Cornell University

CAMBRIDGE
UNIVERSITY PRESS

CAMBRIDGE
UNIVERSITY PRESS

One Liberty Plaza, 20th Floor, New York, NY 10006, USA

Cambridge University Press is part of the University of Cambridge.

It furthers the University's mission by disseminating knowledge in the pursuit of education, learning, and research at the highest international levels of excellence.

www.cambridge.org
Information on this title: www.cambridge.org/9781316505182

© Robert J. Sternberg and Karin Sternberg 2016

This publication is in copyright. Subject to statutory exception and to the provisions of relevant collective licensing agreements, no reproduction of any part may take place without the written permission of Cambridge University Press.

First published 2016

Printed in the United States of America by Sheridan Books, Inc.

A catalogue record for this publication is available from the British Library.

Library of Congress Cataloging-in-Publication Data
Names: Sternberg, Robert J., author. | Sternberg, Karin, 1976- author.
Title: The psychologist's companion : a guide to professional success for students, teachers, and researchers / Robert J. Sternberg, Cornell University, Karin Sternberg, Cornell University.
Description: Sixth edition. | New York, NY : Cambridge University Press, 2016. | Includes bibliographical references and index.
Identifiers: LCCN 2016010214| ISBN 9781107139619 (hardback : alk. paper) | ISBN 9781316505182 (pbk. : alk. paper)
Subjects: LCSH: Report writing. | Psychological literature
Classification: LCC BF76.8 .S73 2016 | DDC 808.06/615–dc23 LC record available at https://lccn.loc.gov/2016010214

ISBN 978-1-107-13961-9 Hardback
ISBN 978-1-316-50518-2 Paperback

Cambridge University Press has no responsibility for the persistence or accuracy of URLs for external or third-party Internet Web sites referred to in this publication and does not guarantee that any content on such Web sites is, or will remain, accurate or appropriate

Contents

Preface

The Psychologist's Companion has been comprehensively updated, revised, and extended for this sixth edition. It is intended for students as well as young professionals and writers at all stages of their careers seeking inspiration and definitive guidelines for better scientific communication. The book is a tremendous resource not only for psychologists but for researchers in other fields as well.

- The sixth edition includes the latest style guidelines of the *Publication Manual of the American Psychological Association*, sixth edition.
- A new chapter has been added on preparing a poster presentation.
- A new chapter has been added that presents a checklist before submitting an article for publication.
- A new chapter has been added on doing a job interview.
- A new chapter has been added on doing media interviews.
- The chapter on writing lectures has been substantially expanded.
- We have added boxes called "Experience is the best teacher." The purpose of these boxes is to call out major points about careers in psychology that we have learned from our experiences over the years.
- We have added "Give it some more thought" boxes to encourage reflection.
- We have added boxes called "What's wrong here?" for students to apply what they have learned to figuring out what in the box should be different.
- Many new examples have been added to increase clarity.
- Existing examples have been updated where appropriate.
- Checklists have been added to many of the chapters.

- Advance organizers have been added to provide an overview of the guidelines in a given chapter.
- The revised *Psychologist's Companion* is now aimed not only at students but also at junior faculty and even seasoned professionals seeking guidance.
- All chapters contain enumerated headers for easier use of the book.
- The book is printed in a more reader-friendly format.

Further covered, with vital updates, are topics such as misconceptions about psychology papers; rules for writing literature reviews and experimental papers; how best to make use of the Internet in research; content, language, and style guidelines; commonly misused words; guidelines for data presentation; standards for evaluating papers; guidelines for submitting papers to journals and winning acceptance; how to write grant and contract proposals; how to find book publishers; and how to write lectures and articles. The book is written in a lively and witty style that will make it easy reading for even the busiest student or professional.

Some readers will work their way through this book from cover to cover. Others will read only selected chapters. For the sake of the latter readers, we sometimes have repeated in later chapters material mentioned in earlier chapters. If a point is relevant to a chapter, we include it to ensure that readers can learn it. Moreover, we believe, as do pretty much all our fellow cognitive psychologists, that occasional repetition helps reinforce important points throughout the book.

Acknowledgments

Chapter 9 contains a summary of the guidelines in the *Publication Manual of the American Psychological Association* (sixth edition). We gratefully acknowledge the *APA Publication Manual*'s contribution to this chapter.

Introduction

Most students and even faculty in psychology receive little or no formal training in how to communicate in psychology. Nor do they necessarily learn how to write grant and contract proposals, book proposals, or talks and lectures. Many people believe that writers receive sufficient training in writing through informal channels and thus will acquire the necessary skills on their own. Do students learn the writing techniques for psychology on their own? Our experience reading psychology papers suggests that often they do not. Moreover, this experience is shared by other psychology professors and by professors in other disciplines, as well. Psychologists also need excellent speaking skills.

The purpose of this book is to provide the basic information that students and professionals alike need to speak and write well in psychology. This information is contained in 20 chapters. Although the intent is that you read the chapters in the order in which they are presented, they are for the most part self-contained and hence can be read in almost any sequence.

Chapter 1 presents and discusses eight common misconceptions that students hold about psychology papers. We have found that many of these misconceptions are reinforced rather than extinguished by conventional academic training. Most students come to believe, for example, that journal articles are and should be autobiographical – that the logical development of ideas in a psychology paper reflects their historical development in the psychologist's head. Accepting this notion as a presupposition, students often believe that authors of journal articles can plan their research and predict their findings well in advance, often down to the last detail. Readers will know better after finishing Chapter 1.

One can write good papers only when one has good ideas that constitute the basis for the papers. Chapter 2 suggests alternative ways to generate ideas for papers. Because not all ideas are good ideas, the latter part of the chapter provides guidelines to decide which ideas are good ones that should be pursued. Finally, the chapter also gives tips on how to sell one's ideas to others.

Chapter 3 describes ways to conduct literature research in the best manner possible. We describe diverse reference materials, introduce literature research methods and useful databases, and explain how to use the Internet for scientific research and to evaluate the information found online.

Chapters 4 and 5 present the sequence of steps that psychologists follow in writing papers. Chapter 4 deals with literature reviews, and Chapter 5 with experimental research papers. The sequence of steps begins with the decision regarding a topic and ends with the publication of a finished paper. Many writers have only a fuzzy idea of the sequence of steps and of how to present this sequence to readers of psychology papers.

Consider two examples. First, would the procedure by which participants are assigned to treatment groups be described more appropriately in the "Procedure" section or in the "Design" section of a psychology paper? Second, do journal editors encourage or discourage extensive use of tables and figures in articles to clarify the presentation of experimental data? The answer to the first question is "Design"; the answer to the second question is "discourage."

Chapter 6 discusses several ethical issues and pitfalls that psychologists may face during their careers and gives advice on how to avoid them.

Chapter 7 presents guidelines for writing psychology papers. They are divided into three different subsections, dealing with content, language, and style. The guidelines are ones that many students and even professionals fail to follow. One of the reasons they fail to follow these rules is that they forget what the rules are. The chances are good that you remember learning something about avoiding dangling constructions but that either you don't look for dangling constructions in your writing or you don't even remember exactly what a dangling construction is. Chapter 7 will remind you about dangling constructions and other pitfalls in writing papers.

Chapter 8 contains a list of commonly misused words and describes the proper use of each of these words. The meanings of these words, like the rules of writing, are quickly learned but quickly forgotten early in one's career as a student. For example, probably fewer than 10 percent of the papers [that/which] are published in psychological journals consistently use the relative pronouns *that* and *which* correctly. [While/Although] these papers are certainly publishable, their readability would be enhanced by the proper use of English. Which word belongs in each place where two choices are given within parentheses? In the first sentence, the proper word is *that*; in the second sentence, the proper word is *Although*.

Chapter 9 summarizes the American Psychological Association's (2009) guidelines for writing psychology papers. Regardless of how well you write, you must learn a number of different rules that are specific to the writing of psychology papers. Different disciplines follow different guidelines for writing, and one is expected to learn to write according to the guidelines of the appropriate discipline. Common mistakes occur when writers follow Modern Language Association (MLA) guidelines, which are the ones most students learn in high school. Although these guidelines are appropriate for much writing in the humanities, they typically are not appropriate for writing in psychology. Test yourself. Does one abbreviate *centimeters* as *cm* or as *cm.*? Does one abbreviate *feet* as *ft* or as *ft.*? Does one test 10 subjects or ten subjects? Does one test 8 subjects or eight subjects? The rules of the American Psychological Association lead to answers of "cm," "ft," "10," and "eight." The rules of the Modern Language Association lead to answers of "cm.," "ft.," "ten," and "eight." Learning to write a psychology paper involves learning certain rules that are unique to writing psychology papers.

Chapter 10 provides guidelines for data presentation. It gives rules for presenting data in the form of tables or graphs, as well as guidance on the advantages and drawbacks of different types of presentations. Following these guidelines will aid both your understanding of your data and your ability to communicate them effectively to others.

Chapter 11 is a primer on effective writing of articles for psychological journals. It contains tips on both what you should do and what you should not do.

Chapter 12 gives you some tips on how to make this process as successful as possible. You are not done with your article just because you have finished your first draft. If you intend to write a good article, what follows are proofreading and revisions. After submission to a journal and even after acceptance of your article, you may have to revise and edit your work.

Chapter 13 contains a critical checklist to use before sending an article out for publication. The checkoffs in this chapter are ones writers can use to avoid quick rejections of articles that might otherwise be accepted.

Chapter 14 contains practical suggestions for submitting a psychology article to a professional journal. What considerations enter into the choice of a journal? What happens to an article once it is submitted? What are the possible courses of action a journal editor can take? You will find out when you read Chapter 14.

Chapter 15 describes the parts of a poster presentation and also contains tips on how to make the poster presentation effective. The goal is to prevent novices from making common mistakes, such as cramming in too much information or using complicated figures or tables.

Chapter 16 contains techniques people can use to increase the chances of their getting funding through a grant or contract. Ultimately, the most important determinant of funding is the set of ideas in the proposal. But many proposals are rejected on grounds that have little or nothing to do with ideas. Competition for grants and contracts is extremely stiff. Therefore, every edge can help. This chapter helps grant writers maximize their chances of winning funding, giving them the edge that may make a difference to the outcome.

Chapter 17 describes the steps a person takes in seeking a book publisher. How do you write a book proposal, and what do you do with the proposal once you are done? Despite the importance to scholars of writing books as well as articles, people tend to know even less about how to find a publisher for a book than they do about how to get an article published. This chapter describes from beginning to end the process of finding a book publisher.

Chapter 18 discusses the writing of effective lectures. Many psychologists end up, sooner or later, teaching. For some, it may be in the form of courses for undergraduate and graduate students. For others, it may be in the form of public lectures. And for still others, it may be in the form of occasional seminars. All of us who have gone through school know how important good lectures are to learning. This chapter will help the reader write and deliver such lectures.

Chapter 19 discusses how to present oneself in a job interview. It suggests both what job applicants should do and what they should not do.

Chapter 20 deals with presenting oneself effectively to the media. The goal is to ensure that a psychologist's experiences with media are positive ones rather than one the psychologist quickly comes to regret.

As you progress through this book, you will discover that communicating with an audience of psychologists requires a unique set of skills. For most students and professionals alike, merely reading and writing psychology papers is an insufficient way to acquire these skills. This book is intended for and dedicated to all of you who want to improve your writing, speaking, and other professional skills.

PART I

Macro-Challenges in Writing Papers: Planning and Formulating Papers

1 Eight Common Misconceptions about Psychology Papers

Students and inexperienced writers often have misconceptions about the writing process and characteristics of good papers that effectively prevent them from writing as good a paper as they possibly could. Here are eight common misconceptions you should be aware of before you even begin writing:

1. Writing the psychology paper is the most routine, least creative aspect of the scientific enterprise, requiring much time but little imagination.
2. The important thing is what you say, not how you say it.
3. Longer papers are better papers, and more papers are better yet.
4. The main purpose of a psychology paper is the presentation of facts, whether newly established (as in reports of experiments) or well established (as in literature reviews).
5. The distinction between scientific writing, on the one hand, and advertising or propaganda, on the other hand, is that the purpose of scientific writing is to inform, whereas the purpose of advertising or propaganda is to persuade.
6. A good way to gain acceptance of your theory is by refuting someone else's theory.
7. Negative results that fail to support the researcher's hypothesis are every bit as valuable as positive results that do support the researcher's hypothesis.
8. The logical development of ideas in a psychology paper reflects the historical development of ideas in the psychologist's head.

Misconception 1. Writing the psychology paper is the most routine, least creative aspect of the scientific enterprise, requiring much time but little imagination.

Many students lose interest in their research projects as soon as the time comes to write about them. Their interest is in planning for and making new discoveries, not in communicating their discoveries to others. A widely believed fallacy underlies their attitudes. The fallacy is that the discovery process ends when the communication process begins. Although the major purpose of writing a paper is to communicate your thoughts to others, another important purpose is to help you form and organize your thoughts (Pinker, 2014).

Reporting your findings in writing requires you to commit yourself to those findings and to your interpretation of them, and it opens you to criticism (as well as praise) from others. It is perhaps for this reason as much as any other that many students are reluctant to report their research. But the finality of a written report also serves as a powerful incentive to do your best thinking and to continue thinking as you write your paper. It requires you to tie up loose ends that you might otherwise have left untied. As a result, reporting your findings presents just as much of a challenge as planning the research and analyses that led to those findings.

We have often thought we knew what we wanted to say, only to find that when the time came to say it, we were unable to. The reason for this, we believe, is that in thinking about a topic, we often allow ourselves conceptual gaps that we hardly know exist. When we attempt to communicate our thoughts, however, these gaps become obvious. Organizing and then writing down our thoughts enables us to discover what gaps have yet to be filled.

Misconception 2. The important thing is what you say, not how you say it.

As a college student, Bob was mystified to find that students who wrote well consistently received better grades on their compositions than did students who wrote poorly. Even in his own compositions, he found that the grades he received seemed less to reflect what he had to say than how he said it. At the time, he was unable to decide whether this pattern in grading resulted from the professors' warped value systems or from their inability to penetrate the facade of written prose. Whereas their criteria for grading papers might be appropriate for an English course, these criteria seemed inappropriate for courses in subjects like psychology.

As a college professor, Bob has at last discovered the secret of the mysterious grading practices. The discovery came about in two stages, each one part of the initiation rites that new college teachers must go through. The first stage occurred when he found himself with a large number of students' papers to read and very little time in which to read them. He was then sincerely grateful to students who wrote well because he could read their papers quickly and understand what they were saying. He did not have the time to puzzle through every cryptic remark in the poorly written papers, however, and he resented the authors' presenting their ideas in a way that did not enable him to understand or evaluate them properly. He also found himself with no desire to reward the authors for this state of affairs. If their ideas were good, they should have taken the time to explain them clearly.

The second stage of discovery occurred when he found himself with just a few seminar papers to read and plenty of time in which to read them. Now, he thought, he could be fair both to students who write well and to those who do not. He was quickly disabused of this notion. He discovered that whereas it is usually easy to distinguish well-presented good ideas from well-presented bad ideas, it is often impossible to distinguish poorly presented good ideas from poorly presented bad ideas. The problem is that the professor's comprehension of what the student says occurs solely through the student's way of saying it. Professors can't read minds better than anyone else. If an idea is presented in a sloppy, disorganized fashion, how is one to know whether this fashion of presentation reflects the quality of the idea or merely the quality of its presentation?

The question is not easily answered. In one case, Bob had talked to a student beforehand about what that student was going to say, and he expected an outstanding paper on the basis of these conversations. During those conversations, certain details had not been clarified, but Bob expected these details to be clarified in the paper. Instead, the same ideas that had been inadequately explained in the conversations were inadequately explained in the paper, as well. Either the student was unable to clarify these ideas for himself, or he was unable to clarify them for others.

The outcome for the reader is the same: confusion and disappointment.

A comparable situation exists for researchers. One quickly notices that the best and most well-known psychologists are also among the best writers. Although there are exceptions, they are infrequent: Poorer writers have fewer readers. One reason for this fact is that poorly written articles are usually rejected by journal editors. Although journal editors are willing to make minor editorial changes in the articles they receive, they are usually unwilling to publish or rewrite poorly written articles. Even if a poorly written article is accepted and published, however, psychologists who receive a journal with 5–20 articles in it do not want to spend their limited time reading such an article. It is therefore important that you learn now how to present your ideas in a readable fashion.

In this book, we include three different kinds of boxes. Here are the first examples of each. "Experience Is the Best Teacher" presents points we have learned over the years about careers in psychology. "What's Wrong Here?" boxes give you a chance to apply what you know to problems that occur in the course of psychological research and communication of that research. And "Give It Some More Thought" boxes give readers a chance further to reflect on what they have read.

Experience Is the Best Teacher

If you look at the top psychologists of almost any era, they tend to be strong writers. This is not a coincidence. More people want to read good writing and people also are more likely to be persuaded by strong writing.

What's Wrong Here?

"The results were significant at the $p < .001$ level, proving that the informed group better recalled the test items than the uninformed group."

Answer: The way the sentence is written, the author makes it sound as though it is possible in psychological research to "prove" something because it has a low p level. In fact, low p levels may increase plausibility of conclusions, but they cannot "prove" conclusions.

Misconception 3. Longer papers are better papers, and more papers are better yet.

Until his first year of teaching, Bob believed that longer papers were better papers. Teachers had for years told him and his classmates that they didn't evaluate papers on the basis of length, but he viewed their remarks as a benign ruse designed to discourage length for its own sake. He changed his viewpoint when he started reading students' papers. Evaluating papers on both quality and quantity of ideas, he found little relation between either of these two criteria and the length of students' papers. Sometimes students wrote longer papers because they had more to say; other times they wrote longer papers because it took them several pages to say what could have been said in several sentences. There is nothing wrong with length per se, so long as length is not used as a substitute for tight organization and clear writing.

Rather than writing longer papers, some people have taken the other route of writing more papers. Why say in one paper what can be said in two for twice the credit? This kind of mentality meets the needs of people who count publications but not of those who read publications. An integrated series of related experiments will have more impact if published as a single, tightly knit package than if published as a string of hastily written articles, none of them of much interest in itself.

When it comes to publication, longer is rarely better. Journals have limited space and long articles take away space that might have been used to publish other articles. Books become more expensive as they get longer, resulting in decreased sales and, ultimately, decreased readership. So from the standpoint of publication, shorter is often better than longer. Take the space you need to say what you want to say, and stop there!

Experience Is the Best Teacher

Bob has edited several psychological journals. He has from time to time received papers that are 100, 120, or even 150 pages long. He, like most editors, rarely accepts papers at those lengths. For one thing, they rarely have the informational content to justify their length. For another, they often tend to be

(*cont.*)

loosely organized and rambling. But most important, very few readers have the time to read papers of such length, unless they are simply fascinated by the topic. So try to keep your papers as brief as possible to increase their chances of acceptance and to increase the chances that they will be read.

Misconception 4. The main purpose of a psychology paper is the presentation of facts, whether newly established (as in reports of experiments) or well established (as in literature reviews).

A common misconception among the general public is that the goal of science is the accumulation of facts. This misconception is fostered by popular scientific writing that emphasizes scientific findings, which may be easy to describe, at the expense of explanations of those findings, which may be both diverse and difficult to describe. Diverse explanations, however, are the hallmark of science.

Students in introductory psychology courses are prone to this misconception, and it carries over into their writing. We could cite numerous examples of this carryover, but one in particular comes to mind. We received some years ago a beautifully written paper reviewing the literature on the testing of infant intelligence. This was one case, however, in which flowing prose was insufficient to obtain a high grade. The paper was flawed in two respects. First, the author made no effort to interrelate the various attempts to measure infant intelligence. Each attempt was described as though it had been made in isolation, even though the various attempts to measure infant intelligence have drawn on each other. Second, the evaluative part of the paper consisted of a single sentence in which the author stated that it is still too early to draw final conclusions regarding the relative success of the various infant intelligence tests. This sentence is literally true: It was too early to draw final conclusions. But it will be too early to draw final conclusions as long as new data about the tests continue to be collected. Because data will continue to be collected for the foreseeable future, and because the tests date back to the early part of the twentieth century, it now seems appropriate to draw at least tentative conclusions. In writing a psychology paper, you must commit yourself to a point of view, even if you may change your mind later on. If the evidence on an issue is scanty, by all means say so. But draw at least tentative conclusions so that the reader knows how you evaluate what evidence is available.

Your paper should be guided by your ideas and your point of view. Facts are presented in service of ideas: to help elucidate, support, or rewrite these ideas. They provide a test against which the validity of ideas can be measured. You should therefore select the facts that help clarify or test your point of view and omit facts that are irrelevant. In being selective, however, you must not select only those facts that support your position. Scientists demand that scientific reporting be scrupulously honest. Without such honesty, scientific communication would collapse. Cite the relevant facts, therefore, regardless of whose point of view they support.

Misconception 5. The distinction between scientific writing, on the one hand, and advertising or propaganda, on the other hand, is that the purpose of scientific writing is to inform, whereas the purpose of advertising or propaganda is to persuade.

Successful advertising or propaganda need only persuade. Successful scientific writing must both inform and persuade. Writers often believe that a successful piece of scientific writing need only inform the reader of the scientists' data and their interpretation of the data. The reader is then left to decide whether the theory provides a plausible account of those (and possibly other) data. This conception of scientific writing is incorrect.

When scientists write a paper, they metaphorically have a product to sell. The product is their set of ideas about why certain phenomena exist. Occasionally, it is the only product on the market, and they need only convince the consumer to buy any product at all. Whether or not scientists are successful will depend in part on how persuasive they are and in part on how much the product is needed. No advertising campaign is likely to sell flowers that are guaranteed not to germinate or an explanation of why people don't normally stand on their heads rather than their feet. In most cases, however, there is an already established demand for the product. Because competing salespersons are trying to corner the market, scientists must persuade the consumer not just to buy any product but also to buy their product.

One of the most common mistakes writers make is to push the wrong product: They misjudge the contribution of their work. We recently received a paper that was full of good, original ideas. The presentation of these ideas, and of other people's as well, was unusually lucid. The only major problem with the paper was that the discussion of the original ideas was condensed into one paragraph buried inconspicuously in the middle of the paper, whereas the discussion of the other people's ideas spanned about 10 pages, starting on page 1. The contribution of this paper should have been in its new perspective on an old problem. But the author had deemphasized this potentially significant contribution in favor of a relatively unimportant one: providing a well-written but unexciting review of other people's perspectives. The hurried reader will usually take the author's emphasis at face value. In this case, the reader might conclude that the paper did not have much of an original contribution to make.

There is a difference, we believe, between "selling" in scholarship and selling in the commercial marketplace. Scholars typically truly believe in the integrity of their product and believe that the ideas they have even may be the best ones out there. Much (although certainly not all) of commercial selling is for products that the salespeople know are nothing special or even not very good. And commercial sellers often are as willing to sell one product as another. In academia, most of us, at least, truly believe in the great value of our ideas.

At the opposite extreme, it is possible to dwell so heavily on the contribution of your paper that the contribution is actually muted. Bob learned this lesson the hard way. A colleague and he wrote a paper intended to compare different measures of a psychological construct called subjective organization and to demonstrate that one of these measures is superior to all the rest (Sternberg & Tulving, 1977). They compared the measures on a number of different criteria. One measure proved to be superior to the rest on every one of these criteria. Despite his colleague's warnings, he explicitly called attention to this fact several times in the paper. Leaving nothing to chance, he pointed out the inescapable conclusion that one measure is better than all the rest and therefore should be the measure of choice.

They submitted the paper for publication, and several months later received two scathing reviews. They were attacked for making what both reviewers believed to be exorbitant claims. According to the reviewers, they had by no means developed an open-and-shut case in favor of the measure they claimed was best. Bob thought that the arguments made by the reviewers were weak and in some cases plainly incorrect. He was so annoyed with the whole affair that he let the paper sit on his shelf for about a year. Rereading the paper and the reviews a year later, he still believed the reviewers were on the wrong track. His colleague and he decided to tone down their claims for the preferred measure, however, while retaining the same basic line of argument. They resubmitted the paper, and this time received a very favorable review. They achieved much more effective results by understating their case than they had by overstating it, an outcome the colleague had anticipated from the start. Our subsequent experiences have confirmed repeatedly that, in psychology papers, a soft-selling technique is more successful than a hard-selling technique. By using the latter, you invite a reaction against you as salesperson that is likely to hurt the sale of your product. We can recall numerous occasions on which we refused to buy a product because we detested a pushy salesperson. In writing the first draft of the paper on measures of subjective organization, Bob unwittingly occupied the role of the pushy salesperson, and he received what should have been a predictable response.

Give It Some More Thought

What could you do to make your own writing (and speaking) more persuasive? Are there specific steps you could take so that you could become more persuasive? An example of a way to become more persuasive would be to figure out before writing a paper what message you want to say, and then write the paper in the service of that message.

Misconception 6. A good way to gain acceptance of your theory is by refuting someone else's theory.

A surprisingly common ploy in scientific papers, even some published in prestigious journals, is to resort to explanation by default. Whereas students may not know better, professionals should. Investigators describe two (or more) theories of the well-known XYZ phenomenon. They then present devastating evidence against all theories except one. They conclude on the basis of this evidence that this one theory is correct.

This indirect method of proof is compelling only when the two (or more) alternatives are (a) mutually exclusive and (b) exhaustive. Mutually exclusive alternatives are ones in which one outcome precludes the other(s). If a coin lands heads, for example, it cannot at the same time land tails. Exhaustive alternatives are ones that include all possible outcomes. A flip of a coin can result in heads or tails, but nothing else.

The ploy described above has been used in some (but by no means all) research studying sources of differences between groups in intelligence test scores. A study would be presented in which obtained differences in test scores could not be attributable to environmental factors. The author would conclude on that basis that the differences must be due to hereditary factors. These alternatives, however, are neither mutually exclusive nor exhaustive. First, it is possible – indeed, probable – that both heredity and environment influence intelligence test scores. Second, a further source of influence on intelligence test scores is the interaction between heredity and environment – the effect produced by their nonadditive influence. As an example, certain genes for intelligence may manifest themselves only under favorable environmental conditions.

One other disadvantage of the indirect method of proof bears mention. Criticism of other people's theories often gains one new opponents; it rarely gains one converts to one's own theory. This was another lesson Bob learned the hard way. He once wrote a paper that had two major goals: (a) to show that his theory of a phenomenon was correct and (b) to show that someone else's theory of the phenomenon was incorrect. He presented what he believed was strong evidence in favor of his theory and in opposition to the other person's theory. He submitted the paper to a journal, and it was rejected. The main reviewer of the paper, predictably enough, was the other theorist. It is a common practice to send papers attacking theory X to theorist X, with editors then using their judgment as to whether the review is a fair one. The reviewer criticized not the positive aspect of the paper, but its negative aspect. He argued that the theories actually dealt with somewhat different aspects of the phenomenon under investigation, so that there was no need to attack the reviewer's theory in the process of supporting Bob's own.

In retrospect, the reviewer probably had some valid points, but we believe he overreacted. In papers we've reviewed that attack our work, we've probably overreacted as well. Scientists have a reputation among the general public for being objective seekers and impartial evaluators of the truth. We think this reputation is generally deserved, but only when it comes to each other's work. When it comes to their own work, scientists lose their objectivity. When scientists are attacked, they behave in much the same manner as anyone else under attack. When someone lunges at you with a fist flying toward your face, you don't stop to reflect on the various considerations that may have led your opponent to attack you. You counterattack. Because scientists are personally so involved in their work, they often treat an attack on their work as a personal attack, even if there is no rational basis for treating it as such. The result can be a personal confrontation in which scientific issues are placed on the back burner.

In conclusion, it is wise to stress the positive contribution of your paper. This does not mean that you should forego criticizing other theories. Such criticism may be essential to your point. If it is, keep in mind our earlier admonition that understatement is a more effective means of persuasion than is overstatement. Avoid statements that can be interpreted as contentious but lacking in substance. And if you publish your paper, don't expect investigators you criticize to congratulate you on your cogent refutation of their work.

What's Wrong Here?

"Jones argued that development must occur in stages. However, our data are inconsistent with stages of development, proving that development must be, as we argued in the introduction, continuous in nature."

Answer: The fact that one set of data is inconsistent with a continuous view of development may serve toward discrediting that view, but cannot disprove it. Moreover, even if the data did show that development in some aspect is not purely stage-like, this demonstration does not show that development must be continuous. It might be continuous in some aspects but stage-like in other aspects. For example, some domains might display continuous development, other domains, stage-like development.

Misconception 7. Negative results that fail to support the researcher's hypothesis are every bit as valuable as positive results that do support the researcher's hypothesis.

Because science is a fair game, the scientist wins some and loses some. Novices often believe that the only honest course of action is for scientists to report their losses as well as their wins. To do otherwise would seem to present a false picture of both the scientist and the state of nature.

After reading a diverse sampling of journal articles, the reader is bound to arrive at one of two conclusions – either scientists have uncannily sound intuitions about the way experiments will turn out, or they maintain closets full of unsuccessful and unreported experiments. Although scientists usually have at least fairly sound intuitions about how experiments will turn out, the state of the journals is more a reflection of well-stocked closets than of unerring intuitions.

Scientists' failures to report failures are attributable not to their dishonesty but to the frequent uninterpretability of negative results. Suppose, for example, that investigators predict that giving children rewards after learning will increase their learning. The investigators conduct an experiment with two groups. In one group, children receive rewards after learning; in the other group, they do not receive rewards. The investigators find no difference in learning between groups. What can they conclude? Unfortunately, not much. Whereas a significant difference between groups could have provided good evidence that rewards can facilitate learning, absence of a significant difference could be explained in a number of ways, most of them uninteresting. Consider three such uninteresting explanations:

1. **Weak rewards**: The reward used in the study did not prove a powerful enough incentive. If the reward, for example, was a peanut, then children's cravings for a single peanut might not have been strong enough to increase their efforts to learn.
2. **Sample size too small**: The sample of children might not have been large enough. It is a well-known rule of statistics that, if any treatment effect exists at all, then it can be discovered if one's sample is large enough. A small effect may be detectable only with a relatively large sample. If there were only three children in each group, then the investigators might have failed to detect the effect of the reward.

3. **Inadequate measures**: The measure of learning might have been inadequate. Suppose, for example, that the task was to learn the set of multiplication facts for one-digit numbers and that the measure of learning was a single multiplication fact. This measure probably would have been inadequate to detect learning in either group and hence a difference in learning between groups.

Under two sets of circumstances, negative results can be of interest: when an investigator fails to replicate someone else's results, and when the results change due to some other factors. Let us first consider the failure to replicate results. Suppose someone reports that subjects who stand on their heads for 30 seconds prior to taking a test of visual-motor coordination perform better on the test than do control subjects who do not stand on their heads. Another investigator, suspicious of this result, tries to replicate it with two groups of subjects and fails. Realizing that the failure to replicate the result may be due to sampling fluctuations, the investigator tests two more groups of subjects and again finds no significant difference between groups. At this point, the investigator feels ready to report the result. Whereas one failure to replicate a result is not informative, repeated failures to replicate can be informative. The number of failures needed depends in large part on the strength of prior evidence in support of the result in question. Two failures are probably more than adequate for the "headstand hypothesis," whereas a great many failures would be needed to overthrow a better-established result, such as that under normal circumstances learning increases with practice.

Negative results are also of interest if a significant result vanishes when a methodological weakness is corrected. Suppose that the experimenter who wrote the headstand paper knew which subjects had stood on their heads and which had not. This aspect of the methodology suggests a possible bias in the experimenter's scoring of the coordination test (especially if the experimenter is public relations director of the American Association for the Advancement of Acrobatics). A worthwhile methodological refinement would be to conduct the experiment under circumstances in which the experimenter does not know which subjects stood on their heads and which did not. A negative result would be of interest in this case, because it would suggest that the significant difference between groups in the first experiment was due to experimenter bias.

What's Wrong Here?

"The difference between the treatment and control groups was notably not significant, $p > .50$, showing that the treatment was ineffective and should no longer be used."

Answer: As we learn in statistics classes, one cannot prove the null hypothesis. The fact that a treatment effect was not significant fails to support the effectiveness of the treatment but does not demonstrate that it is ineffective. The sample may have been too small, or biased, or the treatment regimen may have been inappropriate. There are any number of reasons why the results may not have reached significance and it is not possible to know for sure what reason was operative.

Misconception 8. The logical development of ideas in a psychology paper reflects the historical development of ideas in the psychologist's head.

If one were to take journal articles at face value, one would conclude that scientific results come in neat, attractively wrapped packages. Writers often believe that one needs only to go through a uniform series of well-defined steps to ensure delivery of such packages. These steps are outlined, for experimental papers, in the "Myth" column of Table 1.1. However, we doubt that even as many as 1 percent of the papers published in scientific journals developed in a way even remotely resembling the outline given in the "Myth" column. In fact, they develop according to the sequence described in the "Reality" column of Table 1.1. Yet the large majority of published papers are written as though they had developed in the former way, or in some way closely resembling it. Let us compare the series of steps.

Why does the picture of research presented by journal articles correspond so poorly to the actual state of affairs? There are at least three reasons:

1. **Space limitations:** Journals operate under severe space limitations. A large percentage of articles submitted to journals must be rejected for lack of space. In some journals, more than 90 percent of submitted articles are rejected. Those articles that are accepted must be as concise as possible. An "autobiographical" form of

Table 1.1. The steps of writing an experimental paper: myth versus reality

Myth	Reality
1. Scientists start with ideas about a phenomenon, which they explain in the introduction to the paper. These ideas are formulated before the scientist has collected any data; the data serve to confirm (or in rare cases disconfirm) their validity.	1. Before carrying out an experiment, one usually has only a vague and tentative idea of what the outcome will be, if only because there are so many possible outcomes. One's ideas develop along with the experiment.
2. Scientists test these ideas by carefully choosing variables that can be manipulated in a controlled experiment. The scientists' understanding of the phenomenon under observation and of scientific method enables them to choose the correct variables and experimental manipulation on their very first attempt, which they describe in the "Method" section of the paper.	2. One sometimes performs the right experimental manipulation on the wrong variables or the wrong experimental manipulation on the right variables. To avoid wasting resources, scientists frequently conduct small-scale pilot experiments that test the feasibility of the experiment. Adjustments may then be made for the full-scale experiment, or the experiment may be scrapped altogether.
3. Scientists perform the experiment, presenting in the "Results" section of their paper the outcomes of data analyses scrupulously planned in advance.	3. Major data analyses are usually planned in advance, planning that is necessary to ensure that the design of the experiment permits one to analyze the data in the most advantageous way. Minor data analyses are frequently decided on after data collection. Often the results of a planned data analysis will suggest a subsequent unplanned one. A given set of data can be analyzed in an infinite number of ways, some of them more revealing than others. The scientist must select a small number of ways that are likely to yield maximum payoff.
4. Scientists finally reflect on the broader implications of the results, presenting their reflections in the "Discussion" section of the paper.	4. Ideas for the "Discussion" section of a paper usually start forming at the same time the experiment does, not only after its completion. The reason for this is that unless the experiment has some potentially broad and interesting implications, or unless it can lead to some sensible next step in research, it is probably not worth doing.

presentation, describing all one's false starts and initial misjudgments, consumes a great deal of space. That space is more profitably devoted to other articles.

2. **Efficacy of presentation**: An autobiographical account of an experiment tends to be of more interest to oneself than to one's colleagues. An associate recounted to us the way in which he learned this lesson. He submitted a 20-page theoretical article to one of the most prestigious psychological journals. He spent the first 19 pages of the article describing how he had come to his conclusions after a lengthy series of false starts; he presented his final conclusions on the 20th page. The article was rejected, not because the final conclusions were wrong, but because the editor believed that there was only one publishable page in the article – the last one. The editor was interested in the psychologist's conclusions but not in the lengthy soul searching the psychologist had done to arrive at them.

3. **Focus on the phenomenon**: The object of description in a scientific report is a phenomenon and its explanation, not the reporter of the phenomenon and explanation. The focus of the report must reflect this fact. A graduate student and Bob once completed an experiment investigating the development of reasoning skills in children at the second-, fourth-, and sixth-grade levels. Children were presented with reasoning problems, which they were then asked to solve. Because the experiment involved a considerable investment in time and money, we decided to pretest out reasoning problems on some colleagues' children. The original plan had been to use number of problems correctly solved as the dependent measure. We discovered, however, that even the youngest children made almost no errors on the problems once they fully understood the task. We therefore changed the dependent measure when we did the full-scale experiment, using response time to solve problems correctly instead of numbers of problems correctly solved. Had someone else planned this experiment, that person might have realized immediately that the problems were too easy to use number correct as the dependent measure or might have stumbled longer than we did until they discovered that the problems were too easy. A description of this trial-and-error process is slightly informative about the development of the investigator's intuitions, but it is uninformative about the object of the investigation, in this case,

the development of reasoning in children. The scientifically informative statement is that the problems were of a level of difficulty that made response time an appropriate dependent measure.

There is often a fine line between the omission of autobiographical information and the omission of critical details. If a hypothesis is post hoc, then one is obliged to indicate this fact.

In sum, the steps one follows in planning and carrying out research do not neatly correspond to the successive sections of the psychology paper. In the next two chapters, we will consider the steps in carrying out literature and experimental research and how to describe them in the psychology paper.

2 | How to Generate, Evaluate, and Sell Your Ideas for Research and Papers

There is no one foolproof way of getting ideas for papers. You have to find the ways that work for you. In the first part of this chapter, we present you with different ways in which you can develop ideas for your research projects. Of course, it is not enough to have ideas. To be a successful researcher, you also need the ability to evaluate your ideas and find out whether they are good ones. You do not want to waste your time on bad ideas. The second part of this chapter deals with the evaluation of your ideas. And once you have come to the conclusion that yours is a wonderful idea, it will be important for you to sell your idea. How do you convince others that your planned study is one that is worthwhile to conduct, and how do you convince an editor of a journal and reviewers that your paper is worth publishing? Especially creative ideas are often hard to sell. Therefore, the third part of this chapter shows you some ways to sell your ideas.

2.1 GENERATING IDEAS

2.1.1 Generating Ideas by Consulting with Others

In many colleges and universities, the faculty is among the most underutilized of resources. In Bob's first semester of teaching at Yale, he set aside three hours each week for office hours. He encouraged – sometimes he practically begged – students to come see him during those hours for advice on papers, projects, and the like. He left his door wide open to encourage students to enter. For the most part, though, he sat staring at the walls or at the people scurrying by (but not in) the door. He also encouraged students to make individual appointments if they were unable to see him during his prearranged hours, but for the most part, students also failed to take him up on this offer. Later, business picked up, although much more so among graduate than among undergraduate students.

Once, the psychology department faculty at Yale spent the better part of an hour trying to figure out why students are so timid in approaching faculty. Sometimes students try once, are unsuccessful in reaching the faculty member, and give up. Sometimes they don't try at all. Faculty members (as well as postdoctoral students and graduate students) can be a most helpful first avenue of approach in writing a paper for students as well as for postdocs and junior faculty. You should be assertive in seeking their advice.

Give It Some More Thought

Who could you be consulting that could help you in your research or teaching or other work? Are there people who could be helpful to you as resources upon whom you have not yet drawn? An example would be a senior faculty member in your department or a former adviser.

2.1.2 Generating Ideas by Reading

2.1.2.1 What to Read

Ideas often come out of one's reading. Some kinds of reading are more likely to lead to good ideas than are others:

1. **Pursue a small number of topics in depth:** Most undergraduate psychology courses, and many graduate ones, are not well suited to the stimulation of creative ideas for experiments. This unsuitability is because they cover a large amount of material superficially rather than a small amount in depth. To come up with a good idea for an experiment, it helps to have a deep understanding of the issues involved in some relatively small area of psychological research. Find some topic that interests you. Pursue the references that the papers you are interested in cite, and pursue the references most frequently cited in those references. By digging into the literature on a topic, you will acquire a deeper understanding of the issues that are the focus of psychological research.

2. **Acquaint yourself with research at the frontiers of knowledge:** As an undergraduate, Bob once followed the advice of the preceding paragraph, only to find himself acquiring a deep understanding of an issue that had ceased to interest psychologists 20 years before. In pursuing a topic, consider whether it is of current interest. Because of the long time lag between the writing and the publication of a book, most textbooks are somewhat out of date by the time they are published. Within five to 10 years, they usually become hopelessly out of date. As a result, students relying on such textbooks may find themselves generating ideas that someone else thought of several years before. To become acquainted with literature on the frontiers of knowledge, scan recent journal articles and make use of the references described in Chapter 3 of this book.

3. **Start with general readings and proceed to more specific ones:** Because of space limitations, authors of journal articles are often unable to present in detail the previous research that motivated their particular experiments. If you are unacquainted with that previous research, you may find yourself unable to understand the rationale of the experiments. It is therefore wise to start your reading with a review of the relevant literature, if you can find one, or with a theoretical article that compares the major theoretical positions. Reports of individual experiments will make more sense to you if you are first acquainted with the research context in which they were done.

2.1.2.2 How to Read

How you read is as important as what you read. Suppose, for example, that you read an article testing the theory that repeated exposure to persuasive communications results in attitude change toward the viewpoint advocated by those communications, regardless of one's initial attitudes. You might pursue further research taking you in any one of four directions:

1. **Extend the theory:** After reading the article, you may be persuaded that the theory is sound and could be extended. You might want to show that repeated exposure to communications advocating a viewpoint, but in a nonpersuasive manner, also results in attitude change toward the position taken by the communications.

2. **Generate an analogous theory:** If you find the theory and data compelling, you may want to think up an analogous theory. Perhaps repeated exposure to a particular kind of music increases liking for that music. Or perhaps repeated exposure to any kind of communication increases positive affect toward that kind of communication.

3. **Limit the theory:** Perhaps you believe that the conclusion derived from the data is too broad. If the subjects in the experiment were all children, for example, you may wish to show that the theory is applicable only to children. Or if the communications used in the experiment were all health-related ones, you may want to show that the theory is applicable only to arguments related to bodily care.

4. **Challenge the evidence testing the theory:** In reading the article, you may spot a methodological, statistical, or logical flaw in the author's argument. In this case, you may want to test the theory in a way that corrects the flaw. For example, suppose that the author of the paper tested the hypothesis merely by showing that after two hours of listening to a set of three persuasive communications, most subjects agreed with the viewpoint advocated by those communications. If the author has not shown, however, that at least some of the subjects disagreed with the viewpoints of the communications prior to the test, then the conclusion does not follow from the data.

2.1.3 Other Ways to Generate Ideas

The following list provides 10 ways to generate ideas that work at least for some people. We will illustrate each of the ideas with examples from our own research. We use our own research because we know how we got our ideas, but we have no sure way of knowing how other researchers got their ideas! For an additional view on getting ideas, upon which this chapter partially draws, see McGuire (1997):

1. Observe behavior in other people that arouses your curiosity.

2. Observe behavior in yourself that arouses your curiosity.

3. Question researchers' interpretations of their work.

4. Look for anomalies in patterns of behavior, whether your own or others'.

5. Look for patterns of behavior that are themselves puzzling.

6. Think the opposite of what others think.

7. Synthesize disparate existing ideas.

8. Ask yourself what the next question is.

9. Revisit discarded ideas.

10. Look for ideas in everyday models and metaphors.

1. Observe behavior in other people that arouses your curiosity.

Why, sometimes, when you try to help people, do they get angry at you instead of feeling grateful? Why is it that some people, when they shake hands, feel like they are trying to crush your hand, and others give you what feels like a dead-fish grip? Why do some people almost literally drink themselves to death? Why do some people almost always seem to get lost and others almost always to find their way? Why do people like to go on frightening amusement-park rides, and why do they like scary movies? One way to get ideas is to observe the behavior of others and to try to understand why they do what they do.

Some years ago, Bob did a series of papers on conflict resolution (Sternberg & Dobson, 1987; Sternberg & Soriano, 1984). The goal of the studies was to understand consistent individual differences in ways people approach conflicts. The research grew out of the author's observation of some past chairs of his psychology department. In particular, one was excellent at defusing conflicts and seemed to be able to take a conflict and reach some kind of compromise that, more or less, satisfied the participants in the conflict. The other chair seemed to be almost the opposite: He had a real talent for making existing conflicts even worse than they were. It seemed unlikely he was trying to fan the flames, but he nevertheless succeeded in doing so. But what was most notable was the consistency in each of the chair's styles. They seemed always, in the one case, to mitigate conflict, and in the other case, to exacerbate it. The ensuing research ended up finding seven consistent styles of conflict resolution: physical action, economic action, wait and see, accept the situation, step down, third party, and undermine esteem. One of the chairs used a step-down strategy of trying to ease the conflict; the other was personally insecure, it seemed, and ended up undermining the self-esteem of both parties, which made them feel worse and made their conflict worse.

Karin was blissfully working in Key Largo, Florida, when the September 11, 2001, attacks took place. She observed drastic behavior changes in people afterward: They were much more cohesive, made appointments to go to church together even though before the incident nobody had ever even mentioned the church, and kept to themselves and isolated themselves from other groups they did not see as relevant to them. Some of them became suspicious of certain types of out-groups. Amazement at the effects of the terrorist attacks eventually led to Karin's dissertation on hate and to her interest in prejudice and terrorism.

The research would not have been done had Karin not been curious about the behavior of the people around her. So when you observe other people's behavior, look at it as a set of puzzles that psychologists can understand. You can get some of your best ideas right from those observations.

2. Observe behavior in yourself that arouses your curiosity.

Why do you always fall in love with Mr. or Ms. Wrong? Why do you blush when people praise you? Why do you feel afraid when you watch a scary movie, even though you know it is all fiction? Why do you fail to remember information that you just learned a few seconds ago? Why do you sometimes start studying for tests at the last minute, knowing that you are hurting yourself in doing so? You can get many of your research ideas by observing your own behavior and then doing research to try to understand it.

When Bob was young, he did poorly on IQ tests. His problems in IQ testing seriously affected his life. His teachers thought he was stupid; he thought he was stupid; he did stupid work; and the teachers were happy that their predictions about his stupidity were correct; he in turn was happy that they were happy. And so continued a vicious circle that did not end until he had a teacher in fourth grade who saw more in him than his being a poor test taker. As a result of this experience, the author acquired a lifelong interest in intelligence. To this day, he is still trying to understand why he did poorly on the IQ tests!

Bob ended up forming a theory of intelligence according to which there are three aspects to intelligence: creative, analytical, and practical (Sternberg, 2003, 2005b). A person needs creative intelligence to formulate new ideas, analytical intelligence to ascertain whether they are good ideas, and practical intelligence to implement the ideas and convince others of their value. In his case, he probably suffered from test anxiety, but the author also lacked the practical skills to control the anxiety. Fortunately, intelligence is malleable, and he acquired more practical skills later on.

The research ended up being typical of much psychological research in one key way. It set out to answer one question and ended up addressing a different question instead. Bob still does not know for sure why he did poorly on the tests when he was younger. But in the process of trying to find out, he learned a lot of other things about human intelligence.

Karin once had a friend who was intellectually absolutely brilliant. He worked at a bank, where he advised people on their investment options for their money. The friend seemed to know all there was to know about the stock market, was able to come up with the fanciest calculations to indicate the best investments, and even developed ideas for new investment instruments. And still, he had a lot of trouble at his job and was finally fired for underperformance. When talking to the friend and trying to find out what had gone wrong, Karin discovered that he had always had trouble connecting to his clients and was no more popular with his employers than with the clients. Ultimately, he had failed to make his quota because customers came to him only once but rarely returned or invested money with him. This experience led Karin to think about the importance of social and emotional intelligence in people's lives, and she developed a test of emotional intelligence for her diploma thesis at her university.

When you do research, be open to the possibility that your research may end up addressing questions in addition to or even instead of those you initially posed. Often, the greatest findings in psychology are wholly serendipitous.

Experience Is the Best Teacher

Almost all of Bob's ideas come from his failures. He became interested in intelligence because of low scores on intelligence tests; in creativity because at one point he ran out of ideas; in love because he was in a failing relationship; in wisdom because he found himself giving a student bad advice; and in leadership because he felt himself less than fully effective in leadership positions. The bottom line is that, as a psychologist, you can

> turn your failures into successes by studying the things you do
> not do well. Ironically, it often is easier to get creative ideas
> about things you do poorly than about things you do well
> because you may find the things you do easily are opaque to
> you – you just can't see what the difficulties are that people
> would have with them.

3. Question researchers' interpretations of their work.

Do people really do better on successive exposures to information
because repeated exposures strengthen memory traces? When people
act in ways that are contrary to their beliefs, do they really experience
some kind of cognitive dissonance? Do children have autism because
of parents who have acted in ambiguous ways that alternately encourage the children to come closer and then to distance themselves?
Much of the best research in psychology has come out of ambiguities
in the interpretation of past research findings. Very few findings lend
themselves to unambiguous interpretation, even if they initially seem
to be unambiguous.

Bob's first research project in graduate school arose out of his
questioning an empirical finding in the research literature (Sternberg
& Bower, 1974). Unfortunately, the finding was by his own undergraduate adviser (Tulving, 1966)! (He does not recommend picking
holes in your own adviser's work!) In this case, suppose you give
people a list of words to learn, A. Then, after they have learned the
A list fairly well, you give them one of two other lists to learn, either
AB or BC. Half the words on AB are the complete set of words from
list A, whereas BC has no words at all from A. Curiously, after the first
few learning trials, students actually do better in learning the all-new
list (BC) than the part-new list (AB) that partially overlaps with the
original list (A). This is odd, because one would expect it to be easier
to learn a list that is already half-learned than one that has not been
learned at all. Tulving proposed that the difficulty of those learning
the AB list was a matter of the way participants organized the words
in memory. We proposed instead that the difficulty was in discrimin-
ating which words were carried over from the A list to the AB list.
Well, you might say, all the words were carried over. Right! But
participants had not been informed of that. When they were, the

negative transfer between A and AB disappeared. So the problem did indeed appear to be one of list discrimination.

When reading a paper or listening to a talk, you should think carefully about whether the researcher's interpretation of the data matches your own interpretation. If not, could you design a study to test whether your interpretation or the other researcher's is correct? Many of the best studies in psychology have come from people questioning others' interpretations of their data.

Experience Is the Best Teacher

We often are quick to question others' interpretations of phenomena, but slow to question our own interpretations. Be as skeptical of your own – and your teachers' – interpretations as you are of anyone's. We all show a "myside bias," meaning that we are biased toward our own point of view, and look for ways to support it. Therefore always be asking yourself whether you are looking at facts objectively or skewing them to reach the conclusions you want to reach.

---

4. Look for anomalies in patterns of behavior, whether your own or others'.

Why do people who lose weight for long periods of time – perhaps even many months – all of a sudden break their pattern and start to gain weight again? Why do people who seem in their day-to-day life to be quiet and quite unobtrusive sometimes explode and go on rampages? Why do people who have been top students throughout their school careers sometimes go to college and suddenly become mediocre students? You can get ideas for research by looking for patterns in human behavior that are suddenly broken. What caused the break and why?

Bob became interested in this problem of broken patterns as it pertains to intimate relationships. Why is it that some relationships that seem to be going very well and peacefully unexpectedly – at least to outsiders – end in a breakup, possibly an acrimonious one, whereas other relationships that seem rife with conflict endure? How can a relationship that seems so harmonious break this pattern and end up in bitterness and acrimony? Bob developed a theory of relationships that he came to refer to as the theory of love as a story (Sternberg, 1998). According to the theory, almost from the time people are born, they confront many different stories of love. They observe the love stories of their parents, friends of their parents, couples in movies, and couples on television. They read about couples in books. Over time, as the result of an interaction between their experiences and their personality, they start to develop stories of what they believe love should be. These stories then guide their thinking about the kinds of relationships they should or should not be in. Examples of stories are the fairy-tale story, in which one partner seeks a prince and the other a princess; the business story, in which partners each seek a business partner; the war story, in which partners appear to be at war with each other; and the travel story, in which partners seek a traveling companion through life or a part of it.

The research was helpful in suggesting how couples that seem to be doing well can split and couples that seem to be doing poorly can stay together. If two partners both have a war story, for example, then frequent fights may be an integral part of their relationship and even part of what they mean by love. But if one partner has a war story and the other does not, the relationship may not go so well at all. A relationship may seem to be going well but actually be failing. For example, suppose that two partners are happy with each other, in general. They like the way each other looks; they have similar interests; they have similar ethical and religious values; they share political and other beliefs. But one has a fairy-tale story of love and the other a business story. In other words, one is looking for a prince and the other for a business partner. The relationship may initially seem successful because the couple has so much in common, but it may eventually fail because, at a deeper level, each member of the couple is looking for a different thing. So a relationship that can appear to be going well can fail because of conflicting stories, or one that appears to be going poorly can succeed because of comparable stories (such as the war story).

So look for broken patterns in behavior. Often they provide the best ideas you can get for new and exciting research!

5. Look for patterns of behavior that are themselves puzzling.

Why are people repeatedly so optimistic when a new political party comes into power, only soon to be disappointed after the party has a chance to perform? Why do some people repeatedly look for romantic partners who bring out the worst in them? Why do people often remember clearly people they met and things they did when they were young, but then forget people they met and things they did just a few years (or even months) ago? Why do some people almost always seem to learn from their mistakes, whereas others seem immune to learning from experience and destined to repeat their mistakes? Sometimes, it is not the break in a pattern but the pattern itself that can be puzzling and worthy of investigation. So look for patterns of behavior that are puzzling. Often people will not investigate such patterns because they get so used to them.

Bob became interested in anomalous patterns of leadership during a time when corporate scandals seemed to blossom, one right after the other. Scandals at Enron, WorldCom, Global Crossing, Arthur Andersen, Tyco, and other firms all became known at roughly the same time. History repeated itself in 2008 when several major financial institutions, such as Lehman Brothers, Merrill Lynch, and Washington Mutual, all failed around the same time. There was a clear pattern leading to these failures, but what was it, and why had it been hidden until it was too late?

The conclusion Bob came to is that it is possible to be smart and foolish at the same time (Sternberg, 2002, 2004). In particular, smart, well-educated people may be not only susceptible to cognitive fallacies but even especially susceptible because they think they are not susceptible. In other words, the weird pattern is that smart people may act more stupidly than stupid people because they think they are not susceptible to acting stupidly. Bob identified six cognitive fallacies that seemed to characterize people who had spectacular failures (Sternberg, 2005a). The cognitive fallacies include the following: (a) unrealistic optimism, in which they believe they are so smart that whatever they do will work out just fine, regardless of whether it really makes sense; (b) egocentrism, in which they start to view decisions only in terms of how the decisions benefit them; (c) omniscience, in which they think they are all-knowing but don't know what they don't know; (d) omnipotence, in which they think they can do whatever they want; (e) invulnerability, in which they think they are so smart they can get away with anything they do; and (f) ethical disengagement, in which they believe that ethical behavior is important for others but not for themselves.

6. Think the opposite of what others think.

Is the world flat? Will heavier objects fall more quickly than lighter ones? Is it possible that much of what people think is unconscious rather than conscious? Many of the greatest scientists of all time have made their reputations by defying conventions – by questioning assumptions that others routinely make or by asking questions that others do not ask. Bob's undergraduate adviser, Endel Tulving, was a master of this technique (e.g., Tulving, 1966). He repeatedly has published groundbreaking articles that shock readers because they turn on their head assumptions people have held throughout their careers. Daniel Kahneman and his collaborator, the late Amos Tversky, researchers on human decision making, also proved themselves to be masters of turning conventional wisdom on its head in their research on decision-making heuristics (e.g., Kahneman & Tversky, 1971, 1979).

Highly creative people are those who routinely turn things around – who see things in ways others do not see them (Sternberg, 2006a). Such people, according to the theory, buy low and sell high in the world of ideas. They defy the crowd, often thinking the opposite of what most others think. Our tests of the theory suggested that, indeed, more creative people are more likely to think in ways that defy convention (Sternberg, 2003, 2006a).

We came up with this idea not because it defied conventions about creativity but in part because it defied conventions about how to test students in college and other admissions situations. Conventional tests of admissions such as the SAT and the ACT test memory and analytical skills, but they do not test creative-thinking skills. Our hope was that by testing creative-thinking skills, colleges might see students in a whole new light. More than a decade later, our research found that, indeed, including creative tests in an admissions battery could improve the prediction of freshman grade-point average and decrease average ethnic-group differences (Sternberg, 2010). The inclusion of creative tests, contrary to conventional beliefs, did improve prediction of college performance.

What's Wrong Here?

"Every psychologist knows that recall improves with more repetitions of a stimulus so this is one finding that is not open to question."

Answer: This argument is called an "appeal to authority." The fact that a lot of people, even experts, believe something does not make it true. At one time, experts believed that the sun

(*cont.*)

revolves around the Earth. With regard to the finding about repetitions, Endel Tulving showed that in fact it is not always true.

Experience Is the Best Teacher

When Bob was just starting graduate school, his adviser lined up his new advisees and asked them all what they wanted to study. Bob was toward the end of the line. In turn, each of the students said what he (they all were male) thought the adviser wanted to hear. This was an opportunity for Bob to show courage and that he could think differently from the others. When the adviser came to Bob – he took the cowardly way out and said the same thing the others said. He is embarrassed to this day. You won't do your best work if you merely think and do things the way others do. To be creative, you need to strike out on your own, and ask yourself if perhaps the truth or your best course of action is actually in the opposite of what others think or do.

7. Synthesize disparate existing ideas.

Is it possible that love and hate are not opposites or really even wholly opposed to each other but more complexly related? Is it possible that people are not merely intrinsically or extrinsically motivated but some combination of those? Is it possible that people do not use either direct perception or intelligent perception but some combination of those? Are people neither serial nor parallel processors of information but simultaneously serial and parallel processors? Sometimes ideas or concepts are proposed that initially seem incongruent with each other. People assume that the constructs are related to each other in an either–or way. But it may turn out instead that the concepts can be synthesized in a way that is not mutually exclusive.

Bob and Karin have jointly done work on hate that suggests that hate and love are not opposites nor even wholly incompatible with each other; rather, they are more complexly related (Sternberg & Sternberg, 2008). According to this duplex theory, hate and love have in common that they comprise the three components of intimacy, passion, and commitment. Whereas in love, people feel intimacy toward each other, in hate, they feel negation of intimacy. So intimacy is an opposite. But passion is different. Passion is an intense motivational drive, and the same passion can be labeled in different ways depending on one's beliefs about one's relationship. So the same intense passion can be labeled as "love" or "hate" depending on how one perceives the relationship. It is for this reason that someone who intensely loves someone else and discovers a betrayal may instantaneously go from loving to hating the person. The passion still exists but is converted and relabeled. Both love and hate also involve commitments but of different kinds. Commitment in love is to tighten bonds, and in hate it is to harm and possibly destroy the hated person or group. So the duplex theory views love and hate as complexly related, and it synthesizes in a somewhat novel way what had seemed to some to be two opposing constructs.

8. Ask yourself what the next question is.

So if love and hate are complexly related, where do liking and disliking fit in? If there are consistent styles of conflict resolution across people, from where did the styles come – if from experiences, then from what kinds of experiences? If people have stories of love, do they also have stories of hate? A useful way to think of ideas for research is to ask yourself what the next question is likely to be, given the answer to the last question you asked: What is the next thing to know?

This is actually what Bob did when he proposed his balance theory of wisdom (Sternberg, 2003), according to which wisdom is the use of one's abilities and knowledge to achieve a common good by balancing one's own, others', and higher-order interests over the long and short terms through the infusion of positive ethical values. He had previously proposed a theory of intelligence (discussed previously) that had three parts: creative, analytical, and practical. But he would go out and give talks and particular questions would come up: What about Hitler or Stalin or similar monsters? Were they not creatively, analytically, and practically intelligent? Would they score at the top on what the author was calling "successful intelligence"? So the next question seemed to be, is there something wrong with or at least missing in a theory that would seemingly put wretched dictators at the top of the heap? This anomaly led the investigator to study wisdom and eventually to propose a theory of leadership, WICS (wisdom, intelligence, creativity, synthesized), which incorporates wisdom (Sternberg, 2007, 2008).

Note that, in this example, the idea came not from the author but from members of audiences to which the author spoke. It behooves you to share your ideas with others in a variety of forums and actively to solicit their feedback, because your idea about what the next question you should ask is may well come from others rather than from yourself!

There is one other important thing to remember. It is very rare that researchers in psychology reach a final answer to any question. It is rare that the next question is the last one. Only once in the careers of either of the authors has either of us come close to resolving a question in the literature. This opportunity arose for Bob in the Sternberg and Bower (1974) paper on negative transfer cited earlier. Bob was still in graduate school and was very proud that he and his adviser had, seemingly, actually resolved an issue: After that paper, few papers were published anymore on the topic, then called negative transfer in part–whole and whole–part free recall. But Bob then made a dismaying discovery: When you actually answer a question, you lose the option to do further research on that question, because it is answered. You have to find yourself a new topic to investigate! Fortunately, then, perhaps, neither of us ever again reached anything even approaching a final resolution to a psychological problem!

9. Revisit discarded ideas.

Was Sigmund Freud really as off-base as many current clinical theorists think he was? How about Jean Piaget? Behaviorism is not in fashion in many circles, but is it possible that there were ideas there that would still be valuable today? As mentioned previously, very few issues in psychology reach a final resolution. More often, people just get tired of the issues or move on to the next ones. They may reject old paradigms because they find, inevitably, that the paradigms were flawed. But typically, they introduce new paradigms that themselves have flaws, just different ones from the old paradigms. So sometimes it is worthwhile to revisit old ideas and ask whether, when they were discarded, researchers metaphorically threw out the baby with the bathwater.

10. Look for ideas in everyday models and metaphors.

Which is it: Absence makes the heart grow fonder or out of sight, out of mind? Do people really function like hydraulic systems, as was suggested in Freudian psychoanalysis? Or do they think like computers, as was suggested by early information-processing psychologists like Herbert Simon? Everyday models and metaphors rarely provide precise characterizations of how people think or feel. But they may provide a starting point for understanding human behavior.

Bob was once riding on a plane to a meeting in Virginia when, seemingly out of the blue, an idea came into his head: Maybe the way people govern or manage themselves is analogous to the way in which governments govern (Sternberg, 1997). The idea was that some people are more legislative: They like to legislate – to come up with ideas. Other people are more executive. They like to execute – to be told what to do and then to do it. Still other people are more judicial – they like to judge things and people. Some people are more liberal – they like to do things in new ways. Others are more conservative – they prefer tried and tested ways of doing something. In the end, the theory contained 13 different styles based on the notion of mental self-government. Tests of the theory revealed that the styles provided useful characterizations of how people like to utilize their abilities (Sternberg, 1997). But the original idea came from taking a model from everyday life – government – and applying it to styles of thinking.

In the first part of this chapter, we have proposed different ways in which you can get ideas for theories and research studies. We wish to emphasize that no one technique will work for everyone and that different people will find different techniques to be useful. Moreover, these are far from the only techniques. The McGuire (1997) paper, mentioned earlier, provides additional techniques. Moreover, books on creativity and innovation will contain other techniques as well. As you go through your career, you will learn what works for you. The important thing is to find ways of generating ideas and then to use them not only to produce ideas but also to enjoy yourself while doing so.

So far, we have concentrated on how you get new ideas. But the creative process actually includes two more steps: deciding whether a new idea is a good idea and then persuading others of the value of the idea. We discuss these two issues next.

2.2 EVALUATING YOUR IDEAS

Coming up with an idea is hard. Knowing whether it is a good idea is harder. Worse, there is no failsafe way of knowing whether an idea is good. Here are 12 techniques you can try. Not every idea necessarily has to pass all of the following criteria. But if it doesn't pass most of them, you may wish to reconsider:

Is the idea internally consistent?
Is the idea empirically testable?
Do you have the means to test the idea?
Does the idea go beyond what is known?
Does the idea fit with what is known?
Are you enthusiastic about the idea?
Would you be able to persuade other people of the value of the idea?
Have you answered what you anticipate to be possible objections to your idea?
Is the idea the "right size"?
Are others besides yourself likely to find the idea interesting?
What do others whose opinions you value actually say about your idea?
Could you explain your idea to your grandmother?

1. Is the idea internally consistent?

Make sure that the idea coheres internally – that it does not contradict itself. This point is obvious, but nevertheless, you want to check for coherence.

2. Is the idea empirically testable?

Psychology is a science, so its propositions have to be empirically testable. Make sure that there is some way to test the idea you are proposing. If there isn't, it's not science.

3. Do you have the means to test the idea?

An idea may be empirically testable, but testing it may require more resources than you either have or would be able to acquire. Make sure the idea is testable within the constraints of what is reasonably possible for you.

4. Does the idea go beyond what is known?

Be sure to research the literature reasonably thoroughly before you propose an idea so that you do not end up, metaphorically, reinventing the wheel.

5. Does the idea fit with what is known?

Make sure that existing empirical evidence does not contradict the idea, or if it does, be prepared to say why that evidence did not provide an adequate test of your hypothesis.

6. Are you enthusiastic about the idea?

Especially early in your career, there is a temptation to get started on research just so you can feel that you got started on research! Research projects generally take quite a bit of time. If you lack enthusiasm for an idea, you are unlikely to give it your best effort, and even small amounts of time will seem like a lot of time.

Experience Is the Best Teacher

At one point, Bob was doing research on conflict resolution. Two articles emerged and were published in one of the top journals in the field. Bob thought his ideas were good. But he did not have as much enthusiasm for his ideas in this field as he did about his ideas in other fields. His ideas about conflict resolution just did not seem to be leading him anywhere, and he stopped doing research in the area. You always will do your best work when you have enthusiasm for your ideas.

---

7. Would you be able to persuade other people of the value of the idea?

Remember that other people are often going to be more skeptical of your new ideas than you are. Will you be able to persuade others of the value of the idea so you can get their backing and support?

8. Have you answered what you anticipate to be possible objections to your idea?

Elaborating on Point 5, you should ask yourself specifically what kinds of objections others are likely to raise and how you would answer them.

9. Is the idea the "right size"?

Some ideas are very small. They may be reasonable ideas, but they are so narrow or small in scope that they just will not contribute much to knowledge. Some ideas are very large and perhaps complicated. Testing them might require quite a long series of studies. People differ in the size of idea they are comfortable with. Ask yourself whether the idea is too small or too large for your taste.

10. Are others besides yourself likely to find the idea interesting?

Science is public. You need to have an audience for your idea. So you have to ask yourself not only whether the idea interests you but also whether it is likely to interest others.

11. What do others whose opinions you value actually say about your idea?

It is always worth getting feedback from others. You should not view their feedback as definitive. In the end, you are the one who has to decide whether your idea is good. But at the very least, others may be able to help you improve on your idea.

12. Could you explain your idea to your grandmother?

Good ideas may be simple or complex. But if an idea is well formulated, it can be explained, even if in simplified form, to someone without a technical background. If you cannot give a clear and simple explanation of the idea, you need to ask yourself whether you really have a clear conception of what the idea is.

In the end, you are the one who has to decide whether an idea is good and worth pursuing. We hope these techniques are valuable in helping you to decide whether the idea is one that is worthy of your further attention.

Give It Some More Thought

What could you do to simplify your writing? Could you use shorter sentences, less jargon, simpler words, better organization, or what?

2.3 SELLING YOUR IDEAS

The ways in which you persuade others of the value of an idea depend on the idea. However, there are some techniques that tend to be useful in a variety of circumstances. Here are 12 such techniques:

Present your idea in a way that is crystal clear.
Show that your idea is consistent with past research.
Present your own research in support of the idea.
Neither undersell nor oversell.
Don't be dismissive of or insult disbelievers.
Show your audience why the idea should be of interest to them.
Where possible, tie in your idea with the background and interests of the audience.
Be forthcoming about the weaknesses or limitations of your idea as well as about its strengths.
If asked a question you cannot answer, admit you do not know and say that you will try to find out.
Show enthusiasm for your idea.
Be super well organized in your presentation.
If at first you don't succeed, try, try again – don't be easily discouraged.

1. Present your idea in a way that is crystal clear.

Nothing hurts acceptance of an idea quite so much as a presentation of the idea that is vague, obscure, or confusing. Consider in advance how you can present the idea in a way that is so clear that anyone, or at least almost anyone, in your audience can understand it.

2. Show that your idea is consistent with past research.

No matter what your own research may find, people will be interested not just in what you have found but also in the full existing literature. The more you can show that your idea is consistent with past literature, the more likely you are to persuade people of your idea.

3. Present your own research in support of the idea.

It always helps if you have empirical data of some kind to support the idea. And make sure that others, and not just you, will see how the data support the idea.

4. Neither undersell nor oversell.

If you undersell an idea, people may wonder why they should believe in your idea if you seem hardly to believe in the idea yourself. But if you oversell the idea, people may become offended and question whether you are not being merely self-aggrandizing. In general, it is better to err on the side of more modest claims than on the side of inflated ones.

5. Don't be dismissive of or insult disbelievers.

Sometimes, you may find it incredible that others would question your idea. After all, you know it is a great idea – why wouldn't anyone else in his or her right mind see it the same way? But if you are dismissive of or insulting toward disbelievers, you will lose the audience you most want to persuade.

Experience Is the Best Teacher

Many years ago, Bob had his first job interview. A member of the audience asked a question that Bob considered to be stupid and off the point of the talk. Bob gave a dismissive answer, showing the questioner, he thought, that he recognized a bad question when he got one. Unfortunately for, and unknown to Bob, the questioner was the chair of the search committee. Bob did not get the job. Since then, he has made an effort never to be dismissive in his answers to questions.

---

6. Show your audience why the idea should be of interest to them.

It may be obvious to you that an idea is interesting. It may not be obvious to your audience. You have to persuade them that it is interesting. That is your job, not theirs. And do not say that your idea or results are "interesting and important." Let your audience say that.

What's Wrong Here?

"Here is the most interesting finding in our study: In all, 85 percent of the participants agreed with the confederate when she objected to the experimenter's argument."

Answer: Don't tell your listeners or readers what is interesting. Let them decide what is interesting. Present your finding in a way that will make it clear to them that the finding is indeed interesting.

---

7. **Where possible, tie in your idea with the background and interests of the audience.**

A good presentation is targeted at the audience it attempts to reach. There is no one-size-fits-all paper or talk. You need to tailor your presentation to the audience so that it fits their interests and background knowledge.

8. **Be forthcoming about the weaknesses or limitations of your idea as well as about its strengths.**

You will gain much respect from your audience if you show that you recognize the weaknesses of your idea, not just its strengths.

Experience Is the Best Teacher

In Bob's experience as a journal editor, an article is much more likely to be rejected if it fails to acknowledge its weaknesses than if it states the weaknesses forthrightly. Referees take delight in finding flaws; if you find the flaws yourself, the reviewers will be more likely to tolerate the flaws than if they find them and feel they can shove them in your face.

---

9. **If asked a question you cannot answer, admit you do not know and say that you will try to find out.**

When you present your idea, someone may ask you a question you cannot answer. Don't try to brazen your way through an answer, hoping that the interlocutor won't notice that you are faking it. If you don't know, say so, and if possible, find out the answer and get back to the interlocutor.

10. **Show enthusiasm for your idea.**

If you are not enthusiastic, why would you expect others to be?

> ## Experience Is the Best Teacher
>
> When Bob was younger, there was an assistant professor in his department who was doing absolutely terrific work. The work truly upended many conventional views in psychology. But when the faculty member talked about his work, he practically put his audience to sleep. His presentations were stultifying. It was hard to stay awake. The faculty member seemed to have no enthusiasm for his own work, despite its being truly exciting. Bob believes the individual and his work have never had the impact they could have had because the individual came across as so uninspired, and uninspiring, to his audiences.

11. Be super well organized in your presentation.

An idea is more persuasive if it is presented in an organized way, including the idea, past support for it, your new support for it, and so on. When presentations of ideas are disorganized, they tend to be much less convincing.

12. If at first you don't succeed, try, try again – don't be easily discouraged.

We have found that the first time we present a new idea, it often does not fly with our audiences. Give it another try and maybe even a third try. At some point, you may decide that you are not ready to go forward with the idea. But the more creative an idea, the harder it is to persuade others of its value. Persistence makes all the difference.

3 | Literature Research

Whether you are writing a literature review or working on an experimental research paper, literature research is an important factor. Nowadays, you can get the information you need in several ways. First, you can consult journals and books that you can find in libraries and archives. Second, you can conveniently use the Internet from your own home or workplace to retrieve an enormous amount of information.

In this chapter, we first describe different kinds of reference materials. We also provide a list of reference materials that may be useful for your research. We then give you an introduction to literature research and some of the databases that you are likely to use. Afterward, a section on Internet research gives you an overview of search engines, how best to search for keywords, types of information available on the Internet, and how to evaluate the information you find online. Last, we elaborate on the function of bibliographical software and its use for your research.

3.1 REFERENCE MATERIALS

Authors of psychology papers should be aware of the references available to them. There are many different kinds of resources you can consult. Here are some of them:

■ **Almanacs**
Almanacs are annual publications that contain information and statistics on a wide array of topics. *The World Factbook* is an almanac, for example. There are almanacs for many specialized fields, for example, for special education. The entries are sorted according to

general headings, so you may have to think about superordinate topics that belong to your interest to find the information you need.

■ Bibliographies

Bibliographies list the works of a certain writer or focus on certain topics. If you are interested in a particular topic, like the concept of time in psychology, for example, a bibliography can help you find literature on this topic.

■ Dictionaries

Dictionaries show the correct spellings of words and may list synonyms or alternative words to look up. Similar to encyclopedias, they often also contain short entries that explain the word. There are general dictionaries and dictionaries that specialize in one subject area, for example, psychology. There are also specialized dictionaries, such as of synonyms and antonyms.

■ Directories

Directories list resources and contact information for sources that are of interest to you. For example, there are membership directories of organizations or directories that help you get an overview of journals in a field.

■ Electronic search

Much and probably most searching these days is done electronically. Researchers may use Google, or Google Scholar, or a variety of other search engines, such as Yahoo, Bing, Ask, and AOL Search. These search engines can be an efficient way of locating information on almost any topic. In using such search engines, keep three things in mind.

First, whereas published reference materials can be expected to screen material for accuracy, electronic search engines do not. Most published reference materials are peer-reviewed: scholars check the materials for currency, accuracy, and readability. Much electronic reference material is not peer-reviewed. Thus, you need to be especially careful to check the validity of information you acquire electronically. The appearance of material in multiple search engines or in multiple articles does not guarantee the accuracy of the information. Sometimes, sources just copy each other. You need to check for credibility of information, not just repetition of it. Section 3.3.5 discusses the question of validity in much more detail.

Second, each search engine has its own algorithm for ordering information that results from a search. The most relevant material for your search will not necessarily occur at or even near the top of the list. You need to check far enough down in the material to ensure relevance. The more specific your search criteria are, the more likely you are to gather relevant material.

Third, electronic search engines only cover information available on the Internet. Although much material is on the Internet, certainly not all of it is, and classical sources are likely to be missing. Hence, limiting your search for information to electronic search engines may lead you to miss important sources.

■ Encyclopedias

There are both general and specialized encyclopedias in which you can look up keywords of interest. Furthermore, encyclopedias usually have an index in the back that will refer you to related keywords as well. When you look up the keyword "risk," for example, you may find references to "risk assessment," "availability heuristic," "social dilemmas," and more. The use of such encyclopedias can help you expand your views on a topic. Citations to encyclopedias are generally frowned on in professional articles, and often in papers written at the university level as well. Encyclopedias are more useful for beginning your research than for final citations.

■ Thesauri

A thesaurus lists words that are related to a term. This may be helpful, for example, when you encounter words with which you are unfamiliar, or if you want to check whether there are related terms that you have not considered in your research so far.

■ Yearbooks

A yearbook contains information that refers to a specific year. Yearbooks usually pertain to narrow fields. There are yearbooks on sport psychology, child psychology, and communication, for example. Today, the Internet has made yearbooks much less popular and useful: information can be updated continuously rather than annually.

3.2 LITERATURE RESEARCH

Once you have narrowed down your topic, you are ready to search for resources and material at the library. You don't necessarily have to go there in person right away, because most libraries have their catalogs online. In fact, browsing the online catalogs will give you an overview of what is available in your area of interest, help you narrow down your search, and give you a preliminary set of references with which you can begin your research.

Libraries not only have catalogs of the books they own but also can grant you access to many online databases that contain magazines, journals, and newspapers. If you do not know where to start or how to find what you are looking for, you have several possibilities. First of all, you can ask a librarian for help. Today, many libraries also offer several electronic possibilities for you to get in touch with their librarians. You may be able to chat online with a librarian or to submit questions by text message or e-mail. Remember that the more detailed your question is, the more likely it is that the librarian will be able to direct you to the sources that are of help to you.

Generally, the different research tools that libraries offer are the following:

- **A library catalog** in which you can search for the different books, journals, newspapers, and magazines that are available.
- **Databases** in which you can search for keywords, authors, and so on; they usually contain a large number of journals on one particular subject.
- Libraries often grant you free access to **online journals and newspapers** so you can select the newspaper or journal of your choice and browse freely through the table of contents and other publications.

In addition, libraries may have **subject guides** and **online tutorials** that can help you with your research. A subject guide in psychology can direct you to databases that help you find books, journals, or assessment instruments, for example.

3.2.1 Databases for Psychologists

There are a number of databases that are specifically designed for research in psychology and related fields. Here are a few of them:

CINAHL	Contains more than 330 English-language journals of nursing and allied fields like social services in health care and health education. It also includes books.
ERIC	Education database that includes more than 1 million abstracts of publications in educational research and educational psychology.

ProjectMUSE	Database that contains more than 400 journals from more than 100 not-for-profit publishers in diverse fields such as education, gender studies, and cultural studies.
JSTOR	JSTOR comprises more than 1,000 journals and other sources focused on the social sciences but also the humanities and natural sciences.
PsycInfo	Includes more than 1,300 journals, books, book chapters, and dissertations in the fields of psychology, sociology, education, medicine, and others. The referenced publications are in more than 30 languages.
PubMed	This database mainly focuses on medicine and the life and health sciences.

3.2.2 How to Find Psychological Tests

If you are interested in finding a test that has been published, there are several resources you can use to find it:

Tests in Print (*TIP*), 8th edn., 2011 Published by the Buros Institute for Mental Measurements, Lincoln, NE	Bibliographic encyclopedia that contains information on every published (and purchasable) assessment instrument in the field of psychology
Mental Measurements Yearbook (*MMY*), 19th edn., 2014 Published by the Buros Institute for Mental Measurements, Lincoln, NE	Lists all tests that have been revised or newly developed since the publication of the previous yearbook. Information on prices, authors, psychometric properties, and so on

Online resources you can use to find tests are the websites of the Clearinghouse on Assessment and Evaluation (http://ericae.net), the Buros Institute of Mental Measurements (http://buros.unl.edu/buros/jsp/search.jsp), and the Educational Testing Service (www.ets.org/testcoll).

If you need some more information on how to locate tests (both published and unpublished ones), the American Psychological Association has a helpful website that spells out the details on test search. You can find it at http://apa.org/science/faq-findtests.html.

3.3 INTERNET RESEARCH

The Internet can be a powerful research tool. It allows easy and quick access to information about a wide range of psychological topics. This access can be very helpful in exploring potential research ideas as well as in gathering background information for writing papers.

There are also pitfalls in using the Internet for research that can mitigate its advantages. For example, although information may be accessed easily and quickly, much of it may be either irrelevant or invalid. Effective use of the Internet requires knowing how to search for information efficiently and how to evaluate the quality of the information that is found. Taking advantage of the Internet's potential as a research tool requires avoiding its pitfalls, as we will see in the following sections.

Give It Some More Thought

What are some steps you can take to evaluate the credibility of an Internet source? As an example, you might check the information provided against other sources.

3.3.1 The Components of the Internet

When we speak of the Internet, we are referring to a collection of components that constitute different ways of accessing and sharing information across computers. In assessing the usefulness of the Internet for research purposes, it is important to know the characteristics of the major components:

■ World Wide Web
The World Wide Web is a network of computers that allow linking of documents by means of hypertext, links embedded in one document (a web page) that provide instant access to files located on different computers.

■ Usenet/Netnews
Usenet is a worldwide system of discussion groups, with comments passed among hundreds of thousands of machines. Usenet is completely decentralized and nearly uncensored, with more than 10,000 discussion areas, called newsgroups. Messages are discrete postings to the area; therefore, discussions may occur over weeks or months. Most Internet service providers include access to Usenet discussion groups. The list of current groups and messages can be viewed using major web browsers, with instructions for subscribing to discussion groups contained in their help files.

■ **Mailing lists**

Mailing lists, or LISTSERVs, are a system of exchanging e-mail messages among people who subscribe to the same topical forum. When e-mail is addressed to a LISTSERV mailing list, it is automatically broadcast to everyone who subscribes to the list. The result is similar to a Usenet newsgroup or forum, except that the messages are transmitted as e-mail and are therefore available only to individuals on the list. Many psychological organizations maintain LISTSERVs, which can be joined by accessing those organizations' websites. Other public LISTSERVs are cataloged at www.lsoft.com/catalist.html.

■ **Chat groups and instant messaging**

Chat groups and instant messaging are systems that allow the nearly instantaneous exchange of messages among individuals located on computers that are widely dispersed geographically. Chat groups are usually topically oriented and can be joined by anyone. Chat groups on psychological topics can be located through professional organizations and societies, and they are an increasingly common component of online conferences. Instant messaging systems allow private and intimate online discussions among a small number of individuals. Current versions of major web browsers have instant message systems as a built-in component.

3.3.2 Overview of Internet Searching and Search Engines

The information available on the Internet has been likened to all the pages in all the books in a library being torn out and thrown into a huge pile. The information would still be available, of course, but locating and organizing material on a particular topic would be extremely daunting. Fortunately, this view is overly cynical because effective strategies and tools for locating information exist that can make the task more manageable.

The primary tool for finding specific information on the Internet is the search engine, a software program that provides a list of links to documents and Web pages that contain the keywords specified by the user. The most popular search engines include Google, Yahoo!, AOL, Ask, and Bing. Each of these engines can be accessed using a Web browser and entering the Internet address in the format www.searchengine.com, where you replace "searchengine" with the name of the engine you wish to employ. Most users are familiar with one or more of these programs, but few people take full advantage of their features. Here are some tips for effective searching:

1. Carefully construct the search phrase.

The search phrase, or query, can greatly influence the relevance and quality of the results, and creating effective phrases requires careful thought and practice. For example, suppose the topic being investigated was spousal abuse in rural settings. What would be a good search phrase? The following are suggestions from an excellent online tutorial by the Bright Planet Software Company (www.brightplanet.com/deep content/tutorials/Search/):

- use nouns or objects rather than verbs (*abuse* versus *abusing*);
- indicate exact phrases by using quotes ("spouse abuse");
- include synonyms of key concepts, using Boolean operators (which include *and*, *or*, and *not*) if required by the specific search engine ("spouse" OR "intimate partner"; "domestic abuse" OR "violence" OR "assault"); and
- order concepts with the main subject first ("loving spouse" OR "intimate partner"). Note that the syntax for combining words in a search phrase may vary somewhat from engine to engine – consult the help section of the search engine for details.

What's Wrong Here?

Jack, a psychology student, wants to find as many studies as possible that have been done on the topic of close relationships. So he searches several search engines for the term "close relationships" and carefully notes studies that have been done.

Answer: Jack also should have checked related terms, such as "intimate relationships" and "romantic relationships." Without doing so, he may identify the studies that use the exact term in which he is interested, but not other studies that investigate the desired concept.

---

2. Use more than one search engine.

Search engines differ in the breadth of their search, how they order the search results, and how up to date the links are that are listed;

therefore, the same search phrase entered into two search engines may not return the same list of links. Also, consider using a meta-search engine, such as Vivisimo or Dogpile, which automatically queries several search engines and eliminates duplicate links. You can access any of these meta-search engines by using the same address method suggested previously for single-source search engines.

3. Limit your search to certain domains.

Most search engines allow the search to be restricted to certain domains (e.g., .org, .edu, .gov). This restriction can be useful for maximizing the relevance of links that are identified. For example, suppose the researcher wanted to locate government-sponsored reports on the subject of spousal abuse in rural settings. The search phrase could be entered with the restriction that only links with .gov be listed. Check the search engine's help page for the exact format of a restricted search.

4. Search for links to a specific document.

Imagine in the foregoing example that a restricted search of the .gov domain leads to a site that is particularly informative. Other sites that are linked to it might be informative as well, and most search engines allow a search for linked sites. This strategy is the Internet equivalent of using citation indices in searching for printed materials. A related approach involves taking an exact phrase from one document and using it as a search query. For example, a government report on intimate partner violence contained the sentence "Intimate partners committed fewer murders in each of the 3 years 2007, 2008, and 2009." Inserting this phrase as a search query will locate other Internet documents that used the same reference.

3.3.3 Excursion: Internet Search Using Boolean Logic

Many of the databases on the Internet can be searched most efficiently by using the principles of Boolean logic. Boolean logic was named after George Boole, who was a British mathematician and philosopher. It concerns the logical relationships among a number of search terms. There are three operators: AND, OR, and NOT. You can also combine them or use symbols to represent Boolean operators (implied logic). Here is a short explanation of how each of these concepts works:

1. AND

Assume that you are interested in finding out more about how noise impairs concentration. The keywords for your search are therefore "noise" and "concentration." You are not interested in articles that deal with noise alone or that are solely about concentration. In fact, you need search results that include both of your keywords. You can ensure that your results include both "noise" and "concentration" by connecting them with AND, so that you enter into the search engine "noise AND concentration."

2. OR

Imagine that you are interested in the general topic of headaches and migraines. You would like to retrieve any documents that contain either the word *headache* or the word *migraine*. Therefore you enter "headache OR migraine" into the search engine. Your retrieved results will be much broader than if you had entered "headache AND migraine" because in the latter case you would have retrieved only documents that contain both words, whereas a search with OR gets you all documents that contain the words *migraine, headache,* or both.

3. NOT

If you are interested in the general topic of headaches, but not migraines specifically, you can exclude documents in your search that contain the word *migraine*. To do that, enter the search term "headache NOT migraine." This way, no article about headaches that also contains the word *migraine* will be shown in your list of results.

4. Combined operators

You can also conduct more complicated searches by combining several operators. If you are interested in violence in connection with hate or prejudice, you could enter the search term "violence AND (hate OR prejudice)." This search will retrieve any document that contains the word *violence* as well as one or both of the words *hate* and *prejudice*. This search option may be available only on the advanced search page, depending on the search engine you use. If you want to conduct a more specific search, you are well advised to check out the advanced search page of your search engine. It may give you many more options, for example, to search only for web pages with the extension .edu.

5. Implied logic

Today, search engines often use implied logic, meaning that when you enter more than one search term, they automatically default to either the AND operator or the OR operator. To which of the two the search engine defaults depends on which engine you are using; in most cases, the default will be AND. So, if you enter the search term *headache migraine* and the search engine defaults to AND, you will retrieve documents that contain both the words *headache* and *migraine*. If you would like to use the NOT logic, usually you can put a minus sign in front of the word that you want to exclude from your search. The search term *headache–migraine* will retrieve documents that contain the keyword *headache* but not the keyword *migraine*.

3.3.4 Some Specific Types of Useful Online Research Information

There are several types of valuable online information that might not be located using a general search strategy of the sort described previously. Some of these are proprietary but are available through public computer systems at libraries and universities that have paid for access to the information source. Check with a librarian to see what resources may be available in your situation.

■ **Journal articles**
Full texts of articles published in major psychology journals can be searched and viewed online using PsycINFO and other databases. Many of these databases are purchased by universities and some public library systems.

■ **Magazine and newspaper articles**
Most major magazines and newspapers have websites that allow free searches of past articles. The search engines available on these sites function in much the same way as the major search engines, and the same tips for using them effectively apply.

■ **Government databases**
Many online databases are maintained by the US government, including archives of the *Congressional Record*, Supreme Court decisions,

crime statistics, and reports of various government agencies. A number of these databases can be accessed and searched through the US government website FedWorld (www.fedworld.gov). The advanced search option allows searches of federal and specific state government databases.

■ Home pages of specific researchers

A useful source of information can be the individual home page of a researcher in your field of interest. Researchers usually list their own publications and presentations on the topic, and sometimes provide links to other relevant information. You can locate home pages by conducting a general Internet search using a researcher's name as the search phrase or by going to the website of the individual's academic institution and searching there. Alternatively, many directories of professional society memberships, such as the American Psychological Association and the Association for Psychological Science, provide website addresses for their members.

■ Popular Internet sites for research resources

There are a number of organizational websites that have useful information for researchers. For example, the American Psychological Association's website (www.apa.org) can be searched for short research articles on a variety of topics. The Association for Psychological Science's site (www.psychologicalscience.org) contains a compendium of links to university psychology departments, psychology organizations, and sites that provide tips and resources for conducting research and writing reports. The Social Psychology Network (www.socialpsychology.org) maintains links to individual home pages of psychologists, as well as links to research and teaching resources, including tips on writing in APA style, conducting data analysis, and so on.

3.3.5 Critical Evaluation of Internet-based Information

As noted earlier, relying on information obtained from an Internet search without critically evaluating its quality can be very risky. Much of the information on the Internet has not been subject to the same publishing standards or filters as material found in major scientific journals, books, and newspapers.

Almost anyone can post information to the Internet without checks on its reliability and accuracy. The result is that a great deal of misinformation exists on the Internet – information that seems legitimate but is factually incorrect or incomplete. Misinformation is not necessarily intentionally misleading; it is more likely the result of the author's carelessness or ignorance. However, the ease and low cost of creating websites has also led to many sites where the intent is not so much to provide information as to persuade readers to hold a particular belief or point of view, and the lack of checks on objectivity may make it difficult to tell the difference. Information intended to persuade the audience is called propaganda. In some cases, attempts to be persuasive may include deliberate distortions or fabrications of information – often referred to as disinformation. For online examples and comparisons of misinformation, propaganda, and disinformation, see the Information and Its Counterfeits website maintained by Johns Hopkins Library at www.library.jhu.edu/researchhelp/general/evaluating/counterfeit.html.

The existence of misinformation, propaganda, and disinformation on the Internet means that researchers must carefully evaluate material that might be used in a particular project. There are several criteria for evaluating information that can be adapted to the Internet (see Radford & Barnes, 2005). The following is adapted from online material provided by librarians at Widener University (www.widener.edu/libraries/wolfgram/evaluate), New Mexico State University (http://lib.nmsu.edu/instruction/eval.html), and Johns Hopkins University (www.library.jhu.edu/researchhelp/general/evaluating/):

■ **Accuracy**

It is difficult to determine the accuracy of information when you are not an expert on the topic. However, certain indicators can help you assess the likelihood that Internet material is accurate. Does the author indicate the source of the information, and is the source public so that it can be accessed and verified? Are there fact checkers and editors who may have screened the document (probably so for an online journal article or newspaper article but probably not for a personal home page)?

■ **Authority**

Is the author and publishing body of the Internet document indicated? Are the credentials of the author given, or is there a way to locate and evaluate them? If the publishing body is indicated (e.g., an organization or educational institution), is it reputable? If the document is found on a university server (i.e., has an .edu domain), is the page sponsored by the institution itself, or is it the personal home page of the author? If the author is not someone you recognize as an authority on the topic, do others refer to the work in a positive way? Can you find links to the document from authors you do know and trust?

■ Objectivity

What is the point of view or bias of the document or the website? Is the author a person or organization with a stake in the issue you are researching? Does the document reside on the server of an organization that has a political or philosophical agenda? Is the author motivated to present information selectively or perhaps to distort it? Sometimes these questions are easy to answer, but often the motivation and bias in a document may not be clear. For example, do not assume that all documents residing on a university server or authored by doctorate holders are bias free. Academics may have strong points of view that influence their interpretation of information just as anyone else does. Perhaps the question is not whether a document is objective but to what degree the presentation of information is biased and in what ways.

Experience Is the Best Teacher

One would like to think that there are "objective" standards for deciding whether a source is objective. But there aren't. Psychologists argue at great length over whether particular sources of information are "objective." Some years ago, Richard Herrnstein and Charles Murray published a book called *The Bell Curve.* Some psychologists viewed this source as a refreshingly different and objective discussion of class differences in intelligence. Other psychologists viewed the book as blatantly biased. The problem has not gone away. In 2005, Daniel Goleman published a book on *Emotional Intelligence.* Some psychologists saw the book as a breakthrough study of a new way to look at intelligence; others saw it as writing about a largely imaginary construct. You need to figure out for yourself what kinds of criteria you will use to decide whether a source is "objective."

■ **Currency**
How recent or up to date is the information that the site provides? In a fast-moving field of research, articles just a few years old may need to be supplemented by newer findings that change the conclusions about a topic. It can be important, then, to know the currency of the Internet information you are using. Is there a publication or last-modified date indicated on the document? Are there references in the document to the dates on which data were collected? If the author refers to published works, how recent are the dates?

■ **Coverage**
How thoroughly or deeply does the document deal with the topic? Does it provide background information and references that seem appropriately extensive? Has the author demonstrated the connection of his or her work to other research and theory? Assessing coverage allows you to determine the unique contribution and value of the author's document.

It is possible to practice applying these criteria to websites and Internet documents. Alexander and Tate at Widener University have collected examples of Internet documents and websites that illustrate variations on each of the criteria (www3.widener.edu/ Academics/Libraries/Wolfgram_Memorial_Library/Evaluate_Web_ Pages/Actual_Web_Pages_as_Examples/5722/). They also provide examples of special types of websites, such as those that blend advertising with information and those that subtly advocate political or philosophical causes. Another excellent source of examples is Susan Beck's website "The Good, the Bad, and the Ugly" (http://lib.nmsu.edu/instruction/eval.html). Beck provides examples of each criterion, as do Alexander and Tate, but she also presents sets of links to Internet material on four different topics (i.e., smoking and tobacco use, AIDS, immigration, and drugs). The links for each topic vary in quality, and the viewer must decide which criteria are most relevant – it is a very realistic exercise. Research by Dietz-Uhler (2002) has shown that students who work through Beck's examples are significantly more confident and critical evaluators of Internet information.

3.4 BIBLIOGRAPHY SOFTWARE

When you do literature research, it is important for you to keep an overview of all the different sources you have found. After all, when writing your paper, you will need to look up different facts again that you read about but may only roughly remember. You also have to give references in your paper so that interested readers can look up the sources you cited. One way to stay organized while doing literature research and writing your paper is to use bibliographical software. There are several different programs like EndNote, Reference Manager, and CiteULike. The former two are software available for purchase, and the latter one is a free online service to search and manage literature. You may be able to get bibliographical software for free or at a reduced price through your university. Generally, bibliographical software lets you perform a lot of different functions.

You may be able to search the Internet with your software and import the references that are of interest to you. You can insert references from the software into your paper, and the software automatically inserts a complete bibliography at the end of your paper, formatted in the style you choose (e.g., APA style). In many programs, you can also electronically store a copy of the article.

4 | Writing a Literature Review

Most undergraduate research papers, and many graduate and professional research papers as well, are based on literature reviews. The aims of a literature review are different from those of an empirical research paper, and hence the skills required differ somewhat as well. The goals of literature reviews are the following (American Psychological Association, 2009):

1. To define and clarify problems
2. To inform the reader about a subject by summarizing and evaluating studies
3. To identify inconsistencies, gaps, contradictions, and relationships in the literature
4. To suggest future steps and approaches to solve the issues identified

There are five kinds of literature reviews that can be distinguished on the basis of the aim of the review. Reviews can strive to (a) generate new knowledge, (b) test theories, (c) integrate theories, (d) develop a new theory, or (e) integrate existing knowledge.

If you plan to submit your literature review to a journal and have to decide where to submit it, you may want to read some literature reviews that have been published in the journals you are considering to find out whether your paper is a good fit to the journal. Generally, the probability of an article being accepted is highest when you develop new knowledge, a new theory, or integrate several theories (instead of just reviewing and summarizing the literature on a particular topic) (Eisenberg, 2000). In general, the best literature reviews do not merely summarize literature; they also create new knowledge by placing the literature into a new framework or at least seeing the literature in a new way.

The literature review can proceed smoothly if you follow a sequence of simple steps:

1. Decide on a topic for a paper.
2. Organize and search the literature.
3. Prepare an outline.
4. Write the paper.
5. Evaluate the paper yourself and seek others' feedback on it.

4.1 DECIDING ON A TOPIC FOR A PAPER

Your first task is to decide on a topic for a paper. This is, in a sense, the most important task because the paper can be no better than the topic. We have found five mistakes that repeatedly turn up in writers' choices of topics:

1. The topic doesn't interest the writer.
2. The topic is too easy or too safe for the writer.
3. The topic is too difficult for the writer.
4. There is inadequate literature on the topic.
5. The topic is too broad.

1. The topic doesn't interest the writer.

Many writers put off thinking about their choice of topic until the latest possible date. They then find themselves pressed to select a topic and hastily decide on something that is of only marginal interest to them. Procrastination in thinking about a topic is a mistake because interesting topics do not often pop into your head overnight. So allow yourself plenty of time to think of a topic. Then, if you are unhappy with the first few ideas that come to mind, you can try out others before you resign yourself to a topic that doesn't interest you. Unless you are at least somewhat interested in the topic you pick, you will find the exercise of doing literature research a deadly bore, and your paper will probably show it. We are convinced that a major determinant of quality is the degree of interest the writer sustains in the topic about which he or she writes.

Give It Some More Thought

How do you recognize when you are really excited about a topic, as opposed to just mildly interested in it? What kinds of signs do you show when you are enthusiastic? For example, if you are really enthusiastic, you may find yourself thinking about the topic before you go to sleep or in off hours when normally you would be thinking about something else.

---

2. The topic is too easy or too safe for the writer.

The purpose of literature reviews often is for the writer, and especially for student writers, to learn something about some topic. It is therefore to writers' advantage to select a topic with which they are relatively (although not necessarily totally) unfamiliar. Writers sometimes seek to optimize safety (or grades) rather than learning, however, thereby choosing a topic with which they are quite familiar. Bob saw an example of such a choice one year in his Theories of Intelligence course. A student showed in class that she was quite familiar with the literature on creativity in children, perhaps because she had previously written a paper on it. Her remarks in class also showed, however, that she had little background in other areas covered by the course. Bob was therefore disappointed when she proposed to write a paper on creativity in children. Although she probably could learn something from writing such a paper, it was clear that she had more to gain by selecting a topic from one of the many areas in which she had little background.

Experience Is the Best Teacher

Many investigators, from students to professionals, start doing research on a particular topic and then stick to it. It becomes their "safe harbor," their refuge from the possibility of failure. They thereby deprive themselves of the opportunity ever to branch out and explore new ideas. Eventually, they are likely to become boring – and their audiences may become bored too – but they continue with the safe harbor because they are so afraid that if they switch areas, they will be giving up something safe for something unknown. From time to time, Bob meets senior investigators, even

(*cont.*)

in their 60s, who are still following up on their dissertation research. Of course, it may be that they are just fascinated with what they studied in their dissertation. More likely, they just became afraid to move on and try new things. Yet, to have a creative career, people need to explore and try new things.

3. The topic is too difficult for the writer.

The opposite problem from the previous one is the selection of a topic that is too difficult for the writer. In the Theories of Intelligence course, Bob also had a student write a paper on the heritability of intelligence. The student was obviously interested in the topic and wanted to do a good job, but he found that most of the literature went over his head. Understanding the literature on inherited traits requires a knowledge of certain advanced statistical concepts that most undergraduates have not yet encountered. Consequently, it is not easy or perhaps even possible for most of them to write a really sophisticated paper on this topic, unless they are prepared to learn the necessary statistics. This task is both difficult and time consuming. In general, you should make certain that the topic you choose does not require an understanding of concepts that your background does not permit you to grasp.

4. There is inadequate literature on the topic.

For various reasons, some of the potentially most interesting topics in psychology have been little investigated. In some cases, people simply haven't thought much about the topics; in other cases, they have thought about the topics but have found that the topics did not lend themselves to experimental (or other types of) analysis. These topics are not suitable for literature reviews. Before committing yourself to a topic, make sure that there is adequate literature on it. As a student, Bob was interested in how people understand proverbs. The topic seemed to deal with a psychologically important function (one that is tested in several intelligence tests) and seemed to have considerable real-world relevance. He found almost no relevant experimental literature, however. Although there was more literature on related topics, such as metaphor, it was obvious that his tentative choice of a paper topic would have to be changed because there was not sufficient relevant literature.

5. The topic is too broad.

Perhaps the most common mistake that writers make in selecting a topic is to select one that is too broad. This problem is understandable because, before writing the paper, writers often have only a vague idea of how much literature has been published on a given topic. Textbooks usually only scratch the surface. As a result, it is not until one delves into primary sources that one discovers the full extent of the relevant literature.

Once you tentatively decide on a topic, it is a good idea to start compiling a list of references and to scan some of these references quickly before you start taking notes in preparation for writing the paper. By following this procedure, you avoid the pitfall of too broad (or too narrow) a topic. By narrowing your topic before you start note taking, you save yourself the time wasted on taking notes that later will prove of no use in writing the paper.

If you have settled on a topic that proves to be too broad, you should consider ways you can narrow the topic without abandoning it altogether. Consider as an example the topic of problem solving. A search of the available references quickly reveals that this topic is too broad. This topic (and others) might be narrowed in any of several ways:

1. **Restriction by age.** The review is limited to problem solving in adults or children or infants.
2. **Restriction by species.** Only problem solving in humans or in rats is considered.
3. **Restriction by clinical type.** The review deals with problem solving by people who lack mental handicaps or by people with mental handicaps.
4. **Restriction by psychological perspective.** The review is of the behaviorist, information-processing, or psychometric approach to problem solving, or the review compares those perspectives and deals only with issues that are relevant to the comparison.
5. **Restriction by content.** The review deals only with the solution of verbal, mathematical, or spatial problems.

There are obviously many ways in which you can limit the scope of your topic. The best way will depend on the topic, the available literature on the topic, and your interests. Be sure to state in the opening paragraphs of your paper what restrictions you have imposed. A good title will also help the reader understand how you have limited your topic.

What's Wrong Here?

Janine knows that she tends to be a jealous person. She is always keeping an eye on her boyfriend. So she decides she wants to understand jealousy better and decides to do her social-psychology term paper on jealousy.

Answer: Jealousy is just too broad a topic. Janine should decide what aspects of jealousy interest her. For example, she might limit herself to theories of jealousy, or how jealousy develops over time, or how men and women differ in their patterns of jealousy.

4.2 ORGANIZING AND SEARCHING THE LITERATURE

When you conduct a literature review, you obviously will end up with a large number of papers containing much information. You will need somehow to organize that information to write a meaningful review. We have found it useful to organize the collected information in two ways: with regard to authors and with regard to topics.

4.2.1 Author Notes

You can create virtual index cards on the computer that record all the information you will later need to compile the references for your paper. Alternatively, you can use software for the management of bibliographies, such as EndNote (see Chapter 3). The advantage of using such a program is that it contains fields for the necessary information so you cannot forget or lose track of any information about the reference that you might later need. Once you write the paper, the software can also format your references according to APA style (as well as many other styles). In any case, when doing your literature research, you should document each source. The form of documentation differs somewhat depending on the nature of the source. Our information below is based on APA style according to the 6th edition of the *Publication Manual of the American Psychological Association* (2009). Stylistic conventions change in successive editions, so it is important always to consult the most recent version of this or any other publication manual.

1. Journal articles

   Your documentation for journal articles should include (a) the author's last name as well as first and middle initials (or whatever appears in the authorship of the article), (b) the year of publication, (c) the title of the article, (d) the name of the journal, (e) the volume number, and (f) the page numbers of the article. A sample author note would look like this:

   Barden, J., & Petty, R. E. (2008). The mere perception of elaboration creates attitude certainty: Exploring the thoughtfulness heuristic. *Journal of Personality and Social Psychology, 95*(3), 489–509.

2. Books

   Your documentation for books should include (a) the author's last name and first and middle initials, (b) the year of publication, (c) the title of the book, (d) the city in which the book was published, and (e) the name of the publisher. If the city of publication is not well known, include the state as well. Include the country if the city is not in the United States and is not well known. For publishers in Canada or Australia, include the name of the province (e.g., Saskatchewan) in which the work was published. For example:

   Zimbardo, P. G. (2007). *The Lucifer effect: Understanding how good people turn evil.* New York: Random House.

3. Edited books

   Your documentation for articles in edited books should include (a) the author's or authors' last name and first and middle initials (or whatever is used by the author or authors), (b) the year of publication, (c) the title of the book chapter, (d) the editor of the book, (e) the title of the book, (f) the pages of the book in which the chapter appears, (g) the city in which the book was published, and the state if it is not obvious, (h) the name of the publisher. For example:

Keller, P. A., & Lusardi, A. (2012). Employee retirement savings: What we know and are discovering for helping people prepare for life after work. In G. D. Mick, S. Pettigrew, C. Pechmann, & J. L. Ozanna (eds.), *Transformative consumer research for personal and collective well-being* (pp. 445–464). New York: Routledge.

Although this system of documentation may appear cumbersome when you do your research, it will have several advantages later on:

1. **You will have a complete set of references.** There is no possibility of forgetting any sources you need, because you recorded all your sources at the one time when you can't forget them – the time you used them.
2. **You will have complete documentation for each reference.** Researchers sometimes keep a complete list of references but fail to keep complete documentation on each reference. They must then relocate the references later on – if they can find them – to complete the documentation.
3. **The "References" section of the paper will be all but done.** When you are ready to complete this section, simply reorder the author list alphabetically and use the information from the list.

4.2.2 Topic Notes

You should record on each note card (a) the name of the topic at the top, (b) information about that topic, (c) the source of each item of information, and (d) comments.

Sort your notes according to the topic. Each time you encounter a new topic on which you want to take notes, start a new section of note cards. You will save time later on if you avoid multiple entries that express the same topic in different ways. For example, the topics *Rorschach test* and *inkblot test* can be combined (unless more than one inkblot test is used).

Your notes on each topic should be comprehensive enough so that you will not have to return to your sources later. Avoid extraneous words that convey no useful information. In taking notes on arguments, make sure you capture the gist of the arguments so that later you can reconstruct the author's point of view.

For each statement you compile, record the source by writing down the author's last name and the date of publication. If you make a direct quotation or paraphrase, be sure to indicate this fact in your notes and cite appropriate page numbers.

When you make comments on a source or the information supplied in it, indicate clearly in your notes that the comment is yours and not the author's. The best time to make comments on what you read is often when you read it, because at that time, the material and its context are freshest in your mind. These comments will be valuable to you later on, because you will be expected in your paper to evaluate information as well as to summarize it. In reading through psychological literature, you should be constantly evaluating five characteristics of the author's arguments:

1. Validity of arguments

   On what basis does the author make each argument? Are the arguments properly substantiated? How? Almost any psychologist who has reviewed papers for a journal (or read student papers) becomes very sensitive to the question of proper validation. A surprisingly common ploy is for an author to present a theory, which may well be plausible; design an experiment or marshal evidence to test some other theory, which also may be plausible; and then conclude that the original theory is correct. In reading an article or book, therefore, assure yourself not only that a test of a theory is a strong one but also that it assesses the proper theory.

2. Internal consistency of arguments

   Are the arguments consistent, or do they contradict each other? Are the arguments consistent with the author's general point of view? Whereas with validity you are concerned primarily with the relationship between arguments and facts, with internal consistency you are concerned primarily with the relationship between arguments and other arguments. Authors are often unaware of internal inconsistencies in their own data. As a result, readers sometimes spot contradictions that authors have lived with for many years, blithely unaware of their existence.

3. Presuppositions of arguments

   What does the author presuppose in making each argument; especially, what presuppositions does the author make that he or she does not communicate to readers or may not even be aware of? Are the presuppositions realistic? Do the presuppositions strengthen or weaken the impact of the argument? Consider, for example, the statement: "The Bozo theory of cognitive development is incorrect because it is based on the assumption that cognitive development is continuous."

What presuppositions does the statement make? First, it presupposes that the Bozo theory assumes continuity in cognitive development. Second, it presupposes that the theory making this assumption is incorrect. Third, it presupposes (incorrectly, as it turns out) that there is such a theory as the Bozo theory of cognitive development.

What's Wrong Here?

"We administered to all students the Shtungus Test of Moral Development. College students actually had lower scores, on average, than did high school students, suggesting that college actually may have, or at least be associated with, a detrimental effect on moral development."

Answer: The argument assumes that the Shtungus Test of Moral Development is a valid test of moral development. It would be incumbent on the author of the statement to show that the test is indeed a valid measure of moral development. Moreover, the score differences may be due to age rather than any effect of college education.

---

4. Implications of arguments

What are the implications of each argument; especially, what implications does the author overlook? Do the implications strengthen or weaken the impact of the argument? Are these implications consistent with others reached from other arguments, both in the same paper and across the literature? Consider, for example, this statement: "I violently object to violent objections." What is the obvious implication of the statement?

5. Importance of arguments

Is a particular argument an important one, and therefore one you will want to describe in detail in your paper? Or is it unimportant, and hence not worthy of mention, or worthy of mention only in passing?

A common flaw in papers is to emphasize all arguments equally, regardless of their importance. This flaw inevitably reduces the impact of the paper as a whole.

By keeping in mind these five criteria for evaluating the literature you read, and by writing down your evaluative comments immediately subsequent to the relevant argument, you will supply yourself with much of the substance you will later need to write your paper. Later on, of course, you can always expand on or change your evaluation. But you will have your evaluative notes from the topic cards to work with rather than having to start from scratch.

By compiling topic notes, you will gain several advantages: first, when you are ready to write your paper, you will have available to you all the information you need to write it. You won't have to do any more library work at the last minute when you may no longer have time to do it. Second, you will have available to you the source of each argument or piece of information. You won't have to try to remember who said what. Third, you will find it easier to organize your paper than you might have otherwise. The reason for this greater ease is that the topic cards form the input to the next step, preparing an outline.

When possible, save electronic or print versions of original sources, or at least retrieval details for these sources, *in addition to* your note cards. As you start writing your paper, article, book, or whatever, you may find that you need more information from your sources than you put in your note cards. If you have the original sources or retrieval details for them, you more easily can go back to the original sources when you need them.

4.3 PREPARING AN OUTLINE

4.3.1 Use of Topic Notes

After you have finished note taking, you are ready to prepare an outline. The topic notes form the basis of the outline, because they readily can be used as headings and subheadings. Write down all the topics on one or more pieces of paper. Then, cut out strips of paper, one for each topic. Or, if you are using a computer, you can use an outlining feature that is available in most word-processing programs. Your job now is to rearrange the topics to form a logical order of presentation. The various topics need not and should not be at the same level of specificity. Some of the topics form major headings, others form minor headings, and others are nested under these minor headings. You may have to add introductory and concluding sections to the outline, as well as any intermediate headings that are needed for smooth transitions. The lowest level of subordination for each heading should represent a single sentence of the final paper.

4.3.2 Types of Outlines

Once you have ordered the headings of your outline, you must decide on one of three ways in which you can complete the outline (Harris & Blake, 1976). We will discuss the three kinds of outlines with reference to a miniature example in which we will compare two personality tests, the Thematic Apperception Test (TAT) and the Minnesota Multiphasic Personality Inventory (MMPI).

4.3.2.1 The Keyword Outline

In this kind of outline, you restrict yourself to keywords at each level of description. For example:

I. Introduction
II. Content
   A. TAT: pictorial
   B. MMPI: verbal
III. Administration
   A. TAT: pictorial
   B. MMPI: verbal
IV. Scoring
   A. TAT: oral
   B. MMPI: written
V. Conclusion

4.3.2.2 The Topic Outline

In this kind of outline, you use phrases and clauses at each level of description. For example:

I. Comparison between the TAT and MMPI
II. Type of content
   A. TAT: pictures of people in various settings, some realistic and others not
   B. MMPI: statements describing behaviors or beliefs that subjects mark as true or false as descriptions of themselves

    III. Mode of administration

        A. TAT: pictures sequentially presented by examiner to subject, who supplies a narrative of events leading to, during, and following from the pictured scene

        B. MMPI: booklet containing entire set of statements given to subjects, who proceed through the booklet at their own pace

    IV. Method of scoring

        A. TAT: scored subjectively, often using Murray's taxonomy of needs and press

        B. MMPI: scored objectively by means of a separate key for each diagnostic scale

    V. Differences: content, administration, scoring

4.3.2.3 The Sentence Outline

In this kind of outline, you use complete sentences at each level of description. For example:

    I. This outline compares the TAT and MMPI with respect to content, administration, and scoring.

    II. The tests differ in type of content.

        A. The TAT consists of a series of pictures of people in various settings, some realistic and others not.

        B. The MMPI, however, consists of a series of statements describing behaviors or beliefs that subjects mark as either true or false as descriptions of themselves.

    III. The tests also differ in mode of administration.

        A. In the TAT, pictures are sequentially presented by the examiner to the subject, who supplies a narrative of events leading to, during, and following from the pictured scene.

        B. In the MMPI, a booklet containing the entire set of statements is given to subjects, who proceed through the booklet at their own pace.

    IV. Finally, the tests are scored by different methods.

        A. The TAT is scored subjectively, often using Murray's taxonomy of needs and press.

        B. The MMPI is scored objectively by means of a separate key for each diagnostic scale.

    V. In conclusion, the tests differ substantially in content, administration, and scoring.

4.3.3 Choosing a Type of Outline

You should use the type of outline that most facilitates your writing. People vary according to which type of outline they find most facilitates their writing. Some people find a keyword outline most helpful because it organizes their thoughts while leaving them maximum flexibility in actually writing the paper; others find a keyword outline too sparse in content to be of much use. Some people like a sentence outline because it essentially writes their paper for them; others find a sentence outline time consuming to write and of no greater use in organizing their thoughts than a topical outline. By experimenting with all types of outlines, you will learn from your own experience which type is most suitable for you.

4.3.4 Organization of Outlines

Outlines can be organized in many ways, and many decisions regarding organization are unique to each particular situation. Generally, the organization of your paper should be logical and straightforward; you should lead your reader from one point you make to the next, and so on. Don't organize your paper around individual studies but around models or viewpoints. Five principles of organization are common to all outlines and the papers that evolve from them:

■ **The organization should include a beginning, a middle, and an end, in which you say what you're going to say, then say it, and then say what you've said.**

When readers begin a paper, they need some general statements that tell them what the paper is about and how it is organized; without this orientation, they may become lost almost as soon as they start the paper. When readers complete the main part of the paper, they need a summary of the main ideas as well as whatever final comments you want to supply; without this review, readers may not realize what you consider to be your main points.

Suppose that the keyword outline presented earlier consists only of a middle section:

I. Content
   A. TAT: pictorial
   B. MMPI: verbal
II. Administration
   A. TAT: oral
   B. MMPI: written
III. Scoring
   A. TAT: subjective
   B. MMPI: objective

The reader of a paper based on this outline would encounter immediately a comparison between the content of the TAT and the MMPI, without any idea of what the paper intends to accomplish or how it intends to accomplish it. The reader would finish the paper without any idea of what the author believed to be the main points or of what conclusions the author wanted to draw. Although the main body of the paper is well organized, the reader is left with no sense of direction or purpose in the paper.

■ **Once you decide on a principle of organization, stick with it.**

Beginning writers often change their way of organizing papers midstream, usually without first informing the reader that the change is about to take place. The change confuses the reader. If you must change your organization principle, be sure to let the reader know. But avoid the change if possible. Consider the plight of the reader faced with a paper based on the keyword outline on the left here. The original keyword outline is reproduced on the right:

I. Introduction	I. Introduction
II. Content	II. Content
A. TAT: pictorial	A. TAT: pictorial
B. MMPI: verbal	B. MMPI: verbal
III. TAT	III. Administration
A. Administration: oral	A. TAT: oral
B. Scoring: subjective	B. MMPI: written
IV. MMPI	IV. Scoring
A. Administration: written	A. TAT: subjective
B. Scoring: objective	B. MMPI: objective
V. Conclusion	V. Conclusion

Notice that the outline on the left switches its principles of organization, beginning with topic III. Topic II is organized by theme, whereas topics III and IV are organized by test. The outline on the left makes obvious what the careless writer hopes will remain hidden – that the paper is confusing and the author is confused.

■ **Organize your writing thematically.**

Thematic organization enhances the clarity of a paper. The keyword outline as originally presented was organized thematically. The three themes were content, administration, and scoring. The reader would complete a paper based on this outline with a clear idea of how the TAT and MMPI differ in these three respects. Compare this original outline, presented on the right, to the new outline presented on the left. This new outline is organized by test:

I.	Introduction		I.	Introduction
II.	TAT		II.	Content
	A. Content: pictorial			A. TAT: pictorial
	B. Administration: oral			B. MMPI: verbal
	C. Scoring: subjective		III.	Administration
III.	MMPI			A. TAT: oral
	A. Content: verbal			B. MMPI: written
	B. Administration: written		IV.	Scoring
	C. Scoring: objective			A. TAT: subjective
IV.	Conclusion			B. MMPI: objective
			V.	Conclusion

The organization by test in the outline on the left is not confusing, but it is inferior to the thematic organization on the right. In the thematic organization, readers can compare the two tests on each theme as they read through the main part of the paper, gradually developing a perspective on how the tests differ. In the organization by test, readers are unable to begin comparing the tests until they are halfway through the main part of the paper. By this time, readers may have forgotten the characteristics of the first test, because they had no motivation to remember them. In reading the section of the paper on the MMPI, readers probably will have to refer back to the section on the TAT to draw a comparison. If readers are unwilling to spend the time or effort doing what the writer should have done, they may never understand the comparison.

The same principle would apply if, say, one wished to compare the viewpoints of Sigmund Freud and Konrad Lorenz on aggression toward oneself, aggression toward others, and aggression toward objects. The preferred way to organize the paper would be by the successive themes of aggression toward self, others, and objects, not by the successive authors, Freud and Lorenz.

There are two exceptions to this principle. The first arises when there are no well-developed themes in the literature you plan to review. Each theorist, for example, may deal with a different set of issues. The second exception arises when your focus is genuinely on the objects of comparison rather than on the themes along which they are compared. In a book presenting theories of personality, for example, the author's emphasis might be on the individual perspective of each theorist rather than on the themes dealt with in each theory.

■ **Organize your outline hierarchically.**

Beginning writers tend to overuse coordination of ideas and to underuse subordination of ideas. If a paper contains a large number of main ideas, the reader will have some difficulty understanding the ideas and more difficulty remembering them. When you find yourself with a large number of main ideas, try to subordinate some of them. You will then communicate the same number of ideas at the same time that you increase the effectiveness with which you communicate them.

Suppose that the keyword outline for the tests had taken this form:

I. Introduction
II. TAT content: pictorial
III. MMPI content: verbal
IV. TAT administration: oral
V. MMPI administration: written
VI. TAT scoring: subjective
VII. MMPI scoring: objective
VIII. Conclusion

Notice that this outline is much harder to follow than the original keyword outline because all ideas are presented at the same level, with no subordination. The outline therefore is much less effective in comparing the two personality tests.

■ **Organize for your audience.**

In arranging your outline, it is essential that you keep your audience in mind. The level of description for each topic in the outline should be appropriate for the target audience; level of description that is adequate for one audience may be inadequate for another. Consider, for example, the original keyword outline presented earlier. The introductory heading has no subheadings subordinated under it. Because the lowest level of subordination under each heading represents one sentence, the introduction will be just one sentence in length. A brief introduction of this kind may be adequate for a professional seeking a one-paragraph description of salient differences between the TAT and the MMPI, but it probably is inadequate for someone unfamiliar with personality tests. Such a person requires more orientation to the topic of the exposition. An expanded introduction is therefore appropriate:

I. Introduction: personality tests
  A. Purpose
  B. General characteristics
  C. Divergences
    1. Personality tests in general
    2. TAT and MMPI in particular

The general reader will now be able to follow the remainder of the exposition.

4.3.5 Advantages of Outlines

Students often wonder whether outlines are worth the time and trouble. Using outlines has three advantages that more than offset the extra work they require:

1. Outlines help you organize your writing.

In writing the actual paper, organization will be just one of many concerns you have. Because there are so many different things to keep track of in writing the paper, and because your ability to keep track of many things at once is limited, organization will receive only limited attention. Because the organization of a paper is so important, however, it pays to insert a step prior to writing the paper in which you can devote your full attention to organizing the paper.

2. Outlines prevent omission of relevant topics.

In doing your research or in compiling your topic notes, you may have inadvertently omitted a topic that you intended or should have thought to include in your paper. Omissions are much easier for the author to spot in an outline than in a paper. They are also much easier to correct before writing of the paper has begun.

3. Outlines prevent inclusion of irrelevant topics.

Authors sometimes find that a topic that had seemed relevant to the paper in the early stages of research no longer seems relevant when the research is being organized. Irrelevant material shows itself in an obvious way during preparation of an outline, because the material seems to have no place in the outline. By discovering irrelevancies during preparation of the outline, authors can discard the irrelevancies so that later they do not distract them in writing the paper.

Give It Some More Thought

Are there any potential disadvantages to outlines? For example, outlines may create a certain rigidity: they may tie you down to an organization that originally seemed adequate but turns out not to be once you have learned more about the topic on which you are writing.

4.4 WRITING THE PAPER

In writing your literature review, you should keep several points in mind (see also Eisenberg, 2000):

1. The message

Authors of literature reviews are at particular risk of writing long and elaborate papers in which they lose their readers. You have reviewed a large amount of literature that can be confusing at times, so it is all the more important that you provide your readers with a thread throughout your paper and a clear message they can take away from reading your work.

2. Breadth of review

How many publications you include in your review depends on your topic and the goal you want to achieve with writing your paper. Generally, you should discuss a good part of the empirical literature and make sure that different methodological approaches are being considered. You don't have to discuss every study in detail, however.

Just make sure that the literature that you do include is in fact relevant to your endeavor.

3. Accuracy

Always pay attention that you do not misrepresent the results of studies you include in your literature review. It is OK to disagree with the author's interpretation of results, however.

4. Critique

It is important to include in your literature review a critique of methods, conclusions, and strengths and weaknesses of the works you reviewed. You should do so not study by study, however, but rather by evaluating entire bodies of work. Remember to be fair and not merely to derogate other people's work.

Experience Is the Best Teacher

Bob once edited a journal of literature reviews. Perhaps the most common reason for turning down submitted articles was that although they were literature reviews, they were not creatively organized nor were they analytically sharp. That is, they summarized literature without organizing it in a novel and meaningful fashion and they failed to analyze adequately the strengths and weaknesses of the literature being reviewed.

---

5. The end

The ending of your literature review should not only summarize findings but also draw new conclusions, point out new explanations, or suggest further steps for the exploration of the problem.

4.5 EVALUATING THE PAPER YOURSELF AND SEEKING OTHERS' FEEDBACK ON IT

Once you are finished writing your review, think back to the five criteria for evaluating authors' arguments that were described earlier. Readers will evaluate your paper by the same (or similar) criteria to those you used to evaluate the papers and books you read.

1. Validity

Are your arguments consistent with the literature you reviewed? Have you explained inconsistencies? Have you properly substantiated each of your arguments?

2. Internal consistency

Are your arguments consistent with each other? Are they consistent with your general point of view?

3. Presuppositions

Have you made clear to the reader what you presuppose? Are your presuppositions reasonable ones that the reader is likely to accept?

Have you discussed the impact of your presuppositions on your conclusions?

4. Implications

Have you discussed the implications of your arguments? Are these implications realistic? Do these implications strengthen or weaken your arguments?

5. Importance

Have you emphasized your important arguments and conclusions and subordinated the less important ones? Have you explained why you view certain arguments and conclusions as important and others as less so?

By using these five criteria to evaluate your literature review, you will improve its quality. Later, we will consider in more detail some criteria for evaluating the quality of all psychology papers.

CHECKLIST FOR LITERATURE REVIEWS

- ☐ Does your paper have a clear message?
- ☐ Did you discuss the relevant literature (and no more or less)?
- ☐ Have you checked that you did not misinterpret the results of the studies you included?
- ☐ Have you fairly evaluated the bodies of work included in your review?
- ☐ Does your ending include new conclusions, explanations, or further steps for research?
- ☐ Are your arguments consistent with the literature?

☐ Were you able to explain inconsistencies? Are your arguments substantiated?

☐ Are your arguments consistent with each other and with your overall message?

☐ Have you clarified your presuppositions in the beginning, and are they ones that your readers will likely accept?

☐ Have you stated the implications of your arguments, and are they realistic?

☐ Have you organized your arguments and conclusions into more and less important ones, and have you explained why they differ in their importance?

5 | Planning and Writing the Experimental Research Paper

When research psychologists talk about writing a paper, they are talking about a lengthy and complicated chain of events that includes a great deal more than just reporting research results. In this chapter, we outline these events from start to finish:

1. Planning your experimental research project
   - Getting an idea
   - Selecting independent variables
   - Selecting dependent variables
   - Deciding on between-subjects and within-subjects variables
   - Deciding how data will be analyzed
   - Selecting participants
   - Choosing experimental materials
   - Choosing a means of presenting experimental materials
   - Writing directions
   - Deciding on a means of scoring data
   - Writing a consent form
   - Writing a debriefing sheet
   - Getting approval from the institutional review board
   - Conducting a pilot study
2. Executing the experimental research
3. Data analysis
4. Reporting the experimental research
   - Title
   - Author's name and institutional affiliation
   - Abstract
   - Introduction
   - Method

- Results
- Discussion
- References
- Appendix
- Order of sections

5.1 PLANNING EXPERIMENTAL RESEARCH

5.1.1 Getting an Idea

The basis of any good research is a viable idea that results in a study that contributes to the current state of knowledge. However, getting ideas, and especially getting good ideas, often turns out to be one of the hardest parts of research. If you need help forming ideas for your research, please read Chapter 2.

5.1.2 Selecting Independent Variables

After you have come up with an idea, you need a way to test it. To test the idea, you need one or more independent variables. In random-assignment experiments (i.e., experiments in which participants are randomly assigned to groups), independent variables are those variables that are manipulated by the experimenter. In an experiment to test people's susceptibility to persuasive communications, for example, possible independent variables include (a) amount of exposure to persuasive communications, (b) content of persuasive communications, and (c) level of agreement between participants' initial attitudes and the position advocated by the persuasive communications. Once you have chosen your independent variable(s), you must decide how many and what level of them to use. For example, you might include in a persuasibility experiment three levels of exposure to the persuasive communications (no exposure, 10 minutes of exposure, and 1 hour of exposure) and two communications (one message dealing with capital punishment and one message dealing with compulsory use of seat belts in cars).

In most random-assignment experiments, there are a large number of potentially interesting independent variables, but it is possible to choose only a small fraction of them. In many experimental designs (in particular, ones that are "crossed"), each time you add an independent variable to your experiment, you increase the size of your experiment multiplicatively. You must therefore choose your independent variables with care. In a persuasibility experiment, the type of font in which the persuasive communications are presented is not likely to affect the outcome of the experiment, and hence it would be a poor choice of an independent variable. The medium of communication – oral or written – might affect the outcome of the experiment, and hence would be a possible choice. The amount of exposure to the persuasive communications is almost certain to affect the outcome of the experiment, and hence is a very good choice.

In selecting independent variables in random-assignment experiments, there is usually a trade-off between experimental control and ecological validity. Experimental control refers to the ease with which the experimenter can manipulate and later monitor the effects of the independent variables. Ecological validity refers to the generalizability of the obtained results to real-world situations. Total loss of experimental control can lead to uninterpretable results. Disregard of ecological validity can lead to trivial results. Researchers differ widely in the importance they assign to each of these items: everyone must strike some sort of balance between the two.

5.1.3 Selecting Dependent Variables

In addition to choosing one or more independent variables, you must select one or more dependent variables. The dependent variable is the variable affected by (dependent on) the independent variables. It serves as the outcome to be measured. Whereas it is common to choose more than one independent variable in a single experiment, it is relatively less common to choose more than one dependent variable. When multiple dependent variables are used, they are usually studied separately, without much attempt to interrelate the outcomes. The major reason for psychologists' reluctance to deal with multiple outcomes is the greater difficulty involved in statistical analysis, not the inability of multiple outcomes to provide more meaningful data than single outcomes. However, multivariate methods do make it possible to test hypotheses regarding multiple dependent variables.

In most experiments, there are at least several possible dependent variables of interest to choose from, so the choice must be made carefully. In the persuasibility experiment, two possible dependent variables are (a) response to an opinion questionnaire administered at the end of the experimental session and (b) willingness one month later to join a citizens' lobbying group devoted to the cause advocated by the communication. Note that the first dependent variable measures immediate, overt opinion changes within the context of the experiment, whereas the latter dependent variable measures delayed covert opinion change outside the context of the experiment. Ideally, an experiment will include both kinds of measures. If only one is to be chosen, the experimenter must evaluate an important trade-off that psychological researchers frequently confront. The first measured outcome is much more likely than the second to be influenced by the experimental manipulation, but it is also of much less practical importance. Even if the opinion questionnaire administered at the end of the experiment shows a significant effect of the experimental treatment, one has no assurance that the effect will last for any long period of time, or even for any time beyond the conclusion of the experimental session. The second measured outcome is of considerable practical interest, but in relying on it, the experimenter may be throwing away any chance of an observable experimental effect. The experimenter must therefore decide on a dependent variable that gives a reasonable chance of obtaining an outcome that is both statistically and practically significant.

Not all studies, of course, are random-assignment experiments. Some studies are quasi-experiments or correlational studies. Correlational studies require different kinds of procedures. For example, in many such studies, the variables are pre-existing, as when one correlates scores on an ability test (independent variable) with grades in elementary school (dependent variable), or when one correlates socioeconomic status (SES) (independent variable) with a measure of children's psychological well-being (dependent variable). In such studies, the independent variables for one investigation may be the dependent variable for another. For example, in another study, grades in elementary school may become the independent variable to predict the dependent variable of grades in secondary school.

Moreover, correlational studies may use several independent variables to predict a single dependent variable (or in rare cases, multiple dependent variables). For example, one might predict grades in college (dependent variable) from both an ability test score (independent variable) and high-school grades (a second independent variable).

Thus, in correlational studies, the distinction between independent and dependent variables can at times be less clear-cut, and what is an independent variable in one study may be a dependent variable in another study, or even later in the same study.

5.1.4 Deciding on Between-Subjects and Within-Subjects Variables

Each independent variable can be studied either between subjects or within subjects. A between-subjects independent variable is one in which a given participant receives only one level of the experimental treatment. A within-subjects independent variable is one in which a given participant receives all levels of the experimental treatment.

Return again to the persuasability experiment. If both independent variables were between-subjects variables, then each participant would receive (a) no exposure, 10 minutes of exposure, or 1 hour of exposure to (b) either the communication on capital punishment or to that on the compulsory use of seat belts. Because there are three levels of the first independent variable and two levels of the second, there are 3 × 2 levels in all, or six different experimental groups, each composed of different participants. If both independent variables were within subjects, all participants would receive both persuasive communications and would be tested before receiving the communications, 10 minutes after receiving the communications, and 1 hour after receiving the communications for their current opinions on each.

In some cases, it is easy to decide whether to test a particular variable between subjects or within subjects. In other cases, however, the decision is a difficult one for the experimenter to make, and a potentially consequential one. The experimenter must evaluate a delicate trade-off. On the one hand, earlier within-subjects treatments may spoil the participant for later treatments. In other words, the participants receiving one experimental treatment may have unforeseen consequences for their responses to subsequent treatments. On the other hand, within-subjects designs guarantee the matching of participants across treatment conditions, because the participants are the same. This matching can be particularly important when there are relatively small numbers of participants.

Consider again the design of the persuasability experiment. Suppose we administer the three opinion questionnaires – before treatment, 10 minutes after treatment, and 1 hour after treatment – to the same participants. We run the risk that the mere answering of an earlier questionnaire will influence participants' responses to later questionnaires. This influence can contaminate the results and render equivocal any interpretation of them. Suppose that instead we administer the three opinion questionnaires to three different groups of participants. We then have no way of knowing that our groups are matched in important ways. They may differ in initial level of agreement with the persuasive communication; they may differ in persuasibility (so that some are more susceptible by nature than others to persuasion attempts); or they may differ in the speed at which they assimilate new information, and hence in the speed at which their attitudes are affected by new information. The list can go on ad infinitum. Although random sampling of participants provides some protection against poor matching of groups, the adequacy of this protection depends on the size of the sample. Unless groups are quite large, protection may be inadequate. With six different groups in the full design of the persuasibility experiment, it is unlikely that very large groups can be obtained in a reasonably economical way. In practice, random sampling is often very difficult to accomplish. For example, in school-based research, random samples may be unavailable. One often ends up with a sample of convenience because that is what is available to one.

A compromise can be worked out whereby all participants receive the opinion survey before treatment, but only some receive it after 10 minutes of treatment, whereas others receive it after 1 hour. This compromise, however, does not solve the basic dilemma, because the participants' receipt of the pretest can still affect their performance on the subsequent test. In deciding whether to test a particular variable between subjects or within subjects, experimenters must decide which kind of risk they are more willing to take.

Give It Some More Thought

What are some of the advantages and disadvantages of a within-subjects experimental design? For example, you might point out that an advantage of within-subjects designs is that you need fewer subjects but a disadvantage is that you often have to test them over multiple sessions and they may not show up for all the sessions.

5.1.5 Deciding How Data Will Be Analyzed

Major decisions about data analysis should be made prior to the collection of data. There are two reasons these decisions should be made in advance. First, statistical tests must be interpreted more cautiously if decided on post hoc. As it is sometimes said, everyone has 20/20 hindsight. Second, if major decisions about data analysis are not made in advance, experimenters run the risk of finding later that the experimental design does not permit them to analyze the data the way they want to or to analyze the data at all. Decisions about specific kinds of data analysis require a statistical background that is beyond the scope of this book.

Experience Is the Best Teacher

Unfortunately, different journals have different expectations regarding data analysis, at least in 2016, when this book was being completed. Some insist on conventional significance testing, some prefer other forms of analysis, such as standard-error bands, and others may prefer something different again. Therefore, before submitting an article to a journal, you should make sure that the form of data analysis you are doing is appropriate for the journal. Sometimes, the journals do not publish their data-analytic requirements or preferences so you might want to consult recent articles in the journal to see how data similar to yours have been analyzed.

5.1.6 Selecting Participants

Three major decisions must be made in selecting participants. First, from what population will participants be selected? Second, how will participants be selected from this population? Third, how many participants will be selected?

The population from which participants are selected is the population to which the experimental results will be generalizable. Hence, if one is interested in making generalizations to the general population of the United States or another country, then one must select a sample that is representative of the general population of the United States or the other country. If one is interested in a population of gifted children, then one must select a sample representative of gifted children. The question of generalizability of results is often quietly placed in the background of an experimental report, if it is discussed at all, because most experiments are conducted on samples that are not representative of the population of interest. Many of the experiments conducted today use college students as participants, although the experimenters' intent is to generalize the result to the population of adult Americans (or even to adults all over the world).

One faces a trade-off in deciding on a population from which to draw participants. On the one hand, researchers usually want to generalize their results to as broad a population as possible. On the other hand, participants are much easier to obtain from some populations than from others. College and university students are often readily available, whereas other groups of adults are much harder to corral into the laboratory.

Participants can be selected in any number of ways from the population. The two most common models of selection are the random sample and the stratified sample. In a random sampling procedure, the experimenter selects individuals from the population at random. In a stratified sampling procedure, the experimenter selects individuals in a way that ensures that major subdivisions of the population are represented in some proportion, usually the population proportion. For example, if 30 percent of the general population are Caucasian, then the sample will have about 30 percent Caucasians as well. In practice, it is almost never possible to obtain a purely random or stratified sample, because the entire population is not available to the experimenter. The participants who are available usually form a biased sample of the population from which they are drawn. Even if one's population is college students, for example, the sample of college students at any one university will inevitably be biased.

Decisions about numbers of participants are usually made on the basis of two considerations. First, how many participants can be tested feasibly, given the constraints of time, money, and participant availability? Second, how many participants are needed to show statistical significance for an effect of a certain magnitude? This latter consideration involves statistical concepts beyond the scope of this book. The basic idea, though, is that for a small treatment effect to be statistically significant, a large sample is needed. The greater the magnitude of the treatment effect, the smaller the sample size that is needed to show statistical significance.

What's Wrong Here?

In Jason's college, men and women have separate dormitories. Jason is interested in the college students' views on the possibility of co-ed dorms. The college is planning to hold a meeting of students to discuss whether dorms should go co-ed, and Jason decides to pass out his survey at the meeting, as he believes that the students attending the meeting will be interested in the issue and thus more likely to return his survey.

Answer: Students attending a meeting on the issue of co-ed dorms are unlikely to be anything like a random sample of students at the college. Rather, they are likely to be biased merely because they are so interested in the issue. For example, it may be more likely that students who bother to attend the meeting are those who are less satisfied with the present system.

5.1.7 Choosing Experimental Materials

Four considerations must be taken into account in choosing materials for an experiment:

> Do the materials represent a reasonable sample of the universe of materials to which one wants to generalize?
> Are there enough materials to obtain generalizable measurements?
> Are the materials suitable for the participants to whom they will be administered?
> Are the materials suitable for testing the hypothesis?

Researchers tend to pay too little attention to the generalizability of experimental materials. General conclusions about a broad universe of materials are often drawn on the basis of an experiment or several experiments using just one kind of material. Suppose, for example, that an investigator is interested in how people solve syllogisms.

A participant is presented with two premises, called the major premise and the minor premise, and a conclusion. The participant's task is to say whether the conclusion follows logically from the premises. A simple syllogism would take the form:

1. All B are C.   (Major premise)
   All A are B.   (Minor premise)
   All A are C.   (Conclusion)

As an investigator, you might vary structural properties of the syllogism. For example, you might substitute for the major premise statements like "Some B are C," "No B are C," or "Some B are not C."

Your theory of how people solve syllogisms, however, could not be complete unless you took into account content as well as structure. Suppose, for example, that we leave the structure of the syllogism unchanged, varying only its content. Compare the difficulty of the following two syllogisms with each other and with the foregoing syllogism:

2. All birds are animals.
   All canaries are birds.
   All canaries are animals.

3. All birds are canaries.
   All animals are birds.
   All animals are canaries.

You will probably find, as others have found before you, that the content of the syllogism greatly affects its difficulty. Most people find syllogisms like (2) easier to comprehend than syllogisms like (3) because the premises of the former syllogism conform to real-world experience, whereas the premises of the latter syllogism violate it. A complete theory of syllogistic reasoning would have to take into account these effects of content, something no theory yet does. The general point, of course, is that no theory can be accepted with confidence unless it has been shown to explain data for a wide variety of experimental materials.

It is important to have not only a relatively broad sampling of materials but a relatively large sampling as well. The syllogism experiment would be unimpressive if it had three different kinds of content but only one syllogism of each kind. To obtain reliable measurements, it is usually necessary to have at least several replications of each kind of item.

Investigators must take care that their experimental materials are suitable for the target participant population. Syllogisms such as the preceding ones would be suitable for an adult population, but not for a population of 6-year-old children. If the children failed to solve syllogisms like the foregoing ones, investigators would be unable to determine whether the failure was due to inability to reason syllogistically or to an inability to comprehend the materials. The investigators might use concrete play materials instead of verbal ones. For example, they might show the children plastic replicas of animals and then demonstrate to them that all the elephants are gray and that all the animals with trunks are elephants. The children would then have to indicate whether all the animals with trunks are gray. Special care would have to be taken to ensure that the children understood the nature of the task.

The materials one uses must be appropriate to the hypothesis under investigation. Suppose, for example, that an investigator wants to test the hypothesis that syllogisms with counterfactual conclusions are more difficult to solve than syllogisms with factual conclusions. The following two sets of syllogisms would provide poor tests of this hypothesis:

Factual conclusions	Counterfactual conclusions
1. All integers are rational. All integers are rational numbers. All integers are natural numbers.	1. All rational numbers are natural numbers. All natural numbers are integers. All natural numbers are rational.
2. All sunny days are enjoyable days. All bright days are sunny days. All bright days are enjoyable days.	2. All sunny days are unenjoyable days. All cloudy days are sunny days. All cloudy days are unenjoyable days.

The first syllogism is inappropriate because most participants (except, perhaps, in a population of mathematicians) would not realize which syllogism has a factual conclusion and which has a counterfactual conclusion. The second syllogism is inappropriate because the conclusions (as well as the premises) are matters of opinion; although some people might agree with the first conclusion and disagree with the second conclusion, these agreements and disagreements are not over matters of fact.

5.1.8 Choosing a Means of Presenting Experimental Materials

Experimental materials usually can be presented in many forms. The form of presentation generally is determined largely by convenience, because little is known about the effects of the form of presentation on performance. Investigators usually assume that the effects of form of presentation on performance are trivial. Suppose, for example, that an investigator is interested in the effect of concreteness on free recall of a list of words. The hypothesis is that more concrete words, like *banana*, will be better recalled than more abstract words, like *freedom*. To test this hypothesis, the investigator compares recall of two lists of words, one concrete and the other abstract.

The list of words might be presented either visually or auditorily. If the words are presented visually, they might be presented via flash cards, slides, or a computer terminal. If the words are presented auditorily, they might be presented by a person speaking who is physically present, by tape or CD player, or a by computer. Modality of presentation (visual or auditory) and vehicle of presentation (e.g., computer, CD player) within modality might affect level of recall, but it is assumed that this effect will be constant across treatment conditions. Thus, if on average two fewer concrete words are recalled with an auditory presentation rather than a visual one, it is assumed that, on average, two fewer abstract words will be recalled as well. The investigator is not likely to use both auditory and visual presentations to show generality of the hypothesis to both modalities. In some experiments – for example, experiments on vision or audition – modality of presentation will be a critical variable. In most experiments, however, it is considered relatively unimportant. Investigators turn their attention to variables that are more likely to influence their results. In preparing experimental materials, you may not reproduce copyrighted material, such as tests or reading passages, without permission. Doing so subjects you to the possibility of legal action against you.

Experience Is the Best Teacher

In the past, experimenters, especially those doing studies in elementary and secondary schools, sometimes were reluctant to use computers to present materials because so many students had little or no experience with computers. Today, the opposite is true: so many students are used to using computers that they may find it more difficult to, say, write essays on paper. A problem arises in that a lot depends on the socioeconomic status and cultural background of the children. There still may be groups of students who have little or no experience with computers. In choosing a means for presenting stimulus materials, therefore, it is important to consider the characteristics of the students to be tested.

5.1.9 Writing Directions

Once you have decided on the experimental task and materials, you have to write directions telling participants what is expected of them.

It is essential that the directions be clear and complete, because unclear or incomplete instructions can result in participants doing a task different from the one you intend. The directions may be presented auditorily or visually. We usually have the experimenter present the directions aloud while the participant reads them silently. Participants thereby are exposed to the directions in two modalities. In the free-recall experiment, the following directions might be used:

Directions for Free-Recall Task

In this task, the experimenter will read aloud a list of words. You should listen carefully to these words. After the experimenter has completed reading the list, he or she will pause, and then say the word *recall*. At that point, you should recall as many words as you can from the list in any order you wish. Write your answers on the sheet in front of you. If you are not sure of an item, then guess. Your recall will be scored for the number of words correctly recalled.

If you have any questions, please ask them now.

5.1.10 Deciding on a Means of Scoring Data

Because scoring can be time-consuming, the layout of participants' response sheets or booklets should be planned carefully in advance. An easy-to-score layout can save many hours of work later on. If the participants' responses are simple – letters, numbers, words – their answers usually can be recorded in successive columns of each page. An easily readable format will facilitate scoring, possibly enabling you to devise a stencil key that can be placed either next to or over each column. If responses are made by computer, be sure they are easy for subjects to make.

If the data will be entered for subsequent computer analysis, it is wise to show your answer-sheet layout to the data-entry person. If the layout is easily readable, that person (which may very well be you!) may be able to enter the data directly from the answer sheets, bypassing the time-consuming step of coding the data.

5.1.11 Writing a Consent Form

Some years ago, government and other funding agencies started requiring experimenters supported by their funds to have all participants sign statements of informed consent before participating in experiments. Universities require such statements as well. In the case of child participants, parents are required to sign. Children, if old enough, often can provide verbal assent to participation. Researchers are also required to have their experiments approved by a human subjects committee/institutional review board at their college or university before they conduct the experiments (see below). In view of the widespread concern today with the protection of participants, it is probably wise to use consent forms even for informal class projects. A sample consent form (in this case, for an experiment on decision making in groups) is shown in Figure 5.1.

The consent form must be modified to meet the needs of each particular experiment. The forms must always include, however, (a) a statement of informed consent, (b) sufficient information about the experiment so that the participant's consent is truly informed, and (c) the participant's signature and date.

The consent form here first informs participants about the purpose and procedure of the experiment. If your experiment involves deception, you should still be as truthful as possible in the explanation. Experiments involving deception will be reviewed with special attention by the institutional review board (IRB) to ensure that no harm will be done to the participants. It is then even more important to debrief participants after the experiment. In the case of children,

DECLARATION OF INFORMED CONSENT

1. *Invitation to Participate*

You are invited to participate in this study concerning the perception of other groups. An overview of the procedure is given below.

2. *Purpose*

We are conducting this survey to assess people's attitudes toward various groups.

3. *Description of Procedures*

The survey consists of several questions assessing how you feel toward two groups. It also comprises some personality measures.

4. *Risks and Inconveniences*

The physical, psychological, social, or economic risks associated with participation in this experiment are minimal. The only known inconvenience is the time you spend here today (approximately 30 minutes).

5. *Benefits*

The benefit of participating in this study is purely educational. After you have completed the measures, the experimenter will discuss the procedures and purposes with you further. You will have an opportunity to ask questions about any part of the survey.

6. *Economic Considerations*

You will not be charged for any part of this experiment, nor will you receive financial compensation for your participation. You will receive 1 experimental credit for participation.

7. *Confidentiality*

Your responses are confidential and completely anonymous. You will not be asked to provide any identifying information that will enable your responses to be linked to you. We are not interested in responses from any individual; responses from all participants will be aggregated for analyses. Because all of your responses are anonymous, please feel free to answer all of the questions openly and honestly.

The questionnaires will be locked in a secure area to which only the researchers will have access.

You should also know that the University Institutional Review Board (IRB) and the Office of Research Compliance may inspect study records as part of its auditing program, but these reviews will only focus on the

Figure 5.1. *An informed consent form is required for almost all research that involves human participants*

researchers and not on your responses or involvement. The IRB is a group of people that reviews research studies to make sure they are safe for participants.

8. *Voluntary Participation*

You do not have to be in this study if you do not want to. If you agree to be in the study but later change your mind, you may drop out at any time but will still receive credit. There are no penalties or consequences of any kind if you decide that you do not want to participate. You are free not to answer questions.

9. *Do You Have Any Questions?*

Take as long as you like before you make a decision. We will be happy to answer any question you have about this study. If you have further questions about this project or if you have a research-related problem, you may contact the investigator at 999-9999 (John Doe).

If you have any questions concerning your rights as a research subject, you may contact the University Institutional Review Board (IRB) at 888-888-8888.

Authorization:

I have read this form and decided that _____ will
(name of subject)

participate in the project described above. Its general purposes, the particulars of involvement and possible hazards and inconveniences have been explained to my satisfaction. My signature also indicates that I have received a copy of this consent form.

Signature: _____

Date: _____

_____   _____

Signature of Primary Investigator   Phone

or

_____   _____

Signature of Person Obtaining Consent   Phone

Figure 5.1. (*cont.*)

parents must be debriefed and children should be debriefed in whatever way is age-appropriate for them.

Next, the form describes the risks and benefits of participation in the experiment, as well as economic considerations and whether the collected data will be treated in a confidential way. This information gives your participants the opportunity to consider the overall risks and benefits to help them make an informed decision as to whether they want to participate in your study.

You should also tell participants that their participation is voluntary and that they can drop out of the study at any given time. It is customary to give participants an e-mail address or phone number of one of the investigators in case they have any further questions later.

Emphasis on the technical details of obtaining informed consent can obscure the reason for obtaining it. The important question the experimenter must face is whether the experiment places the participant at risk. If so, then the experimenter must examine the risk–benefit ratio: do the benefits of the research outweigh its risks? Students should consult faculty advisers for additional perspectives on whether participants' rights are being protected, particularly their rights to personal privacy and confidentiality. Often, the research will have to be reviewed further by a departmental or university committee to ensure that participants receive adequate personal protection (see the section on institutional review boards).

Give It Some More Thought

In earlier times, there were no institutional review boards and no informed-consent forms. Why today is informed consent considered so important? For example, you might point out that subjects in the past may have participated in experiments that were harmful to them without even realizing that this was the case.

5.1.12 Writing a Debriefing Sheet

After the experiment is over, participants often want to know the purpose of the experiment and the various experimental procedures.

Experimenters have a moral obligation, and in many universities, a legal obligation, to debrief participants about the experiment. The debriefing should be informative and nontechnical. It should inform the participants of what the experiment is supposed to test, how the experiment tests it, and what the anticipated outcomes are. Debriefing may be oral or written, although we prefer written debriefing

EXPERIMENTAL DEBRIEFING

Decision Making in Groups

The purpose of this experiment was to further our understanding of decision making in groups. The hypothesis tested by the experiment was that groups will make faster decisions if they are explicitly warned in advance that interpersonal frictions, rivalries, and animosities can impede the group decision-making process and that, therefore, group members should take special care not to let these impediments hinder them at the decision-making task.

Four groups participated in the experiment. In two groups, participants were asked to decide whether the United States should sell nuclear material for "peaceful purposes" to countries that have the ability to manufacture atomic bombs. In two other groups, participants were asked to decide in a rational way which two group members would receive a $10 bonus at the end of the experiment. They were informed that the other members would receive no bonus and that the decision could not be made using a random selection procedure (such as drawing lots). In one "nuclear material" group and in one "$10 bonus" group, participants were warned in advance not to let interpersonal frictions, rivalries, and animosities impede their decision-making process. The other two groups received no warning of any kind.

We expected that the forewarned groups would reach a decision more quickly than the unwarned groups, regardless of whether they were making a decision about "nuclear material" or about the "$10 bonus." The purpose of using two different kinds of decisions was to show the generality of the instructional effect. The experiment will be repeated four times with different groups of participants to show that the instructional effect is a reliable one. The four repetitions of the experiment will be combined for data analysis.

If you have any questions, please feel free to ask them of the experimenter. If you would like a summary of the results when the research is completed, please leave your name and address with the experimenter.

Thank you for participating.

_____

(Experimenter's Signature)

Figure 5.2. *Debriefings explain the purpose and procedures of the experiment to the participants after they have completed all measures.*

because participants and experimenters then have a record of having participated in the experiment. Figure 5.2 shows a sample debriefing, in this case for an experiment on decision making in groups.

Before debriefing your participants, it is wise to have your participants debrief you. After the experiment is over, ask your participants to tell you (preferably in writing) how they went about doing the experimental task. Participants' comments can provide you with insights that you otherwise would not have obtained.

What's Wrong Here?

Alyssa runs an experiment that takes almost the full 50 minutes allocated for the experimental session. She knows that students do not like to run over. She therefore asks students at the end if they wish to be debriefed, and if they do not, she lets them go so as not to inconvenience them or give them the feeling that she is forcing them to listen to an explanation in which they have no interest.

Answer: This debriefing procedure would be considered inadequate by today's standards. The reason is that students may be in a hurry but still want to be debriefed. Or they may become interested in the debriefing after thinking more about the study. Therefore she should have a written debriefing that she gives out to everyone, including people in a hurry, with the option of additional oral debriefing for those who want it.

5.1.13 Getting Approval from the Institutional Review Board

When you plan your study, you should allow enough time for your local IRB to approve it. The IRB is a committee of experts from different subjects who discuss every research proposal and decide whether the research can be conducted as proposed or whether amendments must be made to protect the participants. Such boards usually meet at least once a month, and if you have to make changes and need to get them approved, it can easily take you a few weeks, if not longer. Many IRBs offer expedited reviews for low-risk studies. Check with your local IRB if you meet those requirements; the low-risk route may also mean that you have to submit fewer documents than you would for a full review.

To a certain extent, IRBs differ from one place to another in what they consider important when approving research, in the phrases they like to be included in consent forms, and so on. For example, one IRB may want you to include a sentence in the "Risks and inconveniences" section of an informed consent form that identifies the time the participant spends with the study as an inconvenience. An IRB at another university may not consider such a sentence important. Ask other students or professors about their experiences with your IRB and whether they have any tips or even templates so you can get a feel for the formulations used with respect to communications with the IRB. In general, IRB approval for a study is valid only for a certain amount of time (e.g., one year). If you have not completed your study by that time, you may have to resubmit to the IRB for renewed approval.

Often, the IRB requests detailed information about your study. Generally, IRBs ask for information about the following:

1. the purpose of your study;
2. the theoretical background of your study;
3. the design of your study;
4. the instruments you will use (you may need to submit all of your questionnaires and materials);
5. the number of participants and from which population they are drawn (e.g., male students of your university);
6. how you justify the sample size (e.g., if you only need 50 participants to complete your study but plan to have 300 people participate, this sampling design may not be approved);
7. how you recruit your participants (e.g., ads in a newspaper or flyers, and you may have to submit such materials for review);
8. inclusion and/or exclusion criteria (e.g., do you discriminate against potential participants and exclude them from participation for no apparent reason? Why is your group of participants circumscribed as it is?);
9. risks and inconveniences, benefits, and a risk/benefit analysis;
10. economic considerations (e.g., will your participants earn money when they participate?);
11. data safety and monitoring (e.g., are your data locked and inaccessible to others? How do you ensure security of the data? Are the participants anonymous?);

12. informed consent, including your informed consent forms. When writing, keep in mind that some of the reviewers may not be psychologists, so make sure that reviewers unfamiliar with your field of study will be able to comprehend your documents.

What's Wrong Here?

Ellen has received approval from her institutional review board for an experiment measuring people's conscious prejudice toward individuals of races other than their own. After testing the first group of subjects, she discovers, unexpectedly, that some of the subjects find some of her questions offensive so she changes the wording in those questions to be less offensive and starts the experiment over, ignoring results from the first group and using the new questionnaires on subsequent subjects. She finds, to her delight, that the issue of offensive questions does not come up again.

Answer: Ellen failed to seek and obtain approval from her institutional review board for the revised questionnaire. Generally, approval is given for a particular set of materials, and if the materials are changed, approval has to be sought for the revised materials. Although such approval sometimes can delay the execution of the study, it must be sought, nevertheless.

5.1.14 Conducting a Pilot Study

Before starting final data collection, you should consider testing pilot participants. Pilot testing enables you to spot flaws in the experiment before you actually conduct it. You may find that your directions are unclear, that you have not allowed enough time for your participants to complete the task, or that the task is too difficult for your participants. The list of possible flaws is endless. Pilot testing is like an insurance policy. By making a small investment in advance, you can potentially save yourself much greater costs later. The more careful the pilot testing (the larger the insurance premium), the less likely it is that you will end up with disastrous results (i.e., the greater the insurance coverage). We have found that there is almost always some potential problem uncovered during pilot testing.

5.2 EXECUTING EXPERIMENTAL RESEARCH

If you have planned your experiment carefully, then its execution should be straightforward. You should make sure, as much as you possibly can, that extraneous variables are kept constant from session to session. Thus, things like lighting, ventilation, and seating arrangement should not be varied. Outside noise should be minimized. If the experiment involves a number of separate parts, you may want to keep a list so that you do not forget any of them. Experimenters, like participants, sometimes get distracted; and once data are lost, they are difficult or impossible to replace.

Use the experimental sessions as an informal opportunity to gain insights into how participants perform the experimental tasks. Participants occasionally make comments about what they are doing or how they are doing it. Also be on the lookout for nonroutine problems – participants who stayed up the night before writing a paper and can barely keep their eyes open, participants who are not paying attention to the experimental task, a flickering lightbulb, an erratic stopwatch. You should write down notes on any unusual problems, and try to correct them. Participants who stayed up all night should be rescheduled, participants who are not paying attention should be told politely to pay attention, the lightbulb should be replaced, and the stopwatch should be fixed or replaced. You will collect much better data if you are aware of problems and correct them immediately.

In theory, the experimenter should be blind to the assignment of participants to treatments so that any prior expectations about treatment effects will be unable to influence the experimental results. In practice, the experimenter often knows which participants have been assigned to which treatments. In reading the word lists for the free-recall experiment, for example, the experimenter will probably recognize whether the words are abstract or concrete. If experimenters observe the groups in the decision-making experiment, they will know whether they have previously warned the groups about impediments to group decision making. A voluminous literature exists on experimenters' effects on research results, and there is no question that experimenters can influence the outcomes in subtle ways. An experimenter might read the list of abstract words just a little more quickly or less clearly than the list of concrete words or differentially reinforce the decision-making groups with facial expressions. You have a responsibility as experimenter to give your hypotheses the fairest possible test. Subtle and not-so-subtle experimenter effects undermine the interpretability and credibility of your results. It is therefore essential that you take care not to influence the outcome of your experiment through incidental and (presumably) unintended actions.

5.3 EXCURSION: USING THE INTERNET TO CONDUCT ARCHIVAL RESEARCH AND DATA COLLECTION

Clearly, the Internet can be a valuable resource when seeking out ideas for a research project. But even when you have settled on an idea for a study and are confident that enough resources exist to successfully answer your research question, you still need to discover a way to collect data that will allow you to answer your research question. The Internet also can be a valuable tool during the data-collection phase of the research process. In this section, we explore how to use the Internet as a source of data and as a data-collection tool. Specifically, we discuss how to use the Internet to conduct archival research or to collect original data. We also discuss some of the advantages and disadvantages of using the Internet to collect data.

5.3.1 Archival Research

Archival research refers to a method of data collection involving the use of records or previously existing information. For example, suppose you wanted to construct a personality profile of a US president, perhaps to examine whether a president's personality is related to his performance in office. Although this is an excellent research idea, you are likely to have two problems collecting data. First, the president whose personality profile you want to construct might not be living anymore. Second, even if the president is living, it is unlikely that you will be able to interview him or get him to complete a personality survey for you. It turns out that personality profiles of US presidents can be created without ever talking with a president or having him complete a personality questionnaire. Instead, the personality traits of a president can be inferred from such pieces of information as speeches, notes, and papers; conversations with other political leaders; interviews; and press conferences. The advantage for a researcher is that all of this material is archived and made available for public consumption. For example, any research that involves the use of previously existing material, whether public records (e.g., crime statistics, census information) or public documents (e.g., Supreme Court decisions, presidential speeches), is referred to as archival research. Archival research is a particularly useful research strategy for answering research questions that are difficult or impossible to answer via traditional data-collection methods.

The Internet is an especially valuable tool for researchers interested in archival research. As already discussed, the Internet and the World Wide Web contain an abundance of information, much of which can be used to conduct research. Following are some ideas for, and examples of, using the Internet to conduct archival research:

■ Newsgroups

The Internet is full of discussion boards, or newsgroups, on every imaginable topic. Newsgroups allow people from all over the world to engage in asynchronous conversations about a variety of topics. An Internet search of newsgroups yields thousands of virtual discussions (e.g., on a football team's performance, a support group for people who have chronic pain, the best restaurants on Maui). Most newsgroups are accessible to anyone as a participant or as an observer. For the purposes of archival research, newsgroups are typically archived, so that a researcher can access the transcripts of the discussions (although permission of the moderator is often required and always advisable). These transcripts can be a valuable source of data to researchers attempting to answer specific research questions. For example, if researchers wanted to learn whether fans of winning football teams express more pride in their team than do fans of losing football teams, they could analyze the transcripts of a newsgroup of a winning team and the newsgroup of a losing team. Or suppose researchers were interested in examining the extent of depressive symptoms displayed by chronic pain sufferers. They could analyze the discussion board of chronic pain sufferers for evidence of depressive symptoms.

■ Public records

Public records can be an excellent source of data. The Internet allows one to access most public records with incredible ease. The consequence for researchers is that they can answer innumerable research questions with the use of such data. For example, the government's website FedWorld (www.fedworld.gov) includes access to a variety of information, such as the complete transcripts of Supreme Court decisions, transportation fatality statistics, and a list of currently endangered species. Similarly, every state in the United States has a web page, and each can be accessed by using the format www.state.SA.us, where "SA" stands for the state abbreviation (e.g., www.state.oh.us is Ohio's web page). A state's web page makes available information such as statewide incidence of cancer by type, year, and county; results of family health surveys; and the number of live births by county and year.

■ Websites

The format of and information contained on a website can also be a source of data for researchers. Suppose a researcher was interested in examining whether females are more likely than males to disclose personal information about themselves. One method of answering this question is to analyze the websites of males and females, paying attention to the amount and type of personal information included on the sites. Or imagine that researchers want to investigate the correlation between the success (in net profit) of small businesses and the appearance of those businesses' websites. They could analyze the appearance of small business websites and then determine whether it is related to the success of the business.

5.3.2 Data Collection Via the Internet

The Internet can also be a valuable tool for the collection of original data, because it allows researchers to collect survey data or conduct experiments. There are several methods available to researchers who wish to collect data using the Internet. First, a researcher can construct a web page that permits respondents to answer a survey or participate in an experiment. Of course, this technique requires that a researcher have some knowledge of constructing web pages and surveys on the Web and have access to a server. Second, a researcher can send a questionnaire or survey to potential respondents via e-mail, either using one's own questionnaire or a standard survey device, such as Survey Monkey or Qualtrics. Third, a researcher can make use of a LISTSERV to send potential respondents a survey or questionnaire.

Conducting research via the Internet has a number of important advantages and disadvantages (Reips, 2000). Some of the advantages include the following:

1. **Population access.** The number of people using the Internet is increasing every day. Use of the Internet allows researchers to access many more people than would be possible using more traditional methods. Further, the Internet allows access to more diverse populations.

2. **Volunteer bias.** One criticism of most research conducted in universities is that participants may not be invested in the research in which they are participating. On the Internet, people who participate in a study do so because they want to. But they are then a biased sample.

3. **Statistical power.** The large sample size that use of the Internet permits also increases the statistical power of a study.

4. **Experimenter effects.** Face-to-face experiments typically require the presence of an experimenter, but that can sometimes (unintentionally) influence the outcome of a study. The Internet does not require the physical presence of an experimenter, which eliminates any experimenter effects.

5. **Costs.** The costs of conducting a study on the Internet are much less than those of carrying one out in a lab. Internet studies do not require the use of lab space, equipment, experimenters, or paper. The amount of time needed to complete a study on the Internet is also greatly reduced because Internet studies can be conducted 24 hours per day, 7 days per week.

6. **Ethical issues.** Participation in Internet studies is completely voluntary. Respondents can drop out of the study at any time without penalty.

Of course, there are also some *disadvantages* of using the Internet to conduct research. These include the following:

1. **Control issues.** In non-Internet studies, researchers can exercise a great deal of control over many of the practical issues of research, such as who the participants are, when the study is conducted, and where the study takes place. On the Internet, researchers give up this control. Among the control issues that plague Internet research are the fact that people can participate

in the study multiple times and that the researcher lacks control over the experimental situation. It is wise to ask participants not to participate more than once or to ask for personal information that can be verified independently.

2. **Self-selection.** Another issue with Internet studies is that all of the participants are self-selected, rather than randomly assigned. The results, therefore, may not be as generalizable as a randomly selected sample. One solution is to advertise the study widely so that Internet users from a variety of entry points have access to the study. Amazon's Mechanical Turk (MT) provides a source of subjects who will participate for a fee in electronically administered studies, although one often knows neither who the subjects are nor how hard they worked on the materials.

3. **Dropout.** Whenever research is completely voluntary, as is the case in Internet research, there tends to be a high dropout rate. Participants may decide, in the middle of the study, that they do not have the time to complete it. Or participants might decide, after having started a survey, that they are really not interested in the topic. Potential solutions to this problem include offering an incentive for participation, making the website as attractive as possible, and providing participants with estimates of the amount of time needed to complete the study.

4. **Technical variance.** Researchers try very hard to reduce the amount of error variance in their studies. Studies conducted on the Internet can pose some unique challenges to the control of error variance. For example, participants in a study are likely to have different web browsers, different monitor sizes, and different Internet connections, all of which can inflate error variance. However, these sources of variance are likely to be random and may not affect the study in a systematic manner.

5. **Interaction with participants.** If participants in an Internet study have a question, they are unable to ask an experimenter. It is a good idea, therefore, always to include an e-mail address or other means of contacting the experimenter if the participant needs clarification of procedures.

Clearly, the Internet offers a variety of unique ways of conducting research. The Internet can be a valuable source of data to an investigator interested in conducting archival research. Many research questions can be answered via access to public records, public documents, and countless websites. The Internet can also be used as a way to collect original research. Minimal knowledge of web page construction is really all that is needed to collect data via the Internet. And currently there are several websites, such as SurveyMonkey (www.surveymonkey.com), that essentially build your survey or experiment for you. You can find these websites by searching for keywords such as "online survey software." Finally, a review of the research (Krantz & Dalal, 2000) suggests that the results of web experiments often are comparable to non-web experiments, which makes the conduct of research via the Internet even more attractive.

There are sources of subjects available online, the most well known of which is Amazon's Mechanical Turk. Researchers using subjects from Mechanical Turk recruit subjects online and pay them. The subject pool is anyone who has signed up as a subject on this system. The upside of such a system is that it can provide a very quick way of obtaining a large and diverse sample. The downside is that one does not know exactly whom one is testing.

5.4 ANALYZING DATA FROM EXPERIMENTAL RESEARCH

After the experiment is completed, you are ready to analyze your data. Techniques for analyzing data are beyond the scope of this book, although some simple exploratory techniques are presented in Chapter 10. Two especially lucid textbooks covering elementary statistical techniques are those by Gravetter and Wallnau (2012), and Aron, Aron, and Coups (2012). For description and explanation of multivariate statistical techniques, we recommend the works of Tabachnik and Fidell (2012), and Hair, Black, Babin, and Anderson (2009).

5.5 REPORTING EXPERIMENTAL RESEARCH

Once you have analyzed your data and thought about your results, you are ready to report them. In the following sections, we describe all the parts of a manuscript. If you are interested in a more detailed overview, we recommend *Guide to Publishing in Psychology Journals* (Sternberg, 2000). We suggest that you write an outline prior to writing the paper, just as you would if you were writing a literature research paper. A standard format for the outline looks like this:

5.5.1 Title

The title should inform the reader simply and concisely what the paper is about. It is important that the title be self-explanatory. Readers will come across the title in other papers that refer to your paper and in PsycINFO, and they may have to decide on the basis of the title alone whether they want to read your paper. Therefore, you want to catch the attention of your potential readers with the title. It should include, for example, keywords, the theoretical issue that the paper addresses, the dependent variable(s), and the independent variable(s). Keywords are important because the title will be stored in information-retrieval networks that rely on such words to determine the relevance of your study to someone else's research interests. For the same reason, it is important to avoid irrelevant and misleading words, because such words may spuriously lead an investigator uninterested in your topic to your paper. Try not to use abbreviations. The title should not exceed 12 to 15 words in length.

When submitting a paper to a journal, you will also be asked to provide a running title. The running title will be displayed at the top of each page. When readers open a journal in the middle of an article, they will still be able to determine what article they are looking at by means of the running title. As for the regular title, focus on keywords when you formulate your running title.

5.5.2 Author's Name and Institutional Affiliation

Write your name as you wish it to be recognized professionally; for example, John Jones might choose John Jones, John J. Jones, John James Jones, J. Jones, J. J. Jones, or J. James Jones. A first name, middle initial, and last name is the most commonly used form of presentation. Omit titles such as BA, MA, PhD, Lover of Mankind, and so on. Underneath your name, write your institutional affiliation: Podunk College, Frink University. If you have changed your affiliation since you did the research, list the old affiliation under your name and the new affiliation in a footnote. A dual affiliation is listed under your name only if both institutions contributed financially to the study. If you are unaffiliated with any institution, list your city and state. If there is more than one author, you may wish to discuss the order of appearance of names as soon as possible with your collaborators.

Author name might seem like a trivial consideration, but it is not. Always use exactly the same presentation of your name, as electronic indexes cannot recognize, say, that "John J. Jones and "John Jones" are the same person. They will be indexed as different persons. Also, when women (or men) change their names, they may wish to change the way they list their name on articles and books. Be aware, though, that such change may cost one in terms of recognizable citations. One is likely to be separately cited for each name, and individuals looking up your credentials may not realize that they need to look for you under two (or more) distinct names. If at all possible, pick a name at the start of your career for your publishing name, and stick with it.

5.5.3 Abstract

The abstract summarizes your paper. Its length depends on your target journal, but it generally ranges between 150 and 200 words. The abstract, like the title, should be self-explanatory and self-contained, because it is also used for indexing by information-retrieval networks. The abstract should include (a) the major hypotheses; (b) a summary of the method, including a description of the materials, apparatus, participants, design, and procedure; (c) a synopsis of the main results; and (d) the conclusions drawn from the results.

Do not include in the abstract any information that is not included in the body of the paper. Because you will not know until you are done with the outline what information you will include, you are well advised to defer writing the abstract until after you have otherwise completed the outline, or even the paper itself.

Remember that most people will read your abstract only if your title interests them, and they will read your article only if your abstract interests them. It is therefore essential that the abstract interests your reader. You can interest the reader by showing that the problem is an important one, that your hypotheses about the problem are insightful ones, and that you will test the hypotheses in a convincing way. The *APA Manual* (2009) states that abstracts should be (a) accurate, (b) self-contained, (c) concise and specific, (d) nonevaluative, and (e) coherent and readable.

5.5.4 Introduction

The introduction orients the reader to the research. In the paper, it does not receive a heading, because its function is obvious. The task of your opening paragraph is to appeal to readers and to animate them to read on. There are several ways to achieve this goal (Kendall, Silk, & Chu, 2000):

- Ask a **rhetorical question** that inspires readers to consider what they think about a certain issue.
- Mention an **everyday experience** that readers can relate to and that makes the relevance of your topic apparent.
- Use an **analogy** or metaphor to address general principles.
- Mention an **interesting fact** that captures the interest of readers.
- Give some **historical facts** to place the problem in context.
- Point out the **lack of previous research** to highlight the importance of your work.

After the opening paragraph, in which you elicit readers' interest, your introduction should answer four basic questions:

1. What previous research led up to your research?
2. What does your research add to this previous research?
3. Why is the addition made by your research important or interesting?
4. How is the addition made?

The introduction usually contains a brief review of the literature most pertinent to your research. A lengthy literature review is inappropriate, except, sometimes, for theses and course assignments. Focus on integrating the literature rather than on summarizing many single studies. If a voluminous literature exists on the topic, cite a literature review to which the reader can refer for further information if they want it. Assume in your review, however, that readers are familiar with the general area of research. Readers' main interest is in what you have to contribute. They are interested in the previous literature only as it relates directly to your contribution.

Once you have told the reader what is already known, you must relate what still needs to be known, that is, what you intend to find out. Tell the reader not only what you intend to contribute but also what the nature of the contribution is. Does your research resolve an issue that has been unresolved in the past? Does it deal with an issue that others have not thought about? Does it attempt to correct an artifact in previous investigations? This information will give readers a good idea of what you view as the purpose of your study.

Next, you should show readers that the contribution is a potentially interesting or important one. Why have people paid attention to this particular issue? Or why is a new issue one to which people should pay attention? Or does an artifact in previous experimental research really undermine conclusions that previous investigators have drawn? Remember that a major purpose of the introduction is to interest readers in your paper and that your explanation of why your study is potentially important can motivate readers either to continue the article or to toss it aside.

Finally, you should tell readers how you intend to make your contribution. Sketch your experimental design, but leave a detailed description for the "Design" section later in the paper. Show how your design relates to the theoretical issues you address. It is important to convince your readers at this point that your experiment actually does test the hypothesis you want to investigate.

Many APA journals limit the length of the introduction to five to nine manuscript pages. As a rule of thumb, the longer your "Results" section is, the longer your "Introduction" section can be (Kendall, Silk, & Chu, 2000).

What's Wrong Here?

Here is the introduction to a student paper:

"Davis and Moore (2014) found that people are more likely to cooperate with each other if they are not competing for the same goals. This study seeks to replicate and extend Davis and Moore's finding."

Answer: The opening is dull. It focuses on the authors of the study rather than on what they found and it does not specify how the present study will go beyond the past one. A better opening would have been: "People are more likely to cooperate if they are not competing for the same goals (Davis & Moore, 2014). But what about if they are competing for the same goals but do not see each other as a threat? Will they then be willing to cooperate, despite having the same goals?" This opening focuses on the finding rather than the researchers and makes clear what further question the current study is asking.

5.5.5 Method

The "Method" section tells readers how the experiment was conducted. You should include just enough information so that readers can replicate your study. If you include less information, other investigators will be unable to verify your results. If you include more information, you risk boring and possibly losing readers in needless detail. When you are uncertain as to whether a piece of information is essential, it is better to err on the side of including too much rather than too little.

The "Method" section is usually divided into a number of subsections. Although use of subsections is optional, it usually simplifies and clarifies the presentation for readers. The subsections most often used are "Participants," "Materials," "Apparatus," "Design," and "Procedure," although not necessarily in that order. If there is no apparatus, you do not need the section. Use the order of subheadings that best conveys the methods used in your particular experiment.

5.5.5.1 Participants

You should describe in the "Participants" subsection (a) the total number of participants, (b) the number of participants receiving each treatment, (c) the population from which the participants were drawn, (d) how participants were selected, and (e) the circumstances under which the participants participated (e.g., for pay, for course credit, as a favor to the experimenter). In describing the participating population, include any details that might affect the outcome of the experiment, such as sex, ethnic or socially defined racial groups, age, education, and so on. The nature of the experiment will determine what other attributes of participants might be relevant. The term *subject* can be used for nonhuman organisms or when referring to people in the abstract. For example, you can use the term when describing designs, as for a between-subjects design.

5.5.5.2 Materials

In the "Materials" subsection, you should describe the stimulus material used in the experiment. Sufficient detail should be given so that the reader could generate the same or equivalent stimuli. If the stimuli are unconventional, you might reproduce examples in a table or figure.

5.5.5.3 Apparatus

The apparatus used in the experiment should be described in the "Apparatus" subsection. Present a general description of the apparatus, including any details that might affect the outcome of the experiment. If the apparatus is a standard piece of manufactured equipment, the name and model number will substitute for most details, because readers can then learn the details from the manufacturer. If the apparatus is unusual, you might want to photograph it and present it as a figure. This entire subsection can be omitted if no special apparatus is used. If you merely use a standard computer for stimulus presentation, you do not need a section describing the computer.

> **What's Wrong Here?**
>
> Here is the "Subjects" section of a student paper:
>   "Subjects were 100 undergraduates at a large southeastern university. All of the subjects were enrolled in the introductory-psychology course. They all received course credit for their participating in the study. All filled out informed-consent forms and were debriefed after the experiment."
>
> **Answer:** The section does not give sufficient details about the subjects. For example, it does not specify the sex distribution of the subjects, nor does it state their years of study (e.g., freshmen, sophomores, etc.).

5.5.5.4 Design

This subsection should include a description of the following:

1. **The type of design.** Did you use an experimental, quasi-experimental, or correlational design? You should also give information on the number of factors and their levels, and on whether a between-subjects, within-subjects, or mixed design was used. In between-subject designs, every participant is assigned to just one condition, whereas in within-subject designs, each person participates in more than one condition. Mixed designs have at least one between-subject and one within-subject variable. If you employ a within-subject design, the order in which participants are subjected to the conditions can influence the results; therefore, you need to mention if you took action, and if so, the actions you took to counterbalance the order effect (see also Reis, 2000).
2. **The independent variable(s).** Which independent variables were used and what were their values?
3. **The dependent variable(s).** On which variables did you measure the effect of the independent variable(s)?
4. **The way in which participants were assigned to groups.**

The "Design" section is sometimes omitted and the relevant information divided among the other sections. We prefer to include the "Design" section, because it provides readers with a compact overview of how the experiment was put together. If you are interested in a more detailed treatise on how to write the "Design" section, we suggest you consult Harry Reis's chapter "Writing effectively about design" in Sternberg (2000).

What's Wrong Here?

This excerpt is from the "Design" section of a paper:
   "Subjects were randomly assigned to groups. The independent variable in the study was reaction time and the dependent variable was their choice of major, coded as natural science, social science, humanities, or arts."

Answer: The independent and dependent variables are reversed. That is, the stated independent variable is actually the dependent variable, and vice versa.

5.5.5.5 Procedure

The "Procedure" subsection should describe what happened to the participants in the experimental sessions from the time they walked in to the time they walked out. A chronological account is usually best. In the paper, paraphrase directions to participants, unless they were unconventional, in which case you might want to present them verbatim. Because you assume that your readers have a general knowledge of the relevant literature, you can also assume that they are familiar with standard testing procedures. Therefore, describe such procedures more generally, always being sure to include any details that plausibly might affect the outcome of the experiment.

5.5.6 Results

The order in which results are reported is of critical importance. Authors often report first those results that are of most interest or relevance to the hypotheses being tested. Less interesting or relevant results are reported later. You may wish to report first a general conclusion or interpretation, followed by some descriptive statistics that support your assertion, followed only at the end by the inferential statistics that buttress the conclusion. This style of presentation often makes for more interesting reading than does a mélange of facts and statistics followed by an obscurely placed conclusion that bored readers may never even reach if they have given up on your article pages before. Also keep in mind that results should not be reported in the order in which the data analyses were conducted but rather in a way that makes sense to the story you want to tell.

The "Results" section should include (a) descriptive statistics, which summarize the data in a readily comprehensible form, and (b) inferential statistics, which test the likelihood that the results were obtained due to chance alone. Techniques you used for data analysis should be reported with sufficient clarity that someone else could replicate them on the basis of your description. If you had a choice of which statistical methods to employ, give a rationale for what you did. If you plan to present a large number of results, divide the "Results" section into subsections. The particular subsections used will depend on the nature of the experiment.

It is expected that authors provide effect sizes as well as significance values. The field is divided regarding the value of conventional significance testing, but it nevertheless is the most commonly used basis for reporting results. Power analysis is desirable.

As in the previous sections, you should make an effort to report the right amount of information, neither underreporting nor over-reporting your results. Also as in the previous sections, it is usually better to report a result if you are uncertain as to whether to include it. The criteria you should follow are to report (a) all data that are directly relevant to your hypotheses and (b) other data that may be peripheral to your hypotheses but are of particular interest in their own right. Do not present data for individual participants unless (a) you used an $N = 1$ (single-subject) design, (b) the individual data show trends that are masked in the group data, or (c) your hypotheses are relevant to each individual's data rather than to the group data.

It is often convenient to summarize your data in the form of one or more tables or figures. In planning tables and figures, keep in mind that you should not repeat in the text information that is contained in tables and figures and that tables and figures should be largely self-explanatory, although you should certainly discuss them in the text. Two more considerations are relevant, but only if you plan to submit a paper to a journal: (a) large numbers of tables and figures are discouraged (because they are expensive to reproduce in journals), and (b) one or two sentences often can summarize data that initially seem to require a table or figure.

In deciding between presenting data in a table versus a figure, you face a trade-off. On the one hand, figures tend to give the reader a better global sense of the data; on the other hand, tables convey information to the reader more precisely. In general, tables are preferred, but your own judgment of what best conveys your message should be the arbiter of how you present the data.

In reporting tests of statistical significance, include (a) the name of the test, (b) the value of the test statistic, (c) the degrees of freedom (if relevant), and (d) the significance level of the test. Readers should also be informed of whether or not the test is directional and what the direction of the effect was. Assume that your reader is knowledgeable about basic statistics, but describe briefly the assumptions and theory underlying unconventional tests, if possible giving a reference to which readers can refer. Editors may also require you to indicate the power of the significance test.

Experience Is the Best Teacher

In our experience, there are three very common mistakes in "Results" sections. The first is to lose sight of the goal. Authors present data analysis after data analysis and readers get lost because they lose the connection between the data analyses and what the authors ultimately are trying to show. The second is poor organization. The "Results" section is presented haphazardly so that it is hard to follow the storyline. The third is over-interpreting the data – inferring stronger conclusions than the data justify because the authors want the study to have impact and they view it as more likely to have impact if they make strong claims. Sometimes over-interpretation occurs not in the "Results" section, but rather in the "Discussion" section, which is discussed next.

5.5.7 Discussion

The "Discussion" section should include the following: (a) an explanation of how well your data fit your original hypotheses, (b) an explanation of how your data fit in with the existing body of literature, (c) a statement of your conclusions, and (d) a discussion of theoretical and, if relevant, practical implications of the results.

It is appropriate to include in the discussion a consideration of why the findings are important; why the topic itself and the problems within it are important; why you chose the level of analysis you did; and how, if at all, the findings can be applied.

You may open the discussion with a paragraph that summarizes the purpose of your study, your hypotheses, and most important findings.

Then continue with a general statement of how well the data fit your hypotheses. If the data fit your hypotheses, your task is straightforward. If the data do not fit your hypotheses, then you can approach the data from either of two angles. One angle is an acceptance of the data as uninterpretable; the other angle is an interpretation of the data as fitting hypotheses different from the ones you originally suggested. In either case, you should be as clear in describing lack of fit as you are in describing fit. Typically, authors reconceptualize papers that originally were designed to show one thing but end up showing another, thereby writing up the papers in a way different from that originally planned.

If your data are uninterpretable or only partially interpretable, say so. Convoluted explanations of unexpected data are easily recognized as rationalizations of failures. If you have good reason to believe that some aspect of your experiment was responsible for the uninterpretable results, say so briefly, and let matters stand there. Do not, however, waste space listing possible reasons for the uninterpretable results: Such lists can go on forever and are boring to read. If there were weaknesses in the study, note them.

As a guideline, use about one paragraph or more for each main point in your discussion. Make sure that you do not merely reiterate results but also integrate them somehow (Calfee, 2000).

If your data are unexpected but interpretable, it is permissible to interpret them in light of new, reformulated hypotheses. You must make clear, however, that your explanation is post hoc and speculative. There is a fine line between reformulation of hypotheses and empty rationalization, so you must convince your readers that your post hoc explanation provides a compelling account of the data.

Afterward, comment on how your data fit into the existing literature. Where do your results differ, and where do they fit right in? What do the discrepancies and parallels suggest?

After you have discussed the fit of your data to the original hypotheses as well as existing literature, and any new hypotheses you might have, a concise statement of your conclusions should be presented. Because the conclusions are the major message of your paper, you should phrase them with great care, thereby ensuring that readers will interpret them as you intended.

Finally, discuss theoretical and possibly practical implications of the results. Consider internal and external validity in your discussion. If you have drawn conclusions different from those of your original hypotheses, you might suggest ways in which the conclusions could be verified in future research. Do not merely say, however, that future research will be needed to clarify the issues, without giving readers any inkling of what form such research might take. Every reader knows that more research can be done on any topic. What readers want to learn from you is what direction this research should take.

What's Wrong Here?

Here is the last sentence of the discussion section of an article, which also serves as the last sentence of the article:

"In sum, further research is needed to untangle the threads underlying this complex issue."

Answer: Further research is always needed. Don't even bother to tell the readers what they already know. Also, this ending is super-boring.

5.5.8 An Alternative: "Results and Discussion"

The "Results" and "Discussion" sections are sometimes combined into one section called "Results and Discussion," especially when each section is relatively short. We recommend this combination even when the individual sections are not short. The problem with a "Results" section standing by itself is that it is difficult to follow and makes for dry reading. The reader is confronted with masses of statistics without being told what the statistics mean or why they are important. Meaningful discussion is deferred until later.

Reconsider our discussion in the previous chapter of thematic versus nonthematic organization. In the present context, one's choices are the following:

Nonthematic organization	Thematic organization
III. Results	III. Results and discussion
A. Presentation of Result A	A. Result A
B. Presentation of Result B	1. Presentation
C. Presentation of Result C	2. Discussion
IV. Discussion	B. Result B
A. Discussion of Result A	1. Presentation
B. Discussion of Result B	2. Discussion
C. Discussion of Result C	C. Result C
	1. Presentation
	2. Discussion

In the format on the left, readers almost certainly will have to refer back to the results from the discussion, unless the results are re-presented in the "Discussion" section, an undesirable redundancy. Readers are unlikely to remember all the results from the "Results" section if they have been presented in an unmotivated fashion with no interpretation to make them meaningful.

In the format on the right, there is no need for paging backward. The results are discussed as they are presented, so that readers can understand why they are important when they are presented. They do not have to wait until later to discover why the author bothered to present those particular results and not others. Consequently, readers can form a more integrated and coherent representation of the author's results–discussion package.

If the thematic organization on the right in the next example is easier to follow than the nonthematic organization on the left, why is the organization on the left the more widely used? We suspect that it is because of a tacit fear that, in a joint presentation of results and discussion, the discussion will somehow contaminate the results – that combining the sections will blur the distinction between objective and subjective information. This argument, although understandable, is weak. Even slightly skilled writers can interweave data and discussion of the data in a way that makes clear the distinction between the two. Writers can, of course, be dishonest and try to pass off their opinions as facts. But such writers can distort their data regardless of the way in which the paper is organized.

Regardless of which organization you choose, related results may be presented and discussed in clusters to increase the meaningfulness of the presentation. For example, Results A and B might be clustered together in the following ways:

Nonthematic organization	Thematic organization
III. Results	III. Results and discussion
A. Presentation of Result cluster (A, B)	A. Result cluster (A, B)
B. Presentation of Result C	1. Presentation
IV. Discussion	2. Discussion
A. Discussion of result cluster (A, B)	B. Result C
B. Discussion of Result C	1. Presentation
	2. Discussion

5.5.9 References

The references provide a complete list of the sources you cite in your paper. Be sure your references are accurate. Incorrect citations are a disservice to readers and show sloppy scholarship.

Experience Is the Best Teacher

One question to ask yourself in making citations is, if you submit your article for publication, who is likely to review it? You want, if possible, to cite relevant work by anyone who is a likely reviewer, as the reviewer is likely to be offended upon seeing his or her own work not cited. Also, avoid duplicative references where possible, such as the first and second editions of the same book. Also remember that encyclopedias, whether in book form or online, are usually not viewed as authoritative references in scholarly papers.

5.5.10 Appendix

An appendix is rarely used in psychological papers, although it is valuable in certain cases. It is appropriate for (a) computer programs designed explicitly for your research, unavailable elsewhere, and possibly valuable to others, (b) unpublished tests, (c) mathematical proofs that are relevant to your paper but would distract the reader if included in the text, and (d) lists of stimulus materials, if the materials are unusual or particularly important to your conclusions (American Psychological Association, 2009). The appendix should be included only if it is especially enlightening or helpful to others in replicating your study. Sometimes multiple appendices are used. In this case, label each appendix with a capital letter (e.g., Appendix A, Appendix B).

If you have only one appendix, name it *Appendix*. Multiple tables per appendix must be labeled with the capital letter of the appendix and a number (e.g., A1, A2, A3, B1, B2). Note that even if you have only one appendix, you still have to label your tables in the appendix A1, A2, and so forth, to indicate that they are located in the appendix. Appendices sometimes are presented via the Web.

5.5.11 Order of Sections

Once you are ready to write your paper in final form, you should order the sections in the following way:

1. Title page (including your name and affiliation)
2. Author identification notes
3. Abstract
4. Text
5. References
6. Footnotes
7. Tables (one table per page)
8. Figure captions
9. Figures (one figure per page)

This ordering is to facilitate editing and printing. It is not the order in which the various parts will appear. Pages should be numbered consecutively using Arabic numerals, beginning with the title page and ending with the figure captions. Place page numbers in the upper right corner of each page. Immediately above the page number, write the first few words of your title, or the whole title if the title is short. This way, the pages can be returned to the manuscript in case they are temporarily misplaced.

The preceding ordering applies to papers written for submission to journals. For course papers, the following exceptions should be noted. First, footnotes usually should be placed at the bottom of the page on which they are cited. Second, tables and figures should be placed near where they are cited in the text rather than at the end. Third, figure captions should be placed immediately below the appropriate figures rather than in a separate section.

Once you have finished ordering and numbering your pages, the paper is complete. Once you have proofread it (see Chapter 12), you are ready to hand it in or send it off.

CHECKLIST FOR EXPERIMENTAL PAPERS

☐ Is your title simple, concise, and self-explanatory? Does it contain keywords?

☐ Have you decided on a name under which you will publish all your professional publications?

☐ Is your abstract self-explanatory, and does it include major hypotheses, a summary of the method, the main results, and the conclusions?

☐ Will your introduction appeal to readers and animate them to continue reading?

☐ Does your introduction state what previous theory and research led to your own research, what your research adds and how, and why your research and the question it answers are important?

☐ Does your "Method" section contain all necessary information concerning subjects, materials, apparatus, design, and procedure?

☐ Does the "Design" subsection, in particular, include information on the type of design, the independent and dependent variables, and how participants were assigned to groups?

☐ Have you presented your results in a way that makes sense and supports your story rather than in the order in which you conducted the data analyses?

☐ Have you made an effort to report the "right" number of results – neither too many nor too few? Have you ensured that your data are directly relevant to your hypotheses, or that they are at least interesting in their own right?

☐ Does your discussion include (a) an explanation of how well your data fit your hypotheses, (b) how your data fit with the literature, (c) your conclusions, and (d) a discussion of theoretical and practical (if applicable) implications of your results?

☐ Have you used about one paragraph per main point in your discussion?

☐ Have you named all sources and listed them in the references list?

☐ Are the parts of your manuscript in the right order?

6 Ethics in Research and Writing

Ethics are of utmost importance when doing research and later writing about it. There are many ways to get tripped up ethically in both research and writing. This chapter summarizes some of the pitfalls and gives you advice as to how to avoid them.

6.1 RESEARCH ISSUES

A number of ethical issues arise in psychological research (as well as in medical and other research). Some of the main issues involve deception, pain, the ethics of research on animals, and confidentiality.

6.1.1 Deception

Sometimes, for research to work, participants must be kept unaware of the purpose of the research until it is completed. In some cases, however, psychologists have used extreme forms of deception. Stanley Milgram (1974) led participants to believe that they were delivering painful electric shocks to another person, when in fact they were not. When Milgram carried out his studies, researchers were generally not required to obtain advance approval of their plans to conduct a psychological investigation. Another ethical issue arises when researchers pay participants to indulge in a vice, as when researchers pay alcoholics to drink to study their drinking behavior. Today, deception is permitted in research only when the benefits clearly outweigh the costs.

6.1.2 Informed Consent

Before participants begin their involvement in a study, they are required to give informed consent to participate in the research. In the informed-consent procedure, the individuals are told what kinds of tasks they may be expected to perform and what kinds of situations they may expect to encounter, with specific qualifications on the use of deception. They are also told that they may withdraw from the study without penalty. It is unethical to run a study without informed consent. For children or others who are not capable of giving fully informed consent, it is necessary to obtain informed consent as well from a parent or other guardian.

Experience Is the Best Teacher

Bob knows a tenured faculty member who planned a series of experiments and decided informally to test some pilot subjects in order to fine-tune his materials in advance of submitting them to his institutional review board. The board caught wind of what the faculty member was doing and made a formal accusation of academic misconduct against him. He ended up losing his privilege of testing subjects for an extended period of time. The moral of the story is that before you begin testing subjects, even in a pilot, you should get IRB approval. Don't risk your academic reputation on collecting data, even pilot data, without IRB approval. If a study is a pilot study, you should say so in your IRB application.

6.1.3 Debriefing

After the research is completed, the participants are fully debriefed about it. They are told exactly the nature of the experiment, informed of any deception that may have been involved, and given the reason for the deception. Minor deception is usually permitted if the value of the proposed research justifies the deception. But the deception must be necessary for the purpose of the experiment, and it must be fully explained afterward.

6.1.4 Pain

In the past, it was not uncommon for experiments to involve mild electric shocks to participants. These shocks were slightly painful but not harmful. In addition, studies sometimes have had the potential to cause psychological damage, because many experiments are stressful. How stressful a study is often depends on the individual as much as on the experiment. What is difficult for one person may be relaxing for another and neutral for yet another. Still, researchers generally try to anticipate and to minimize distress (unless distress itself is the construct under study). Institutions will generally not permit studies that are likely to cause any long-lasting pain or harm. If participating in a study might cause short-term pain or stress, participants must be fully informed in advance about possible consequences, via the informed consent procedure. Moreover, informed consent requires that participants be told that they are free to leave the experiment at any time without fear of any negative repercussions. Thus, if participants thought that they could tolerate the conditions of an experiment beforehand but then found out in the course of it that they could not, they could leave at once.

6.1.5 Confidentiality and Anonymity

Most experiments in psychology are conducted on an anonymous basis – participants' names are not associated with their data. Occasionally, however, complete anonymity is not possible. For example, if an experimenter wants to compare students' scores on some standardized test of ability to their freshman grades in college, the experimenter needs to have some means of identifying individual students. Even when participants cannot be anonymous, however, experimenters go to great lengths to ensure that participants' names are known only to the experimenters. Confidentiality can be a particularly important issue when researchers are studying basic characteristics, such as health status. Confidentiality means that results will not be disclosed to anyone not connected with the research where identification of the participant would be possible. One needs to guarantee that information about their health, for example, will not later be used against them, such as in employment situations. If you ensure anonymity and/or confidentiality in your informed consent form, then you must be certain you have the means to provide it.

6.2 ISSUES IN RESEARCH WITH NONHUMAN ANIMALS

Issues become murky when nonhuman animals – such as rats, pigeons, rabbits, dogs, or even simple multicelled organisms – are involved instead of people. Nonhuman animals cannot sign informed consent forms, for example. Most institutions vigorously attempt to ensure that animals are protected and that they have all they require in terms of food, shelter, and freedom from harm or discomfort. Furthermore, in recent years, the government has increasingly regulated scientific research and the appropriate treatment of animals. However, nonhuman animals sometimes are exposed to painful or even harmful procedures. In such cases, institutions attempt to weigh the potential benefits of the research to humans against the potential harm to the nonhuman animals.

Questions regarding how to guard animal rights are not easily answered. On the one hand, no scrupulous researcher actively wishes to cause harm to animals. On the other hand, some of the most important discoveries in both medicine and psychology have come from research in which laboratory animals were sacrificed to advance our knowledge about and our ability to help humans. Given the choice of testing new drugs that may be beneficial but whose side effects are unknown first on laboratory animals or first on people, society has opted for testing of laboratory animals. Those whose lives have been saved by such testing, or who have had relatives whose lives have been saved, understand at first hand why the testing has been accepted by much of society. Review boards and policymakers attempt to weigh the costs and benefits involved in all research, whether it employs human or laboratory-animal participants. Still, the controversy over use of laboratory-animal participants is far from over. Fortunately, there is much less controversy regarding another ethical issue, that of faking data.

6.3 FAKING OF DATA

Probably the single greatest research sin is faking of data: either making the data up entirely or collecting data but then inventing data that you did not actually collect. The faking of data is viewed as sufficiently grave that one can lose one's job or position as a student over it. Whereas some ethical issues can be gray – was a person's contribution of ideas great enough to merit coauthorship – faking is viewed as an absolute black-and-white issue. Don't ever even think about it. Those who have been caught doing it are disgraced, and there is not likely to be any redemption. It is not something that other scientists will forget, and they are not likely to forgive it either.

> ## Give It Some More Thought
>
> Investigators, even professors at top institutions around the world, have been caught faking data – either inventing whole data sets or tampering with the data sets in order to achieve the results they want. Why would investigators, even some with big reputations, risk their careers in this way? For example, you might point out that some investigators seek a lot of attention, including from the media, and may conclude that the only way they can get that attention is by having super-compelling findings (including falsified ones).

6.4 INSTITUTIONAL REVIEW BOARD APPROVAL

Do not under any circumstances run a study without written approval from an institutional review board (IRB), unless you have a written document stating that your research is exempt. Researchers can get into serious trouble if they run studies that are not approved. Sometimes, it is frustrating waiting for approval, and many researchers have complaints about the handling of their proposals to IRBs.

Nevertheless, you must make sure that you have written approval before you go ahead and collect data.

6.5 FINANCIAL MANAGEMENT AND MISMANAGEMENT

Rules regarding financial management are extremely strict. If you are given funds for a particular purpose, you must use those funds for that purpose. You cannot redirect them without permission. So if money is for payment of participants, it must be used to pay participants. If you want to redirect it to another use, you need permission to do so. You cannot use funds allocated for one research project to fund another project. Universities have been fined, sometimes millions of dollars, when funds were redirected from one project to another. These days, many and probably most grants and contracts are audited, sooner or later. So you need to keep a clear paper or digital trail of where money is going. Be extremely careful of how you manage funds because there is essentially no tolerance for diversion of funds from intended purposes.

Experience Is the Best Teacher

When Bob was in graduate school, faculty members were much "looser" in their spending of grant money than faculty members are today. No one thought much about shifting small sums of money from the research program of one grant to the research program of another grant. Today, this is no longer the case. A number of mechanisms have been put into place to ensure that money allocated to a particular grant is spent *only* on work related to that grant. It therefore is important *never* to shift funds allocated for one project to funds allocated for another – unless you have prior approval from the relevant funding agency or agencies.

6.6 WRITING ISSUES

In our experience, there are 12 areas in which ethics issues become salient when writing a paper: accuracy of reporting, inclusion/exclusion of data and data analyses, interpretation of data, authorship, origins of ideas, plagiarism, citations, permissions, reanalysis of data sets, piecemeal publication, simultaneous submission, and duplicate publication.

6.6.1 Accuracy of Reporting

Who among us can say he or she is never sloppy? Probably none of us. But writing a psychology paper is not the place to be sloppy. Sloppiness may not sound like an issue of ethics, but when your sloppiness results in people drawing wrong conclusions and possibly designing future research based on your inaccuracies, it becomes an ethical issue. Even worse would be treatments designed to help people based on inaccurately reported data, for which there would be a risk that the intervention designed to help people actually harms them.

There are many ways in which accuracy of reporting can be impugned in particular instances. Errors in reporting are especially possible because computers will analyze your data, even if you give them the wrong data to analyze. Are you sure you gave the computer the right data set? Are you sure that you distinguished clearly between values of "0" and missing values in each data cell? Are you sure that you have labeled the various data points correctly? Are you sure the columns and rows of tables are properly labeled?

Are you sure that figures give an accurate rather than a misleading picture of the data? The basic point, then, is to be sure that your reporting is correct and as nearly complete as possible.

6.6.2 Inclusion and Exclusion of Data and Data Analyses

It is sometimes appropriate to exclude data from an analysis. For example, you may exclude outliers from data analysis, or data from participants who obviously did not take the task seriously (e.g., they responded randomly or failed to respond to many questions), or who did not understand the task. However, there is sometimes a fine line between concluding that someone did not understand the task or did not take the task seriously and concluding that someone just did poorly on the task because it was too hard or inadequately explained to him or her. You have a responsibility as a researcher not to bias your analyses or your reporting of the data.

For example, if you exclude participants from the data analyses, you have to say how many were excluded, why they were excluded, and if possible, how you knew that they fell into the category you claim they fell into. You also have an obligation to include data analyses that do not support your hypotheses or what you hoped to find, not only ones that support your views. It is tempting to include data analyses that support your idea and to exclude those that do not, but it is not ethical. You do not have to describe in detail every analysis you did that fails to reject the null hypothesis. But you have to indicate that you did these analyses and that no significant results turned up.

6.6.3 Interpretation of Data

Occasionally, data are self-evident and self-explanatory, but not often. Usually they can be interpreted in multiple ways. Because we are all susceptible to confirmation bias, our tendency is to interpret data in a way that best suits what we had hoped to find.

A problem is that reviewers often have a very different mind-set and look for alternative interpretations of the data. If authors are too one-sided, reviewers may come to believe that they are purposely biasing the interpretation of the data in a way that may even become unethical.

Recently, we have been involved both in seeking to sell a house and in trying to buy a house. We have been taken somewhat aback by the difference in perspectives. When you are trying to sell a house, you concentrate on all the really fine features of the house and tend to ignore or discount the negative features. When you are seeking to buy a house, you tend much more to notice all the flaws. It is the same with a journal article. When you write the article, you are the "seller" and your temptation is to ignore the weaknesses in your data and your article. To maximize your chances of success with reviewers and an editor, try your best to put yourself in the "buyer" state of mind. What weaknesses will the buyers see, especially those who tend to be critical of the particular kind of house you are selling? Editors often deliberately send papers out for review to scholars whose views are different from your own. So keep those reviewers in mind and write with the notion that they are likely to be reviewing your work.

6.6.4 Authorship

Authorship is sometimes simple and other times remarkably complex. If the paper is sole authored and no one else has contributed scientifically to it, then your situation is perhaps simple. But often a number of people work on a project, and it becomes more of a challenge to decide who should be a coauthor and in what order coauthors should be listed.

We have found that, although there are no easy answers, seven general principles are worth keeping in mind.

1. If multiple individuals are involved, issues of coauthorship should be discussed before the study is even started. You may not know in advance in exactly what order coauthors will be listed, but to the extent possible, it is better to clarify issues before the research is conducted rather than after it is done.
2. Anyone who has contributed meaningfully to the scientific ideas in the paper should be a coauthor. Obviously, there is ambiguity in what constitutes a "meaningful" contribution. But that is the nature of the enterprise. People who had ideas for the conceptualization, hypotheses, methods, data analysis, and interpretation are typically coauthors. We have had situations in which we talked to someone about the data and that person then demanded to be a coauthor. So you need to think carefully about what others will interpret as "meaningful scientific contribution," not just what you think about it.

3. Simply collecting data or preparing stimulus materials does not qualify a person for coauthorship. If all someone does is collect data or prepare materials, then that person is usually acknowledged in a footnote. But even here, things can get tricky. If the person not only prepared the stimulus materials but also designed them, then the designing of the materials may well qualify the person for coauthorship.

4. It is better to be over-inclusive rather than under-inclusive in inclusion of coauthors. You are much more likely to find yourself in conflict with people over exclusion than over inclusion. Recently, one of us worked on a paper for which it was ambiguous whether a particular person should be included. The person was invited to be a coauthor and declined but greatly appreciated the consideration of being asked.

5. The order of authorship generally reflects level of scientific contribution, except that the last position is often reserved for someone who has also contributed in a special way, such as through providing the funding through a grant or being integral in forming the team. However, simply providing grant money alone does not qualify individuals for coauthorship unless they have made a meaningful ideational contribution to the work.

6. If you find yourself in a dispute that is not resolving itself, rather than letting it get ugly, it is better to agree to a means for resolution of the conflict. For example, you might appeal collectively to the chair of a department or a dean. In general, administrators do not relish getting involved in such disputes, but they typically would rather get involved than see them turn ugly.

7. If you have greater seniority in the field (e.g., if you're a professor rather than a student), please remember what it was like when you were more junior. More junior people, in general, need credit to progress through the field. You may need the credit less. Sometimes, when people's promotions are on the line, their sense of ethics can be strained by the realization that if they do not have sufficient professional credit, they may lose a promotion or even a job. But if one acts unethically in coauthorship matters, it not only speaks ill of one, but also gets around. Soon other people will not want to work with you because they believe you are a credit hog.

> ## What's Wrong Here?
>
> Ellen spent almost a year collecting and entering data for a large scientific project with over a dozen coauthors. She is therefore miffed when she learns that she will not be granted coauthorship on the resulting article, but rather, only a footnote. She plans to file a formal complaint with her university.
>
> **Answer:** Although collecting and entering data can consume a lot of time and energy, these activities are not in themselves bases for coauthorship. Ellen might have become a coauthor if, say, in the course of collecting data, she realized that there was something wrong with the experimental protocol and she made a suggestion that resulted in a substantial change to the scientific protocol. Coauthorship is determined on the basis of intellectual contribution to the final product, not on the basis of contribution of time or effort.

6.6.5 Origins of Ideas

Usually, when we think we have an idea, it is indeed our idea. But the origins of ideas can be complex. Sometimes we may have had a conversation with someone and an idea came out of that conversation. In such cases, the person with whom one had the conversation may (legitimately) expect to be involved in and to have coauthorship of subsequent research based on the conversation. The conversation may be in a professional office, but it also may be at a cocktail party. Sometimes, an idea may evolve in a research seminar with a number of people in it, and it will not be feasible for all of them to be involved in the study, although it may be appropriate to acknowledge them in a note. It behooves you to be careful in thinking about the origins of your ideas and to make sure that anyone who would have a legitimate claim to coauthorship is included.

6.6.6 Plagiarism

Plagiarism is basically a failure of attribution. There are few academic sins that are viewed more gravely than this one. Plagiarism takes two general forms: plagiarism of others' work and plagiarism of one's own work. We discuss both sequentially.

6.6.6.1 Plagiarism of Others' Work

Plagiarism of others' work occurs when you fail adequately to cite the work of others, or fail to cite it at all. Plagiarism applies both to ideas and to actual words used to express ideas. Never quote others without putting the material in quotation marks and giving a correct citation. Never use the words of others without citing them. If you paraphrase, that is fine, but then say you are paraphrasing and give the correct citation. Do not use material from tables or figures without citation and do not just copy tables or figures and use them as your own. When in doubt, cite!

Whereas once it was somewhat difficult to detect plagiarism, today there are electronic programs that can check a piece of work for plagiarism. These programs rely on enormous databases, and you should assume that whatever you are using as a source is in the databases. Moreover, even a simple search engine such as Google or Bing can be used to detect plagiarism. If you quote extensively, you may need to get permission, as discussed in Chapter 9.

6.6.6.2 Self-Plagiarism

Self-plagiarism occurs when you fail adequately to cite your own work. It is totally understandable that you may wish to cite or draw on past work you have done. But doing so becomes a problem when you fail to cite that past work. In extreme cases, someone might attempt to publish exactly the same paper twice without noting that the paper has been previously published. Be sure when you draw on previous work of your own that you accurately cite it.

Experience Is the Best Teacher

Just as increasing numbers of teachers are using plagiarism software to detect plagiarism in student papers, so are increasing numbers of journal editors submitting journal submissions to such software to check for plagiarism, whether of others or oneself. One therefore needs to be very careful that one's submissions represent original work, and where they do not, to quote and cite original sources appropriately.

6.6.7 Citations

On the one hand, when you write a paper you cannot possibly cite every past work that has been done on the topic you are discussing. On the other hand, if you do not cite work that reviewers see as directly relevant, you are likely to be called on it and criticized for not including it. In particular, you have an ethical obligation to cite not only work that supports your hypotheses but also work that runs contrary to them. Reviewers tend to get annoyed when you put together either a one-sided presentation or a presentation that seems to ignore everyone who has done relevant work except you and perhaps a handful of collaborators. So be sure to cite all work likely to be seen as directly relevant. In our experience, it also pays to cite, where possible and relevant, researchers who are likely to review your paper.

6.6.8 Permissions

If you use the work of others, you must get permission. Permissions can be for tables, figures, photographs, or long quotations. Failure to receive permission can hold up publication of your work or can even potentially put you in legal jeopardy if the work is published without needed permissions.

6.6.9 Reanalysis of Data Sets

If you reanalyze a data set that previously has been published, make sure you are clear that you are presenting a reanalysis of an existing data set rather than an analysis of a new data set.

6.6.10 Piecemeal Publication

There is increasing pressure to publish fairly large quantities for hiring, tenure, and promotion. Such pressure creates a temptation toward piecemeal publication, which is the publication of one's work in small bits rather than as a more integrated whole. There are two other kinds of pressure that can lead to piecemeal publication. The first is that studies often are done sequentially, and one cannot always wait until all possible studies one might do are completed until one publishes. The other is that journals generally prefer shorter articles to longer ones because of scarce numbers of pages. In general, you should try to publish your work in meaningful wholes rather than bits, remembering at the same time that you do not want to wait too long to publish because, if you do, you risk the work's getting out of date or being scooped. You also risk its not being at least in press by the time you really need it to appear on your curriculum vitae (CV) either as in press or as published.

Experience Is the Best Teacher

Although piecemeal publication can be a problem, so can holding onto a data set for too long. You not only have the risk of being scooped, but also the risk that, by the time you are evaluated (as a graduate student, faculty member, or whatever), the work on which you have spent so much time will not be published, or possibly even accepted by a scientific journal. You therefore need to balance the need to avoid piecemeal publication with the need to have your work come out in a timely way.

6.6.11 Simultaneous Submission

You are not permitted to submit the same article to more than one journal simultaneously. Hence, in making a submission, you need to take into account the journal's typical review time as well as your chances of acceptance, as you have to wait until the process is completed before resubmitting the piece.

If your article is rejected with resubmission allowed, you do not have to resubmit to the same journal. You can instead choose to submit it to another journal if you prefer.

You are generally permitted to submit a book proposal to more than one publisher simultaneously. If you do so, however, you should inform the publishers that you are multiply submitting the proposal.

6.6.12 Duplicate Publication

You are not permitted to publish the same work twice unless the second publication is clearly labeled as a reprint. You also may not publish a second work that is essentially the same as another without making clear to the editor of the second journal what you are doing, and then letting the editor decide if the piece is sufficiently newsworthy.

We cannot possibly include in this chapter every ethical issue that can arise in the life of researchers. In most cases, the best thing to do is to follow common sense and not rationalize unethical behavior. Nothing quite destroys a career the way unethical behavior does, so start and maintain your career the right way by scrupulously avoiding it!

PART II

Micro-Challenges in Writing Papers: Presenting Your Ideas in Writing

7 | A Word about Content, Language, and Style

In the previous chapters, we have described what belongs in a literature review or an experimental paper. You have learned how to do literature research, what the goals of the two different kinds of papers are, and how to report your findings. To write an appealing paper that maximizes your chances of getting your research published, it is important not only that your studies have substance but also that you well explain about that substance. This chapter provides you with some guidelines on how to write a paper that conveys your findings in an attractive, easily readable, and convincing way. We have divided the guidelines into three parts: Part 1 explains how to present your content in a way that is compelling and convincing. Part 2 deals with style issues, and Part 3 deals with language and grammar issues.

7.1 CONTENT GUIDELINES

1. State clearly the problem you are addressing, and then organize the article around the problem.

2. Start strong.

3. Make clear up front what the new and valuable contribution of your article is, and make sure you are right.

4. Tell readers why they should be interested.

5. Make sure the article does what it says it will do.

6. Make sure that the literature review is focused, reasonably complete, and balanced.

7. Make clear how your work builds on that of others.

8. Check your data analyses and interpretations.

9. Always explain what your results mean – don't force the reader to decipher them.

10. Make sure that your conclusions follow from your data.

11. Make clear what the limitations of your work are.

12. Be sure to consider alternative interpretations of the data.

13. End strongly and state a clear take-home message.

1. State clearly the problem you are addressing and then organize the article around the problem.

Sometimes it is hard to figure out exactly what problem authors of an article thought they were trying to solve. This phenomenon can occur because an author does not know what problem the article is supposed to solve or because the nature of the problem was not clearly communicated. It is the author's responsibility to make clear early in the article what problem or problems the article tackles.

Once you have stated the problem, organize the article around it. Show why the problem is important, why it should matter to anyone beside you. If you do not know, why should a reviewer? In the literature review, use relevance to the problem tackled as the major basis for deciding what to cite. In the "Methods" section, tell the story of how the successive analyses help solve the problem that you originally posed. And then, in the "Discussion" section, summarize what you did and discuss its implications.

A clearly focused, tightly organized article has a great advantage in the review process. You are helping the referee understand what your goals are and how you are trying to reach them. If you leave it to the referees to figure these things out, there is a good chance that the conclusions they come to will differ from your own.

2. Start strong.

"Smith and Jones (2009) found that 83 percent of readers never got beyond the first paragraph of the majority of articles they began to read." This opening is an example of how to be boring, as are these opening sentences: "Past research shows..." or "It is interesting to note that... "(says who?). A stronger start asks a question or states a problem pertinent to the theme of your article: "Why are so many psychology articles safe and cheap substitutes for sleeping pills?" for example, or "Dullness blunts the impact of many potentially interesting articles." Tell readers what the article is about in a provocative way that catches their attention.

3. **Make clear up front what the new and valuable contribution of your article is, and make sure you are right.**

Our conversations with journal editors suggest that the No. 1 reason for rejection of journal articles is lack of substance – there just is not enough new information in the article to justify its publication in a journal. Reviewers, too, are on the lookout for articles that have little or nothing new to say.

It therefore behooves you to ask yourself what the new and valuable contribution of your article is and to make clear near the beginning of the article what it is. Do not expect reviewers to figure it out for themselves. If you cannot figure it out, you cannot expect them to. If you cannot find such a contribution, either do more research or do more thinking before you submit the article.

4. **Tell readers why they should be interested.**

"These findings are interesting and important. Therefore, you should support my promotion to tenure." Don't expect readers to know why you find a topic interesting or why they should find it interesting. Show them! Keep your audience in mind: The more you can relate your topic to concerns of your readers, the more interest you will generate. If you are writing for perceptual psychologists, make contact with the theoretical issues that concern people in that field. If you are writing for teachers, show how your findings can be used to improve teaching.

Give It Some More Thought

Why has the expression "interesting and important," such as in "The results are interesting and important," become such an awful cliché? One possible reason is that it is much easier to say results are interesting and important than actually to demonstrate it.

---

5. **Make sure the article does what it says it will do.**

"In this article, I will characterize the meaning of life, solve the problem of world hunger, and reveal at long last Richard Nixon's secret plan to end the Vietnam War." Many articles are rejected by journals because they do not deliver what they promise. They claim much but deliver little. For example, experiments should follow from the theory you present. Make sure that you frame your article in terms of what you have really accomplished, not in terms of what you wished you had accomplished.

6. Make sure that the literature review is focused, reasonably complete, and balanced.

"Thus, both studies showed that high levels of reasoning performance require people to wear propeller beanies on their heads. Other studies, showing that high levels of reasoning performance require pocket protectors, are irrelevant." Reviewers are infuriated by literature reviews that are biased in favor of a single point of view, especially if it's not their own (and chances are good that at least some of the reviewers will have views different from your own). Reviewers are even more upset when their own work is clearly relevant but not cited (you can say *Sayonara* to your acceptance). And reviewers do not want to read about every marginally relevant study ever done. Make your review complete and current, but also keep it focused and concise so that it encompasses but does not overwhelm what you are studying.

Experience Is the Best Teacher

It is tempting, in a literature review, to cite or at least use secondary sources that refer back to original articles of interest. If you are lazy or cannot easily find the original reference, using a secondary source can save you time and bother. There are several problems with doing this, however. First, if you cite the secondary source as your basis of information about a primary source, you are advertising that you were too lazy to look up the original material. Second, whether you cite the secondary source or not, often secondary sources misrepresent primary sources, so you inadvertently may be propagating an error. Third, sometimes you end up in a truly embarrassing situation. For example, Richard Atkinson and Keith Wescourt published an influential paper many years ago. A scholar mistakenly cited it as "Atkinson and Westcourt." Other scholars then started citing it as "Atkinson and Westcourt." In doing so, they trumpeted to the world that they were too lazy to look up the original article and were relying on a secondary source that in fact incorrectly spelled Keith's name.

7. Make clear how your work builds on that of others.

No one likes a credit hog – someone who makes a contribution and then acts as though no one else has ever had any idea of value in the area of work. Sharing credit goes beyond citing potential reviewers. It involves showing how your work builds on their work and the work of many others. Scholarship always requires drawing connections between what is new and what is old.

It also is important in citing references that you are up to date. Referees generally are not happy to see reference lists that would have been up to date a decade earlier. So check recent literature in the area in which you are working. In this way, you also are less likely to repeat what someone already has done.

Some authors may feel that, in setting out in a bold new direction, they really owe almost nothing to anybody else. But it is important to realize that, even when you oppose old ideas, you still are using those ideas as a base from which to map your campaign of opposition. And even when you move away from what others have done, had they not done what they had done, you would not have had their work to move away from. Thus, it is important to show how you build on, not just how you go beyond, past work.

8. Check your data analyses and interpretations.

If your article makes a substantial contribution, there is a good chance that someone will ask for your data, which you are obliged to provide. This "someone" may be a referee or someone who later reads the article. One of the more embarrassing events in the life of an academic is to have the interpretation of one's data analyses demolished. It is therefore important to check that you have used the correct forms of analysis and to ensure that you have transcribed the statistics correctly.

Also, make sure that your interpretations are correct. For example, more stringent levels of significance do not indicate stronger effects but rather decrease likelihoods that a given result would have been obtained under the null hypothesis.

9. Always explain what your results mean – don't force the reader to decipher them.

"Finally, we obtained a seven-way interaction among the independent variables, clearly showing that the variables need to be considered in terms of their interactive as well as their additive effects." Interpret your results. With enough time, readers could figure out the meaning for themselves, but who has time? Don't leave the interpretation for the "Discussion." Speculation and ideas that relate your work to that of others should go in the "Discussion" section. Basic interpretations should accompany the results – while people still remember what they are.

Experience Is the Best Teacher

Sometimes even experienced investigators fail to explain what their results mean. Bob just read an article by a senior investigator. He presented a series of complex results with hardly any interpretation at all. When asked to provide an interpretation, he said that he preferred to present "just the facts." But science is not merely a collection of facts. The facts are only meaningful to the extent they fit into an interpretive framework. It is your job, as an investigator, to provide that framework, not to let your readers guess what it might be.

---

10. Make sure that your conclusions follow from your data.

High up on the list of annoyances to referees are authors whose claims go well beyond their data. Such authors are all too common. They may have a modest finding and then write about that finding as though they have changed the face of the earth. If your conclusions go beyond your data, chances are that referees will notice this and lash out at the conclusion and at you.

There is a place in most articles for speculation that goes beyond the boundaries of the data. This place is the "Discussion" section. But when you go beyond the boundaries of the data, make clear that you are speculating. Do not assume that referees or other readers will know that you are in a speculative state of mind.

11. Make clear what the limitations of your work are.

Any good "Discussion" section includes at least some frank acknowledgment of the limitations of the study. Did you use just a single methodology or type of stimulus material? Did you use a restricted range of types of participants? Did you look at behavior only in one kind of situation, perhaps an artificially contrived one? Referees and all readers appreciate honesty. Most important, referees are less likely to mention in reviews limitations that you already have mentioned, unless the referees see them as fatal flaws.

Many authors nurse the hope that referees will not notice the flaws. Such a hope is likely to be wishful thinking. Moreover, it is a misguided wish. Worse even than getting a paper rejected before publication is having to retract it after publication or having to resist an onslaught of published criticism for flaws that you should have noticed. Save yourself the trouble by acknowledging the flaws yourself.

Give It Some More Thought

Why do you think referees of articles tend to be less forgiving if authors leave it to the referees to figure out the weaknesses of a study rather than if the authors point out these weaknesses themselves? For example, you might point out that if referees have to figure out weaknesses for themselves, they may feel like the authors are hiding the truth and thus may feel miffed.

---

12. Be sure to consider alternative interpretations of the data.

"Thus, the data overwhelmingly support the XYZ theory, and if you can't see it, you need to have your head examined." No data set is unequivocal. Sooner or later, someone will see one or more alternative interpretations. You are much better off recognizing and trying to discount the alternatives yourself than leaving the task to the reviewers or to your potential readers. Even if you cannot discount every alternative, readers will appreciate your honesty in recognizing that other explanations may exist. If the results are too inconclusive, your article may be turned down. But even published articles are not fully definitive, and readers expect you to admit as much.

What's Wrong Here?

"The high correlation (.64) between scores on the test of extraversion and people's tendency to seek out others for help

> (*cont.*)
>
> showed that, indeed, being extraverted leads one to have greater willingness to seek aid from others."
>
> **Answer:** Correlations do not demonstrate causation. Both the high scores on the extraversion test and people's tendency to seek help, for example, might be a result of some third unknown factor. Also, a correlation of .64 is a moderately high level of association, but certainly should not lead one to make any kind of causal attribution, in whatever direction.

13. End strongly and state a clear take-home message.

"In sum, there is a need for further research to clarify the issues." What a snooze! There's always room for further research; readers don't have to be told that. Readers want a punch line. They want to go away from a paper with a clear conclusion, preferably a snappy one (which may or may not be in the last sentence). When readers later try to remember your article, they will probably do so by means of your conclusion. Leave readers with what you most want them to remember.

7.2 STYLE GUIDELINES

In this section, we first give you an overview of the guidelines and subsequently explain them in more detail:

1. Your article should interest, inform, and persuade your readers.

2. Place yourself in the background.

3. Write for your readers.

4. Emphasize logical flow and organization.

5. Be creative, and give concrete examples.

6. Write sentences that are clear, readable, and concise.

7. Prefer simpler to more complicated sentences.

8. Use summary statements.

9. Use transitions.

10. Avoid digressions.

11. Don't overexplain.

12. Don't assume that people will know what you mean or be familiar with abbreviations or jargon.

13. Write for a somewhat broader and technically less skilled audience than you expect to read the article.

14. Avoid overstatement.

15. Eliminate unnecessary redundancy.

16. Don't bother to say that your results are "interesting" or "important."

17. Cite sources as well as findings.

18. Don't end your article by saying, "More research is needed."

19. Proofread your article.

20. Request a critical reading of your article from an adviser or colleague.

1. Your article should interest, inform, and persuade your readers.

Psychological writing should not be dull or stuffy. An article tells a story. Like a story, it should capture readers' interest. You must interest your readers in your article; otherwise, readers will find something else to do. Even teachers reading course papers will often read boring papers more quickly and less carefully than they will read interesting papers. Although you can lose a reader at any time, the major decision points for the reader are the title, abstract, and introduction.

An optimal title is one that concisely informs readers of what the article is about. Such a title will minimize the number of people who start the article only to find that the topic doesn't interest them and maximize the number of people who start the article because the topic does interest them. The abstract should summarize the article while conveying to the reader why the topic, hypotheses, and results are of theoretical or practical interest. The introduction should further motivate readers by pointing out why the research is a necessary next step in putting together the pieces of an as-yet-unsolved puzzle. The reader should finish the introduction believing that you have (a) put together one or more pieces of the puzzle and (b) pointed the way toward further pieces being put together. The second accomplishment is as important as the first. No one likes to come to the end of an article only to find that the research has hit a dead end.

The best way to inform your readers is to tell them what they are likely to want to know – no more and no less. Experienced writers acquire a knack for knowing what to include and what not to include. Ask yourself which points are central to your main arguments and which are peripheral details possibly of interest to you but not to your readers.

The major means of persuasion is tight logic. Tight logic is more convincing to readers of psychological papers than rhetorical devices. Remember that you must sell your ideas but not oversell them, and you must be persuasive without being condescending. In attacking alternative positions, stick to substance, avoiding ad hominem or irrelevant attacks. (People who disagree with this advice don't know what they're talking about!)

2. Place yourself in the background.

There was a time when it was considered bad form for writers to place themselves anywhere near the foreground of a article. Writers avoided first-person references at all costs. When strictures against first-person references started to ease, sole authors often started referring to themselves as *we*, even though they were sole authors of papers. Today, references to oneself as *we* are discouraged. If you are the sole author of an article and use the word *we*, you should use it only to refer to yourself and your readers, not just to yourself. If you mean *I*, then use *I*. Overuse of the first-person singular, however, tends to distract the reader, calling attention to you rather than to what you are saying. Stay in the background, surfacing only when you have good reason to draw attention to yourself, as in emphasizing that an idea is your own speculation rather than a conclusion closely following from a set of data.

In some schools, you are expected to tell the story of your life when you write a paper, especially a dissertation. This story includes all your false starts, blind alleys, and tales of woe. You even may be expected to explain all the reasons your manipulation didn't work out the way it was supposed to. Journal space is precious, however, and there just isn't room for these autobiographical details. Therefore, journal articles are usually written in a manner that bears little resemblance to the way the research was actually conducted. This difference is not dishonesty: Professionals simply know how the system works.

(Bob first learned this fact when he was in graduate school. It was a dark and stormy night. He'd just received an editor's letter. For further details, see his *Complete Life and Works*, Vol. 21, published by Narcismo Press.)

3. Write for your readers.

Writing for your readers means keeping in mind four things. First, take into account the extent of their technical vocabulary. Terms that are familiar to professional psychologists may be unfamiliar to members of a general audience. Even within the field of psychology, specialists in different fields have different technical vocabularies. Whenever you can replace a complicated word with a simple word, do it. If you must use technical words, define them. It is most annoying to find a technical term used repeatedly without first having been defined. Second, maintain a level of formality in your writing that is appropriate for your audience. A book addressed to students can be more informal than a book addressed to professional psychologists. Remember, though, more formal writing need not and should not be stilted. Formality is not a substitute for readability. Third, include only those details that are appropriate for your audience. Readers of a popular journal such as *Psychology Today* will probably be less interested in methodological and statistical details than will readers of the scholarly journal *Psychological Review*. Fourth, avoid abbreviations. They can be annoying, and often interfere with the reader's comprehension of the text (QED!).

Experience Is the Best Teacher

In our experience, writers far more often tend to overestimate the background knowledge of their readers than they do to underestimate it. Perhaps it is because they have forgotten how recently concepts and terms that are familiar to them once were unfamiliar. You therefore are better off assuming less rather than more background knowledge on the part of readers (and listeners).

---

4. Emphasize logical flow and organization.

Don't expect readers to decipher the logical sequence of your ideas. It is important that the prose flows and that the organization emerges clearly. Write your ideas down in a sensible sequence. Readers should concentrate on what you say, not on how you say it. Logical organization can mean the difference between confusion and clarity.

5. Be creative, and give concrete examples.

Some academic writers harbor the illusion that the more abstract and highbrow their writing is, the more readers will be impressed. On the contrary, most readers need concrete examples or analogies to understand other people's ideas. The more abstract the points, the more it is that readers need examples. Readers are busy: Don't expect them to generate the examples. It's your responsibility. You have all read papers that have left you drowning in abstractions. We'll leave it to you to think of specific examples.

6. Write sentences that are clear, readable, and concise.

You know an unclear sentence when you read it. Why, then, don't authors know unclear sentences when they write them? A major reason is their personal involvement in their own work. If authors omit or poorly describe certain details, they can subconsciously insert or clarify them. Because readers do not share authors' cognitive structure, readers cannot do the same. A large amount of unclear writing would never pass beyond authors' eyes if all authors were willing to reread their papers in the role of naive readers. A major reason for lack of clarity in writing is an author's unwillingness to go back over what has been written and rewrite it. One reason for this unwillingness is a delusion that readers won't notice unclear sentences. Authors hope that the imperfections in their writing will pass by readers unnoticed. Unfortunately, the typical outcome is the opposite of what authors desire. Readers stumble over the unclear sentence and then reread it, trying to make sense of it. Instead of the sentence blending into the background, it sticks out like a sore thumb. If there are enough unclear sentences, what started out as temporary confusion may become permanent. Hence, do not succumb to the delusion that you will get away with poor writing. Assume that your readers are as likely to detect an unclear sentence as you are to write one. (For the ideation of unclarity is the worst form of self-indulgence, and an ideological facsimile!)

7. Prefer simpler to more complicated sentences.

Sentence structure is largely a matter of style, and you should write in a style that is comfortable to you. Some major writers, like Ernest Hemingway, preferred short sentences; others, like William Faulkner, preferred long sentences. The advantages of short sentences, from a journalistic point of view, are that they are (a) easier to understand and (b) less likely to contain errors of grammar or diction. When you find yourself becoming bogged down in a complicated construction, try to restate in two or more sentences what you had planned to state in one. You will probably find that you are able to say better what you wanted to say. (Having thought about this, you will realize as you read this sentence at the end of the paragraph why complexity in an already long sentence creates bewilderment!)

What's Wrong Here?

"After the subjects entered the room, they were given a questionnaire to fill out, which required them to provide basic demographic information and which served as an entrée to the main assessment, which was a test that measured their various personality traits, and this test in turn was preliminary to an intelligence test that measured their verbal, mathematical, and spatial-reasoning abilities."

Answer: The sentence is much too long and convoluted.

---

8. Use summary statements.

Explain what you're going to say, say it, and then restate what you've said. In this way, you provide an advance organization for the reader, explicate the main content, and emphasize to readers what you want them to remember.

Psychologists frequently divide long papers into sections and subsections. It is often helpful to include one or two brief summary statements at the end of each section or at the end of a long argument. Such statements improve comprehensibility at very little cost in additional space. Summaries help readers (a) quickly absorb the main point of each section as they complete it and (b) keep track of where they are. A long summary in the middle of a paper is unnecessary and inadvisable, because it is redundant with the abstract and possibly the conclusions. (To summarize, a summary at this point in the chapter is unnecessary!)

9. Use transitions.

Have you ever noticed that some people write clear sentences, and yet their writing nevertheless appears disjointed? A common cause of disjointed and choppy writing is missing transitions between ideas. Missing transitions are sometimes caused by careless thinking: The writer goes from Step A to Step C without thinking of the necessary, intervening Step B. More often, though, missing transitions are caused by quick thinking: Authors think faster than they write. As authors write Sentence A, they are already thinking about Sentence B. By the time they finish writing Sentence A, they have started thinking about Sentence C and so proceed to write Sentence C, forgetting to insert the necessary transitional Sentence B. No matter how clearly Sentences A and C are stated, readers will pause in reading Sentence C, wondering whether they missed something in Sentence A or even in some sentence further back. You can insert missing transitions if you reread your paper and check carefully whether each sentence follows logically from the sentence immediately preceding it. (The price of rice also increased in China during this past year!)

10. Avoid digressions.

Papers are usually difficult enough to follow without the added encumbrance of digressions. Digressions lead readers away from the main points of your paper. Once readers' attention is diverted from the main points, there is always a risk that their attention will never find its way back to the main point. Occasionally, a digression may be needed to clarify a point. Minor digressions of this kind can be incorporated into footnotes. Major digressions can be incorporated into an appendix. But keep the digressions out of the basic text, where they will distract readers unnecessarily. (It's off the subject, but all this reminds us about a joke we heard. Two guys walk into a bar, and the first one says...)

11. Don't overexplain.

Students learning how to write psychology papers often explain too much. This problem is especially apparent in their "Method" sections.

Students doing a simple free-recall experiment can end up explaining (a) why they used visual rather than auditory presentation of words, (b) why they used nouns instead of other parts of speech, (c) why they used 18-word lists rather than lists of some other length, (d) why they presented words at a rate of one word per second rather than some other rate, and so on. Assume that readers of your paper (if they are professionals) are familiar with standard procedures and will be interested only in explanations of nonstandard ones. Exclusive use of people's names, for example, would be nonstandard in a free-recall experiment.

The same warning is relevant to the presentation and discussion of results. If your experiment has only a few results, then you need not select among them. If your experiment has many results or if you have analyzed the same data in many different ways, select the important results or analyses and concentrate on those. Your selection procedure must be honest: It would be unethical and unscientific to report and discuss only those results that support your hypotheses. The importance of a result should not be determined by its fit to your preconceived notions. (All of this will become clearer when we write our 1,000-page tome on how to avoid overexplanation!)

12. Don't assume that people will know what you mean or be familiar with abbreviations or jargon.

Sometimes when we're writing an article, we notice a sentence or paragraph that isn't clear. Occasionally, we're too lazy to change the offending text and hope no one will notice. We're particularly likely to hope that people will know what we mean when we're not sure what we mean ourselves, so that perhaps later they can tell us. Almost without fail, however, readers don't understand what we've said any better than we do. Reviewers complain about what they don't understand – and that includes abbreviations or jargon. (QED!)

13. Write for a somewhat broader and technically less skilled audience than you expect to read the article.

Writers tend to overestimate the knowledge and technical sophistication of their readers, as well as the extent to which readers share their exact interests. You should therefore write for a slightly broader and less knowledgeable audience than you expect will read the article, keeping in mind that you don't want to insult your audience, either. Somewhere between *Visualize Maculation Decamp* and *See Spot Run* lies both your audience and the Land of Acceptance Letters.

14. Avoid overstatement.

Scientific writing should be conservative in its claims. By overstating your case, you undermine your credibility and put your readers on guard. Once on guard, readers may cease to accept at face value anything you say. Consider, for example, the psychological phenomenon of writing a letter of recommendation for an undergraduate applying to graduate school or for a graduate student applying for a job. On the one hand, you want to do what you can to ensure that a good student obtains the best possible placement. On the other hand, you know that if your claims sound extravagant, you run the risk of damaging your case. Hoping that the major strengths will sell the candidate, writers of letters frequently look for minor weaknesses in their candidates so that their letters appear impartial. Persons writing and reading letters know that some letter writers have reputations for writing inflated letters, and as a result, their letters are taken less seriously than the letters of others with greater credibility. The same reputations can be acquired by writers of psychology papers. Authors who are known to overstate their case will find others taking their claims less seriously than they would have taken the identical claims coming from someone else. (Everyone caught overstating their case ought certainly to be hanged on the spot!)

15. Eliminate unnecessary redundancy.

Elimination of redundancy from a paper is a difficult task, because one is never certain of how much redundancy should be eliminated. On the one hand, redundancy can reinforce your points. Readers may comprehend the second time a point that had eluded them the first time. On the other hand, redundancy can obscure your points. When a paper is highly redundant and readers become aware of its redundancy, they may start reading the paper more quickly and less carefully, assuming that they will have read before and will read again much of what they are reading. Readers assume that if they do not quite understand a point the first time, they will have another chance when the author repeats the point in a slightly different way. Readers may then fail to understand the point because it is not in fact presented again or because its second presentation is no more enlightening than was the first.

Because redundancy is a double-edged sword, you are better off attaining emphasis through other means. There are three alternative means you can use. First, you can discuss in more detail the points you wish to emphasize. Instead of repeating the points several times at different places in the paper, you give them additional space the first time you make them. Second, you can make important points at strategic places in the paper. People tend to remember best what they read at the beginning or the end of a paper. Third, you can state explicitly that one or more points are of special importance and thus merit more careful attention. It may be obvious to you which points are your important ones, but it may not be obvious to your readers. Simply telling readers which points are important can help guide their attention in an optimal way.

Writers usually find it much easier to spot redundancy in others' writing than in their own, because they have difficulty distinguishing what they have thought about from what they have written about. They may repeat a point for a second or third time, unaware that they have made the point before. Even in rereading their work, they may have trouble distinguishing their thoughts from their writing. It is therefore a good idea to have someone else read your paper and deliberately seek out repetitious material. (Because other people usually will not have thought about your topic in the same way you have, they are more likely to recognize redundancy, repetition, reiteration, rehashing, restating, and duplication!)

16. Don't bother to say that your results are "interesting" or "important."

Let the results speak for themselves. (By the way, keep in mind that this point is both interesting and important!)

17. Cite sources as well as findings.

When you cite a finding, cite its source. There are four reasons why you should supply this information. First, readers can check whether you have cited the source accurately. They may doubt the finding and want to verify that you properly cited it. Second, readers can check whether the source is credible. If you merely cite a finding, readers have no way of checking the quality of the evidence in support of that finding. Third, readers can learn about a reference that they may have been unaware of and that they then want to read. Fourth, you show your readers that you are familiar with the literature on your topic, thereby increasing your own credibility as a source of information. (In fact, research has shown that citing sources of research findings does improve credibility!)

18. Don't end your article by saying, "More research is needed."

This statement has become a cliché. There is almost always room for further research.

19. Proofread your article.

We estimate that fewer than half the articles we receive have been proofread by their authors. Fewer than one quarter are proofread carefully. We think that authors often fail to proofread their work because they are afraid they won't like what they read. But other readers of your paper will like it even less if they have to put up with errors that you easily could have corrected. We cannot emphasize enough the importance of proofreading. The time it takes to proofread an article is a small fraction of the time it takes to write it. And there is probably no other thing you can do in so little time that will as much improve others' evaluations of your work.

The best method of proofreading is to have someone read the text to you from the original while you check the final copy line by line. In following the text, read only for errors in spelling, punctuation, capitalization, and the like. Do not read for meaning. You should read the paper an additional time to make sure that you have said what you wanted to say in the way you wanted to say it. (Typografikal erors are uneccesary!)

Give It Some More Thought

Do you proofread your own articles? Why do you think it is that so many people fail to proofread their articles, even though proofreading is probably the easiest aspect of writing an article? For example, you might point out that proofreading takes time, or that sometimes it is painful to read one's own writing.

---

20. Request a critical reading of your article from an adviser or colleague.

Because people are so involved in their own work, they find it much easier to criticize the work of others than to criticize their own work. It is therefore to your advantage to seek the advice of others on any article you write. When asking people to read your article, ask them to read it critically, indeed, ruthlessly. It is a common experience for authors to receive compliments from their colleagues on their articles and then to find them torn to shreds by journal reviewers. One reason for the discrepancy is that colleagues you ask to read your article may not willingly sacrifice the time or risk the loss of friendship that might be involved in a very critical reading of your work. Encourage your readers to be critical, perhaps offering your own critical paper-reading services in return.

7.3 LANGUAGE AND GRAMMAR GUIDELINES

1. Use the precise word.
2. Prefer simpler to more complicated words.
3. Use concrete words and examples.
4. Use the active voice.
5. Prefer affirmative to negative constructions.
6. Avoid unnecessary qualifiers.
7. Avoid dangling constructions.
8. Avoid participles without referents.
9. Avoid pronouns without antecedents.
10. Avoid use of the indefinite *this*.
11. Avoid split infinitives.
12. Avoid gender-biased language.

1. Use the precise word.

In the course of writing your article, you will probably find yourself occasionally stumbling over words, unable to choose a word that expresses the precise meaning you want to convey. Do not settle for an approximate word when a precise word is available. While you are writing, have available both a dictionary and a thesaurus, so that you can search for the optimal word. Settle for a suboptimal one only if you are unable to find the optimal one after diligent searching. (It is to your advance to alleviate use of ill-chosen words!)

2. Prefer simpler to more complicated words.

The main purpose of writing is communication, and simpler words usually communicate more effectively than do complicated ones.

The reaction of readers coming across a complicated word they do not know is not awe for the writer's vocabulary but annoyance that communication has broken down. The reaction of readers coming across a complicated word that they know doesn't fit the context in which it is being used is often one of even greater annoyance. Every year, we encounter at least one author who seems to write papers not to communicate thoughts but to communicate vocabulary. More often than not, this communication is unsuccessful: The writer misuses complicated words. The most important decision regarding words is always to use the one that best expresses your meaning. (If you find that two words express your meaning equally well, use the simpler one, not the more reticular one!)

What's Wrong Here?

"We utilized three measures in our study, each of which tapped a different aspect of personality."

Answer: The author could easily have said "used," which is a simpler word than "utilized" and means essentially the same thing.

---

3. ## Use concrete words and examples.

Much psychological writing is of necessity abstract. Whenever you have a choice, though, between an abstract and a concrete word, choose the concrete one. People will understand you better. When taking your readers through an abstract argument, use examples. If the argument is a long one, don't wait until the end to supply the example. Readers may have gotten lost in your argument a long time before, so that in reading your example they will have to go back through the argument anyway. Your argument will be clearer if you weave examples into the argument, alternating between the abstract and the concrete. Readers will then be able to understand your argument as they read it rather than when (or if) they reread it. (Indeed, this paragraph would have been clearer if it had provided an example of what it was talking about.)

4. ## Use the active voice.

Use of the impersonal third person in psychological articles encourages overuse of the passive voice. Psychology articles are replete with expressions like "it was found," "it can be concluded," "the tests were administered," "the subjects were told," and "the session was completed." Instead, say (in the case of collaborative work) "We found...," ""We concluded...," "We administered the tests...," "We told the subjects...," and "The subjects completed the session..." (If you did the work individually, you can replace "we" with "I." Do not use "we" if you mean "I." You can also use a more formal expression, "The experimenter(s)," but journals are using such formal language less often today than in the past.) Expressions stated in the passive voice are harder to read and make for duller reading than expressions stated in the active voice. Whenever you use a passive construction, try to restate it as an active one. (Although it will be found that this cannot always be done by you, it will be appreciated by your reader, whose understanding of your prose will be enhanced!)

What's Wrong Here?

"The subjects were tested by two different examiners."

Answer: The author could as easily have said the same thing in a more readable way: "Two different examiners tested the subjects."

---

5. Prefer affirmative to negative constructions.

Negative constructions are harder to understand than affirmative ones. Your writing will therefore be easier to understand if you use affirmative rather than negative constructions wherever possible. In some cases, you will have a choice between an implicit and an explicit negation. For example, you might say either "Writers should avoid negative constructions" or "Writers should not use negative constructions." Similarly, you might say either "Six children were absent from school the day the testing took place" or "Six children were not present in school the day the testing took place." Implicit negations like the first example in each pair are easier to understand than explicit negations, and hence are preferred. (Wherever possible, do not fail to avoid explicit negations!)

6. Avoid unnecessary qualifiers.

Qualifiers serve a useful purpose when they honestly limit the scope of a statement. For example, if only some participants showed the effect of a certain treatment, then the effect of the treatment should be qualified as limited only to those subjects. Qualifiers serve no purpose, however, if they do not honestly limit scope. A somewhat noticeable tremor is not distinguishably different from a noticeable tremor; a rather loud pulse is not distinguishably different from a loud pulse. The use of *somewhat* and *rather* in those contexts draws life from the prose without giving anything in return. In using qualifiers such as *somewhat, rather, mostly, largely*, and *for the most part*, check that they make an honest addition to the sentence. If they don't, throw them out.

Sometimes authors use qualifiers to hedge their bets. Because psychology is an inductive science, proceeding from the specific to the general, psychologists can never draw conclusions with certainty. Psychologists may therefore express their uncertainty by qualifying their conclusions. For example, suppose that in a series of experiments, psychologists find that recall of a list of words always increases with practice. They conclude that "at least under some circumstances, certain participants tend to recall more words after more free-recall trials." The qualifications are correct: There are indeed circumstances under which recall will not improve with practice; there are some participants who will not show increasing recall over trials (e.g., dead ones); and because a given participant's recall may occasionally decrease from one trial to the next (if only by chance), one is safe in referring to a tendency toward increasing recall. The psychologists' successive qualifications, however, have left the statement moribund and have not told readers anything they don't already know. Had the authors simply stated that "the results indicate that free recall generally increases over trials," they would have made the point without bogging readers down in excess words. (For the most part, it is usually true that, in most cases, absolutely unnecessary qualifiers can often impede communication!)

Experience Is the Best Teacher.

As academics, we learn to be careful. So we end up often using qualifiers like "rather," "somewhat," "fairly," and "quite." These qualifiers sometimes serve a purpose, but often they add nothing to the text. They just make it harder and more time-consuming to read. Ask yourself whether you really need each of the qualifiers you use.

7. Avoid dangling constructions.

Dangling constructions make sentences ambiguous, including this one. The preceding sentence is ambiguous because it is not clear whether *one* refers to dangling constructions or to sentences. The source of the ambiguity is the phrase "including this one," which dangles at the end of the sentence. Suppose a "Method" section informs you that "the participants were falsely debriefed by the confederates after they finished their task." You cannot be certain whether *they* and *their* refer to the participants or to the confederates. This sentence could be improved by eliminating the dangling construction. Depending on who finished the task, authors might write either "after they finished their task, the confederates falsely debriefed the participants" or "after they finished their task, the participants were falsely debriefed by the confederates." Consider another example from a "Discussion" section: "The result would have been more easily interpretable if all the participants had answered all the questions affirmatively, not just the first five." In this sentence, it is not clear whether just the first five participants answered all the questions affirmatively or whether all the participants answered just the first five questions affirmatively. The sentence should be rewritten in one of two ways, depending on the author's intent: (a) "The result would have been more easily interpretable if all the participants, not just the first five, had answered all the questions affirmatively" or (b) "The results would have been more easily interpretable if all the participants had answered all the questions, not just the first five, affirmatively."

8. Avoid participles without referents.

Suppose you read in an article, "The rat was found dead while cleaning the cage." You probably would be correct to assume that an experimenter or a technician, not the dead rat, cleaned the cage. The sentence is ambiguous, however, because it lacks a referent for the participle. Less extreme examples of participles without referents abound in psychological writing. Consider the following sentence from a "Method" section: "While monitoring the participant's heartbeat, adrenaline was injected into the participant's left arm." The sentence is unacceptable because it does not state who monitored the participant's heartbeat. Obviously, it wasn't the adrenaline that did the monitoring. But who did? The sentence should be revised to read, "While monitoring the participant's heartbeat, the experimenter injected adrenaline into the participant's left arm." In general, if you use active constructions when you use participles, you will eliminate participles without referents.

9. Avoid pronouns without antecedents.

Early in their schooling, students learn the rule to avoid pronouns without antecedents, and yet they continue to violate it, usually in subtle ways. For example, many people will not recognize the following statement from a "Method" section as ungrammatical: "After the participant's task was completed, he or she was free to leave." To whom does "he or she" refer? Obviously not to *task*, but there is no other noun in the sentence, and the antecedent of a pronoun must be a noun. The author could reword the statement to say, "After the participant's task was completed, the participant was free to leave," or better, "After the participant completed the task, he or she was free to leave."

A possessive pronoun needs an antecedent as much as does any other pronoun. Consider, for example, a slight variant of an earlier sentence: "While monitoring the participant's heartbeat, the experimenter injected epinephrine into his or her left arm." The grammatical antecedent for *his* is *experimenter*, although it is obvious that the author intended otherwise. The author should rephrase the sentence: "While monitoring the participant's heartbeat, the experimenter injected epinephrine into the participant's left arm."

10. Avoid use of the indefinite *this*.

A common problem in writing is use of the word *this* without a definite antecedent. You will find this even in otherwise well-written prose, such as this sentence. The first use of *this* in the preceding sentence is indicative of sloppy prose. Note that there are two possible antecedents of *this* in the second sentence of this paragraph, *problem* and *use of the word*. The ambiguity is eliminated by changing *this* from a pronoun to an adjective: "You will find this problem even in otherwise well-written prose."

11. Avoid split infinitives.

Split infinitives (such as "to thoroughly examine") seem to evoke two reactions. Some people use them regularly and barely notice when they read them. Other people never use them and wince every time they see or hear them. Usually, split infinitives make sentences less graceful without adding any clarity. "To carefully weigh the evidence" is the same as "to weigh the evidence carefully," but the latter way of expressing the idea is more readable than the former. If the adverb with which you want to split the infinitive seems to fit nowhere else, consider rewriting the sentence in a different way. (Try to always follow this advice!) There is no rule against using split infinitives, though. If you like using them, be assured no one is going to reject your article because you have used them.

12. Avoid gender-biased language.

Do not use the pronoun *he* when you mean *he* or *she*. Excessive use of *he or she* is awkward and can be irritating as well. Use of plurals and rephrasing of sentences can often help eliminate both sexist language and excessive use of *he* or *she*. Another option is to alternate "he" and "she" when referring to indefinite persons.

CHECKLIST FOR CONTENT

- ☐ Have you stated the problem clearly?
- ☐ Is the article organized around the problem?
- ☐ Have you made clear early on what the contribution of your article is?
- ☐ Have you told readers why your article is of interest to them?
- ☐ Is your literature review focused, reasonably complete, and balanced?
- ☐ Have you checked your data analyses and interpretations?
- ☐ Have you explained the meaning of your results?
- ☐ Do your conclusions follow from your data?
- ☐ Have you made the limitations of your work clear?
- ☐ Have you considered alternative interpretations of the data?
- ☐ Have you provided a take-home message?

CHECKLIST FOR STYLE

- ☐ Have you placed yourself in the background?
- ☐ Is your article logical and organized?
- ☐ Have you given concrete examples?

☐ Are your sentences clear, readable, and concise?
☐ Are your sentences as simple as possible?
☐ Have you used summary statements?
☐ Have you used transitions?
☐ Have you avoided digressions?
☐ Have you explained abbreviations?
☐ Have you avoided jargon?
☐ Have you eliminated unnecessary redundancy?
☐ Have you cited sources and findings?
☐ Have you requested a critical reading of your article by a colleague or adviser?

CHECKLIST FOR LANGUAGE AND GRAMMAR

Whenever possible, have you
☐ used precise words?
☐ used simple words?
☐ used concrete words and examples? used the active voice?
☐ used affirmative constructions?
☐ avoided unnecessary qualifiers?
☐ avoided dangling constructions?
☐ avoided participles without referents?
☐ avoided pronouns without antecedents?
☐ avoided use of the indefinite *this*?
☐ avoided split infinitives?
☐ avoided gender-biased language?

8 | Commonly Misused Words

This chapter explains the meanings of some of the most commonly misused words in student papers. The chapter is divided into two parts. The first part deals with meanings of nontechnical terms. Dowling (2008) provides an extensive overview of misused words, and Garner (2009) provides a complete dictionary of American usage. The second part of the chapter deals with meanings of technical terms. The psychological dictionaries and encyclopedias described in Chapter 3 provide much more extensive lists of psychological terms.

8.1 NONTECHNICAL TERMS

1. **adapt, adopt**. To adapt is to accommodate, to adjust, to bring into correspondence. To adopt is to embrace, to take on, to make one's own.
   a. Organisms adapt to their environment.
   b. Children adopt the attitudes of their peers.
2. **adopt**. See (1).
3. **affect, effect**. Both words can be used either as nouns or as verbs. An affect is an emotion or something that tends to arouse an emotion. An effect is a result or outcome of some cause. To affect is to influence or to have an effect on something. To effect is to accomplish or to bring about.
   a. His display of affect in response to the TAT (Thematic Apperception Test) picture seemed artificial and contrived to gain the psychologist's sympathy.
   b. The effect of the experimental treatment was negligible.
   c. Shoddy procedures affect the outcome of an experiment.

    d. She was able to effect a change in behavior by desensitizing the patient to snakes.

4. **aggravate, irritate.** To aggravate is to intensify, to heighten, or to magnify. To irritate is to annoy, to inflame, to provoke.

    a. Don't aggravate his frustration by telling him that he answered all the questions incorrectly.

    b. Experimenters who deceive subjects often irritate the subjects.

5. **allusion.** An allusion is an indirect reference. An explicit statement about X is not an allusion to X.

    a. The first experimenter made an allusion to a reward for exceptional performance, but she never came out and directly told the subject that the subject would receive a reward.

    b. The second experimenter told the subject he would receive a reward for exceptional performance. (He did not allude to a reward.)

6. **among, between.** *Between* refers to a relation between two things and *among* refers to a relation among more than two things. The term *between* can be used for a relation involving more than two things if reciprocity is involved in the relation. When in doubt regarding relations among more than two things, use *among*.

    a. The subject had to decide between the button on the left and the button on the right.

    b. The subject had to decide among the left, middle, and right buttons.

    c. The agreement between the three members of the group broke down quickly when the experimental manipulation was introduced.

7. **amount of, number of.** An amount of something is a sum total or aggregate. A number of something is a quantity of it. Use *amount of* when dealing with quantities that can't be counted. Use *number of* when dealing with quantities that can be counted. Monetary terms are exceptions to this generalization.

    a. The amount of liquid in the tall jar was the same as the amount in the fat jar.

    b. The number of stimuli was too small.

    c. The subject was dissatisfied with the amount of money she received for participating in the experiment.

8. **and/or.** Avoid this expression, which means that a relation is either conjunctive (*and*) or disjunctive (*or*). The expression disrupts the flow of prose, is ambiguous, and often indicates that

authors couldn't decide which conjunction to use, so they used both.

9. **as to whether.** Avoid this expression. Say *whether*.

10. **between.** See (6).

11. **bring, take.** To bring something is to carry it toward the speaker or listener. To take something is to carry it away from the speaker or listener.

a. Take this incomprehensible book back to the library.

b. Bring me a better book from the library.

12. **certainly.** Use the word *certainly* only if you mean "with 100% probability." Don't use the word loosely to connote near certainty.

She certainly won't eat her hat.

13. **compare to, compare with.** To compare *to* is to point out or emphasize similarities between different things. To compare *with* is to point out or emphasize differences between similar things.

a. The student compared the predictions of the continuous learning model to those of the discrete learning model and showed that they were indistinguishable.

b. The student compared Freud's conception of the ego with Erikson's conception and showed that the two conceptions differed in fundamental respects.

14. **comprise.** To comprise is to consist of or be made up of. This word has the dubious distinction of being misused more often than it is properly used in student papers. A whole comprises its parts; parts constitute (form or compose) a whole.

a. This book comprises 15 fascinating chapters.

b. The group comprises a range of fascinating characters.

15. **continual, continuous.** Continual means often repeated. Continuous means without stop.

a. Continual interruptions forced the experimenter to terminate the session early.

b. Continuous background music improved employees' morale.

16. **continuous.** See (15).

17. **data.** *Data* is a plural noun and should take a plural verb. Today, however, many people use *data* as a singular. The singular form is *datum*, which is used infrequently.

a. The professor's data were far from perfect.

b. One datum was inconsistent with all the rest.

18. **different from, different than.** If two things differ, they are *different from* each other. The expression *different than* is nonstandard.

19. **discover, invent.** To discover something is to find something that was there before. To invent something is to create something new.
    a. No one has discovered a single gene for intelligence.
    b. Some people would like to invent a pill to increase intelligence.

20. **disinterested, uninterested.** To be disinterested is to be impartial. To be uninterested is to lack interest. Today, many people use *disinterested* to mean *uninterested*.
    a. There seem to be few disinterested investigators studying the heritability of intelligence. Most of them have obvious biases.
    b. Psychoanalysts are generally uninterested in stimulus–response explanations of behavior.

21. **effect.** See (3).

22. **enormity, enormousness.** The former word refers to extreme wickedness, the latter to extreme size or volume.
    a. The enormity of the tyrant's crimes could not be simulated in an experimentally controlled setting.
    b. The enormousness of the giant scared the children.

23. **enormousness.** See (22).

24. **fact.** A fact should be directly verifiable either empirically or logically. Do not refer to judgments or probable outcomes as facts.

25. **factor.** Because this word has at least two technical meanings in psychology (see the next part of this chapter), it is best not to use it in a loose, nontechnical sense. Instead of saying, for example, that "several factors contributed to the subject's euphoria," say that "the subject was euphoric for several reasons."

26. **farther, further.** The word *farther* should be used to refer to greater distance; the word *further* should be used to refer to quantity or time.
    a. Further jokes were to no avail; the subject refused to laugh.
    b. The patient explained to the psychologist that the farther he traveled from his home, the more anxious he felt.

27. **fewer, less.** *Fewer* refers to number, *less* to amount or degree.
    a. The patient had fewer nightmares after she began therapy.
    b. The patient's nightmares became less frightening after she began therapy.

28. **former, latter**. *Former* refers to the first item in a series, *latter* to the second. These words are applicable when the series consists of just two items or when a longer series is divided into two parts. In series with more than two items, refer to the end points of the series as the first and last items.

    a. The male and female confederates entered the room together, the former carrying a live alligator and the latter carrying a dead rattlesnake.

    b. Of the three people who interviewed for the job, only the first was qualified but only the last was willing to take the job after finding out what it entailed.

29. **fortuitous, fortunate**. A fortuitous event is one that occurs by chance. A fortunate event is one that is favored by fortune.

    a. The simultaneous appearance of the two rivals was made to appear fortuitous, but it was in fact contrived.

    b. The appearance of all the subjects at the testing session was most fortunate because the machine controlling the testing exploded at the end of the session and thereafter was incapable of further use.

30. **fortunate**. See (29).

31. **further**. See (26).

32. **hopefully**. This word means *full of hope*. It does not mean *it is to be hoped*. Today, this word is more often used incorrectly than correctly.

    He started the experiment hopefully but ended it discouraged.

33. **imply, infer**. To imply something is to suggest it indirectly. To infer something is to conclude or deduce it from the information available. The two words are not interchangeable.

    a. The patient implied that she still felt like strangling anyone who got in her way.

    b. The therapist thus inferred that the patient was not yet cured.

34. **infer**. See (33).

35. **interesting**. This word is overused. Saying that something is interesting is not a substitute for making it interesting.

36. **invent**. See (19).

37. **irregardless**. This word does not exist in English. The proper word is *regardless*.

    The rat receives a sugar pellet after pressing the bar regardless of how long the rat takes to press it.

38. **irritate**. See (4).

39. **its, it's.** The word *its* is a pronoun that indicates *belonging* or *pertaining*. The word *it's* means *it is* or *it has*.

    a. The investigator knew the fear manipulation had failed when the monster shook its tail and the children laughed in response.

    b. After seeing the children's response, the investigator thought to himself: "It's all over."

40. **latter.** See (28).

41. **lay, lie.** *Lay* and *lie* both have a number of meanings. Confusion regarding which word to use arises from one meaning of each word. For *lay*, that meaning is *to put or place something*. For *lie*, that meaning is *to recline*. The past tense of *lay* is *laid* and the present perfect is *has* (or *have*) *laid*. The past tense of *lie* is *lay* and the present perfect is *has* (or *have*) *lain*. *Lay* always takes an object; *lie* never does.

    a. i. When the experimenter enters the room, he lays the booklets on the table.

        ii. The experimenter laid the booklets on the table.

        iii. The experimenter has laid the booklets on the table.

    b. i. The patient lies down on a couch when she enters the therapist's office.

        ii. The patient lay down on a couch after she entered the therapist's office.

        iii. After the patient has lain down, the therapist begins the session.

42. **less.** See (27).

43. **lie.** See (41).

44. **literally.** If something is literally true, then it is true in fact. Use *literally* only if you mean it. Do not use the expression *literally true* if you mean figuratively true or almost true.

45. **number.** See (7).

46. **one.** Do not follow *one* by *his*. Follow it by *one's*.

    To communicate effectively, one must organize one's papers carefully.

47. **only.** Imprecise placement of *only* in a sentence can change the meaning of the sentence. Place *only* immediately before the word or clause it modifies. Do not say, for example, "I only tested five participants" if you mean, "I tested only five participants." Consider how the meaning of a sentence changes depending on the placement of *only*:

    a. Only I will treat the patient in my office tomorrow.

    b. I only will treat the patient in my office tomorrow.

    c. I will only treat the patient in my office tomorrow.

    d. I will treat only the patient in my office tomorrow.

    e. I will treat the only patient in my office tomorrow.

    f. I will treat the patient only in my office tomorrow.

    g. I will treat the patient in only my office tomorrow.

    h. I will treat the patient in my only office tomorrow.

    i. I will treat the patient in my office only tomorrow.

    j. I will treat the patient in my office tomorrow only.

48. **principal, principle**. Used as an adjective, *principal* means *chief, dominant, main, major*. Used as a noun, it means a *person* or *thing of* importance or rank. *Principle* can be used only as a noun, and it refers to a general truth or law.

    a. The principal of the school wondered why the student's data were not scored. The principal reason for not scoring the student's test was that the subject had cheated in answering the last two problems.

    b. This book presents many principles for writing psychology papers.

49. **principle**. See (48).

50. **relevant**. Use this word only if you can specify a precise relationship. Do not use it to express a vague connection to everyday life or your experience, as in "clinical psychology is relevant." If you make the connection clear, then the word is appropriate:
Clinical psychology is relevant to everyday life.

51. **since**. APA recommends that in formal writing for its journals, authors use this word only in its temporal sense, not as a substitute for *because*. If you mean *because*, use *because*.
Since leaving therapy, the patient has shown no recurrence of symptoms.

52. **take**. See (11).

53. **that, which**. *That* is used for restrictive clauses, *which* for nonrestrictive clauses. Restrictive clauses limit the possible meaning of a preceding subject of a sentence. For example, "The paper that he wrote was a great success." Here, "that" refers to a specific paper. Nonrestrictive clauses contain information regarding a preceding subject in the sentence, but they do not limit (restrict) the meaning of that subject. For example, "The paper, which he wrote, was a great success." Note that here, in this second use, the

fact that he wrote the paper tells us more about the paper rather than pointing to a specific (restricted) paper. Clauses using *which*, therefore, are surrounded by commas. The use of *which* for *that* is common in psychological (and other) writing but is inadvisable. Excessive use of *which* makes sentences cumbersome and difficult to read.

    a. The experiment that he designed is a gem. (This sentence tells which experiment is a gem. It was his experiment, not someone else's.)

    b. The experiment, which he designed, is a gem. (This sentence tells something about the one experiment in question.)

54. **try.** Say "try to," not "try and."

    Before she showed the picture of the snake to the patient, the therapist told the patient to try to relax.

55. **uninterested.** See (20).

56. **unique.** Something that is unique is one of a kind. It is not merely unusual or extraordinary. There can be no degrees of uniqueness.

    The psychologist employed a unique combination of therapeutic techniques in treating his patients.

57. **utilize.** *Use* is simpler, and usually serves just as well.

    The participant used the process of elimination to answer the multiple-choice test questions.

58. **which.** See (53).

59. **while.** This word is best used to mean "at the same time that." It is frequently used as a substitute for *whereas*, *but*, and *although*. The word does not serve well as a substitute, because it is not clear whether the author intends to imply simultaneity. The sentence, "I went east while he went west," is unambiguous if the reader knows that the author uses *while* only to mean *at the same time that*. But if the author sometimes uses *while* to mean *whereas*, the sentence is ambiguous: The reader does not know whether the two individuals went in opposite directions at the same time. Similarly, in reading the sentence "the subject answered test questions while the examiner scored them," readers will want to infer that answering and scoring occurred simultaneously.

    The experimenter appeared nonchalant while the subject finished the task.

60. **whom.** This word is often used incorrectly before expressions like *he said*, when *who* should serve as the subject of the verb following the expression.

a. The graduate student who the professor said would come to Cornell went to Squeedunk instead. (*Who* is the subject of *would come*.)

b. The graduate student whom the professor telephoned was not at home.

61. **whose**. This word can serve as the possessive case of either *who* or *which*. Hence, it can refer to inanimate as well as animate objects.

a. The subject was upset when the machine whose buttons she pressed disintegrated in fewer than five seconds.

b. The experimenter, however, knew whose fault the disintegration was and had trouble holding back a smile.

8.2 TECHNICAL TERMS

1. **ability, capacity**. Capacity is innate potential. Ability is developed capacity. One's ability may not reflect one's capacity if environmental circumstances have been unfavorable to the development of that capacity. Only ability can be measured; hence, we cannot assess the degree to which one's ability reflects one's capacity.

a. The child's test scores indicated only marginal ability to succeed in school work.

b. The child's unhappy childhood suggested to the psychologist that the child's capacity for school work might not be reflected in his scores on ability tests.

2. **algorithm, heuristic**. An algorithm is a systematic routine for solving a problem that will eventually solve the problem, even if the solution involves consideration of all possible answers to the problem. A heuristic is a short cut or informal routine for solving a problem that may or may not eventually solve the problem. An algorithm may be slow, but it is guaranteed eventually to reach an answer. A heuristic is relatively fast but does not guarantee solution. Some problems can be solved only by heuristics. No algorithm is available, for example, that guarantees that a given move in a game of chess is the optimal move.

a. The subject discovered an algorithm for solving the jigsaw puzzle, but the algorithm required 752,964 arrangements of the pieces of the puzzle to guarantee a solution.

b. Another subject discovered a heuristic for solving the puzzle that she estimated gave her a 75 per cent chance of solving the puzzle after only 55 arrangements of the pieces.

3. **anxiety, fear.** Anxiety is a state (or trait) of apprehension or uneasiness with no well-defined object. Fear is a state of apprehension in response to a well-defined threat.
   a. The executive felt a constant sense of anxiety, and yet was unable to pinpoint anything in his environment that threatened his well-being.
   b. The hunter was filled with fear when her rifle failed to fire and the bear started charging toward her.
4. **applied research, basic research.** Applied research strives for findings of practical value, regardless of whether or not they have theoretical value. Basic research strives for findings of theoretical value, regardless of whether they have practical value. Applied research may yield findings of theoretical value, and basic research may yield findings of practical value, although such findings are incidental to the major goals of each type of research.
   a. Research on consumer preferences for different kinds of cosmetic products has been almost exclusively applied research.
   b. Research on serial learning of nonsense syllables has been primarily basic research.

Give It Some More Thought

Is the distinction between basic and applied research always clear? For example, you might point out that basic research often has practical implications that researchers do not recognize at the time they conduct the research.

---

5. **artificial intelligence, simulation.** Artificial-intelligence researchers seek to build machines or instructions for machines that solve in an optimal way problems usually thought to require intelligence. Little or no attempt is made to have these machines or instructions correspond to the human mind or to the strategies used by the human mind. Simulation research seeks to build machines or instructions for machines that solve problems in ways analogous to those used by humans. Little or no attempt is made to achieve optimal performance. Indeed, if human performance is suboptimal, then an attempt is made to imitate this suboptimal performance.

a. Using the techniques of artificial intelligence, the computer scientist was able to program a computer to solve algebra problems far more efficiently than human beings solve them.

b. The psychologist wrote a simulation program that closely matched the techniques of Algebra I students in solving algebra problems.

6. **average**. As a statistical term, this word is used in two ways. The more specific way is as a synonym for *mean*. Used in this way, the average is the sum of a set of values divided by the number of values. The more general way is as a generic term for all measures of central tendency (cf. *mean, median, mode*). Used in this way, the average is the central value, however defined. In order to avoid confusion, the word *average* is best used only in its more specific meaning.

The five children taking the test had scores of 2, 4, 4, 6, and 14, giving an average of 6.

7. **avoidance learning, escape learning**. Avoidance learning is motivated by avoidance of punishment. The learner is punished only if learning does not take place. Escape learning is motivated by escape from punishment. The learner is punished until learning takes place.

a. After being suspended from school for a third time, the mischievous child learned not to play practical jokes on his classmates. (This situation provides an example of avoidance learning.)

b. The rat learned to jump on the pedestal whenever the floor to its cage was electrified. (This situation provides an example of escape learning.)

8. **basic research**. See (4).

9. **classical conditioning, operant conditioning**. In classical conditioning, an originally neutral stimulus is repeatedly paired with a stimulus that evokes a certain response. This latter stimulus is called the *unconditioned stimulus* or *US*. The response given to the stimulus is called the *unconditioned response* or *UR*. As a result of the repeated pairing, the originally neutral stimulus eventually starts to evoke the same response as the unconditioned stimulus, even if it is not paired with the *US* any more. At this point, the originally neutral stimulus becomes a *conditioned stimulus* or *CS*. The response given to this stimulus is called the *conditioned response* or *CR*. In operant conditioning,

a learner is rewarded (reinforced) when a desired response takes place. Eventually, the learned response occurs even without paired presentation of the reward.

   a. Every time the salesman visited his Southeast Asian client, the salesman became ill from the change in climate; the salesman was surprised, though, when the client came to visit him and he became sick again without any change in climate. (This situation provides an example of classical conditioning.)

   b. As a child, she was given a lollipop every time she took her vitamins without complaining, and as an adult, she continued to take her vitamins without complaining, even though the lollipop no longer accompanied the vitamins. (This situation provides an example of operant conditioning.)

10. **compulsion, obsession.** A compulsion is an irresistible urge to perform repeatedly a stereotyped act that serves no apparent purpose. An obsession is a recurrent thought that the thinker is powerless to control.

   a. The therapist suggested to the patient that the patient's desire to wash her hands every 15 minutes might be a compulsion rather than a reasonable wish for cleanliness.

   b. As a soldier during the Gulf War, he had seen a little girl shot to death on the battlefield. Since then he was obsessed: A vision of the little girl being shot plagued him at least twice every waking hour.

11. **control group, experimental group.** A control group is one that does not receive the experimental treatment of interest. An experimental group is one that does receive the treatment. The effect of the treatment can then be assessed by comparing performance in the experimental group with that in the control group. The term *experimental group* is sometimes used in a more general sense to refer to any group in an experiment. In order to avoid confusion, the term is better restricted to the more limited, contrastive usage.

   a. Members of the experimental group were told that they had been selected because their teachers had rated them as unusually likely to succeed in difficult reasoning tasks.

   b. Members of one control group were told that they had been selected at random, whereas members of a second control group were not told anything about selection procedures. The first group served as a control for telling subjects that they were rated as unusually likely to succeed, and the second group served as a control for telling subjects anything at all about selection procedures.

12. **culture-fair test, culture-free test**. A culture-fair test is one that attempts to minimize the *differential* effects of different cultural experiences upon performance. A culture-free test is one that attempts to minimize the *absolute* effects of any cultural experiences upon performance. Construction of a culture-fair test is a sensible goal, although one that probably only can be approached. Construction of a culture-free test is not a sensible goal, (a) because the very act of taking a test is culture-bound and (b) because we have no culture-free baseline against which to assess the success of a culture-free test. In other words, we have no way of knowing what *culture-free* means.

   a. By using only pictures of naturally and commonly occurring objects, the investigator hoped to attain a culture-fair test.

   b. The investigator set out to make a culture-free test by stripping away from her culture-bound test everything that in any way reflected cultural experiences; when she finished her task, she realized she had nothing left.

13. **culture-free**. See (12).

14. **deduction, induction**. Deduction is reasoning from the general to the specific. Given general principles, one deduces specific outcomes. A characteristic of deduction is that one can attain certainty in one's conclusions. If the premises are valid and the reasoning correct, then the conclusions must be valid. Mathematical and logical proofs are usually deductive. Induction is reasoning from the specific to the general. Given specific outcomes, one induces general principles. A characteristic of induction is that one can never attain certainty in one's conclusions. One can disconfirm but never confirm with certainty an inductive argument.

   a. From just a few basic axioms, Euclid was able to deduce all the theorems that constitute what we now call Euclidean geometry.

   b. A jeweler observed that all emeralds he had ever seen were green. He induced on the basis of his extensive observations that all emeralds are green, regardless of whether he had ever seen them. He realized, though, that the induction could be disconfirmed by the subsequent appearance of just a single nongreen emerald, but that the induction could not be proven because the next emerald he saw might be nongreen.

15. **delusion, hallucination, illusion.** A delusion is a false belief. A hallucination is a sensory experience in the absence of an appropriate external stimulus. An illusion is a misperception of a stimulus.

   a. The psychologist tried to convince the patient that her belief that her friends were secretly plotting against her was a delusion.

   b. After three days without water in the desert, the explorer saw an oasis ahead; but when he reached the point where he had seen the oasis, and saw only dry sand, he realized he had suffered a hallucination.

   c. The clever student knew that her perception of the train tracks as meeting each other on the horizon was an illusion.

16. **dependent variable, independent variable.** A dependent variable is one whose value is affected by (is dependent upon) the value of some other variables. These other variables, which are the variables under experimental control, are the independent variables.

   a. The dependent variable in the experiment was reaction time to a visually presented stimulus.

   b. The independent variables in the experiment were length of stimulus presentation and clarity of the visual stimulus.

17. **descriptive statistics, inferential statistics.** Descriptive statistics summarize data. They include indices such as the mean, median, standard deviation, and correlation coefficient. Each of these statistics tells us some important property of the data under consideration. Inferential statistics provide tests of hypotheses about data or simply permit generalizations about populations from sample data. They include such indices as t, z, and F. Each of these statistics is used to test hypotheses about differences between one value (or set of values) and another.

   a. The author first presented descriptive statistics so that readers could get a feeling for the data.

   b. Then he presented inferential statistics so that readers could see the extent to which the data were consistent with his hypotheses.

18. **deviation IQ, ratio IQ.** The IQ, or intelligence quotient, was originally conceived of as a ratio of mental age to chronological age. This ratio (or quotient) was soon perceived to have several

disadvantages. First, it seemed to assume that mental age kept increasing as long as chronological age increased, whereas in fact mental age increases very slowly after a person reaches a chronological age of 16, and eventually it begins to decrease. Second, the ratio assumed that increases in mental age are continuous in the same way that increases in chronological age are continuous, although the research of Piaget (1952) and others indicates that this assumption is not the case. In order to correct for these undesirable properties of the ratio IQ, deviation IQs were introduced. These IQs are not actually quotients, although the designation "IQ" was retained. The concept of mental age is not used in the calculation of deviation IQs. Instead, the IQs are fixed at a certain mean, usually 100, as is a certain standard deviation, usually 15 or 16. IQs are then computed on the basis of each person's standardized deviation from the mean. If the mean IQ is set to 100 and the standard deviation to 15, the deviation IQ is equal to {[(Raw Score – Mean Score)/(Standard Deviation)] × 15} + 100.

   a. The child's raw score on the intelligence test was 50. Because the mean on the test was 40, and the standard deviation was 10, her deviation IQ was {[(50 – 40)/10] × 15} + 100, or 115.

   b. The child's raw score of 50 corresponded to a mental age of 12 years, 0 months. Because her chronological age was 10 years, 0 months, her ratio IQ was (12/10) × 100 = 120.

19. **empiricism, nativism.** Empiricism is a view that behavior is learned primarily as a result of experience. In its extreme form, it claims that all behavior is acquired through experience. Nativism makes the claim that most behavior is innately determined. In its extreme form, it claims that all behavior is innately determined.

   a. Empiricists such as Skinner have claimed that language acquisition can be explained by operant conditioning.

   b. Nativists such as Chomsky have claimed that language acquisition can be understood only if one postulates an innate competence for learning (sometimes called a language acquisition device).

20. **escape learning.** See (7).

21. **experimental group.** See (11).

22. **experimental psychology.** This term is used in two different ways. Properly used, it refers to a methodology – the use of experiments to collect data. Thus, psychologists who collect data

via experiments are referred to as experimental psychologists. A second and less desirable use of the term is as referring to a substantive area of psychology embracing sensation, perception, learning, memory, and thinking. This latter usage developed because researchers interested in these processes have long (although not always) used experimental methods. Because investigators in other areas of psychology (e.g., personality, social, developmental) may also use experimental methods, the term *experimental psychology* is better used in its first meaning.

Using experimental methods, the investigator concluded that introverts were more likely to complete his boring task than were extroverts.

23. **extrinsic motivation, intrinsic motivation.** Extrinsic motivation is motivation controlled by the possibilities of reward or punishment other than those directly achieved by engaging in a behavior or by the outcome of that behavior. Intrinsic motivation is motivation controlled by the possibilities of reward or punishment that are achieved directly by engaging in a behavior or by the outcome of that behavior.

   a. The student's motivation to learn geometry was extrinsic: She wanted to receive an A in her geometry course.

   b. Her friend's motivation to learn geometry was intrinsic: He enjoyed learning how all of geometry could be deduced from a few simple axioms.

24. **factor.** This word has two common technical meanings in psychology. First, it can refer to an independent variable in an experiment. A three-factor experiment is one with three independent variables. In such cases, you may be better off referring to *variables* rather than *factors* in order to avoid confusion with the second meaning of *factor*. Second, the word can refer to a mathematical representation of a hypothetical psychological construct. This mathematical representation is obtained through a statistical technique called factor analysis.

   a. The student manipulated two factors in her experiment, attractiveness and sex of the confederate.

   b. According to Spearman's theory of intelligence, intelligence comprises one general factor common to performance on all intellectual tasks and many specific factors, each limited to performance on a single intellectual task.

25. **fear.** See (3).

26. **fixation, regression.** Fixation refers to arrested development at some stage, usually a stage earlier than the one an individual should be in. Regression refers to a return to an earlier stage of development.
    a. The 5-year-old child's continual sucking of anything she could get into her mouth suggested to the psychologist that the child had fixated at the oral stage of development.
    b. The soldier seemed perfectly normal until he entered the battlefield, at which time he showed regression toward infantile behaviors that he had not exhibited for more than two decades.
27. **genotype, phenotype.** A genotype is a set of inherited characteristics that may or may not be displayed. A phenotype is the set of characteristics that is displayed.
    a. The woman's phenotype revealed brown eyes.
    b. When the brown-eyed woman had a child with blue eyes, it became apparent that her genotype included the recessive gene for blue eyes as well as the dominant gene for brown eyes.
28. **hallucination.** See (15).
29. **heritability.** Heritability is the proportion of the total variance of a trait in a population that is attributable to genetic differences among individuals in that population. Heritability is thus the ratio of (variance due to genetic causes)/(total variance). (See item 70.) Height is a characteristic with high heritability, whereas temperament is a characteristic with low heritability.

Experience Is the Best Teacher

We have seen even experienced professionals refer to a heritability of, say, .60 as stating that 60 percent of a trait is heritable. This statement is incorrect. A heritability of .60 means that 60 percent of the variation in the trait in a population is heritable.

---

30. **identification, imitation.** In identification, a person (often a child) acquires the social role of another person by modeling the behavior of that person. In imitation, the person models the behavior of another person, not necessarily acquiring that person's social role.

    a. Because the man identified with his lazy and irresponsible father, he found himself unable to cope with any of his family responsibilities.

    b. The young boy often imitated the actions of his mother, but he eventually identified with his father.

31. **illusion.** See (15).

32. **imitation.** See (30).

33. **independent variable.** See (16).

34. **induction.** See (14).

35. **inferential statistics.** See (17).

36. **intrinsic motivation.** See (23).

37. **latent content, manifest content.** The latent content of a dream is its deeper, hidden meaning. The manifest content of a dream is its apparent meaning.

    a. The manifest content of the dream consisted of the patient's being chased out of a luxurious palace across a moat by an angry older man wielding a big stick.

    b. The psychologist believed the latent content of the dream was sexual, and that the man exhibited through the dream an unresolved Oedipal conflict.

38. **learning, maturation, performance.** Learning is often distinguished both from maturation and from performance. Learning is an increment in knowledge that occurs as a result of practice. Maturation is a change in behavior resulting from a growth process that is independent of practice. Performance is overt behavior. Note that *learning* takes place only with practice; *maturation* takes place regardless of whether or not it is preceded by practice. Note also that learning may occur without showing itself through a change in performance.

    a. The child repeatedly failed to understand that the amount of liquid in the tall jar was the same as the amount obtained when the contents of the tall jar were poured into the fat jar. Eventually, her cognitive abilities matured to the point at which she could understand the principle of conservation, and thus the equality between the two amounts of liquid.

    b. Although the subject had learned all the words in the list, his recall performance was far from perfect; it was not until the subject was given a test of recognition performance that he showed that he was familiar with all of the words.

39. **manifest content.** See (37).

40. **maturation.** See (38).

41. **mean, median, mode.** The mean (average) is the sum of a set of values divided by the number of values. The median is the middle value: Half the values are higher and half are lower. The mode is the most frequently occurring value.
    a. The mean of the numbers 2, 2, 4, 6, and 16 is 6.
    b. The median of the numbers 2, 2, 4, 6, and 16 is 4.
    c. The mode of the numbers 2, 2, 4, 6, and 16 is 2.

Experience Is the Best Teacher

In scientific papers, the mean is usually the preferred measure of central tendency. However, you almost always should provide the standard deviation corresponding to any mean because it is difficult to interpret the mean without knowing the variability of the data around the mean.

---

42. **median.** See (41).
43. **mode.** See (41).
44. **nativism.** See (19).
45. **nature–nurture.** The nature–nurture distinction refers to the relative proportions of variance in traits or behaviors attributable to heredity (nature) versus environment (nurture).
    In the nature–nurture debate, hereditarians favor nature and environmentalists favor nurture as the primary source of differences in behavior. In reality, nature and nurture work together.
46. **neurosis, psychosis.** A neurosis is a minor disorder in which a person exhibits maladaptive behavior patterns (symptoms) that avoid rather than cope with underlying problems. A psychosis is a major disorder in which a person exhibits severely maladaptive behavior patterns that usually require treatment in a hospital.
    a. The neurotic woman counted her money every hour on the hour to make sure it hadn't fallen out of her pocket.
    b. The psychotic man continually saw robbers reaching out to grab his wallet, but when he chased the robbers, they always disappeared into thin air.
47. **null hypothesis.** The null hypothesis is a hypothesis of no difference. It is not *no* hypothesis.
    The investigator's null hypothesis was that the treatment would produce no effect on the experimental group relative to the control group.

48. **obsession.** See (10).

49. **operant conditioning.** See (9).

50. **parameter, statistic.** A parameter is a constant value that describes a characteristic of a population. A statistic is a variable value that describes a characteristic of a sample from a population.

     a. A psychologist tested the IQs of all 25 students in Ms. Blakeley's 2009 fourth-grade class. He found that the mean IQ was 105. If this class were the population of interest, then the mean of 105 would be a population parameter. (See item 54 for definition of *population*.)

     b. If, in the above example, Ms. Blakeley's 2009 fourth-grade class were viewed as a sample of fourth-grade classes throughout the United States, then the mean of 105 would be a sample statistic. (See item 54 for the definition of *sample*.)

51. **participant, subject.** At various times, the word "subject" or "participant" has been preferred in referring to human beings involved in studies. Currently, the words are used largely interchangeably, except when testing animals other than humans, in which case the term "subject" should be used.

52. **performance.** See (38).

53. **phenotype.** See (27).

54. **population, sample.** A population is the universe of cases to which an investigator wants to generalize his or her results. A sample is a subset of a population.

     a. If an investigator views Ms. Blakeley's 2009 fourth-grade class as a population, then any generalizations he makes from data obtained from the class will be limited to that class only.

     b. If an investigator views Ms. Blakeley's 2009 fourth-grade class as a sample, then generalizations he makes from data obtained from the class will be to the population of which Ms. Blakeley's class is a subject. The more diverse the population, the less likely is Ms. Blakeley's class to be representative of the population and, thus, the less likely are the data to be generalizable. One could have more confidence in generalizations to the entire fourth grade at Ms. Blakeley's school than in generalizations to the fourth grades of the entire United States.

55. **preconscious, unconscious.** The preconscious contains cognitions that are not conscious but can be brought into consciousness with little or no effort. The unconscious (subconscious)

contains cognitions and feelings of which we are unaware and that can be brought into consciousness only with difficulty.

  a. As she completed the first sentence of her paper, the ideas for her second sentence glided from her preconscious to her conscious thoughts.

  b. The girl's desire to excel over her three sisters was unconscious and showed itself only in her behavior and in her repeated dreams of athletic conquests over three familiar but not quite recognizable opponents.

56. **primacy/recency.** Primacy effects are effects that occur at the beginning of some temporal sequence. Recency effects are effects that occur at the end of some temporal sequence.

  a. The primacy effect in free recall is the tendency for people to remember items from the beginning of a list better than they remember items from the middle of a list.

  b. The recency effect in free recall is the tendency for people to remember items from the end of a list better than they remember items from the middle of a list.

57. **ratio IQ.** See (18).

58. **recency.** See (56).

59. **regression.** See (26).

60. **reliability, validity.** Reliability refers to how well or consistently a test measures whatever the test measures. Validity refers to how well a test measures what it is supposed to measure. Thus, a perfectly reliable test can be completely invalid if it measures something well but not what it is intended to measure. A perfectly valid test, however, must be perfectly reliable, because if the test measures what it is supposed to measure perfectly, it must measure what it does in fact measure perfectly.

  a. The test of finger-tapping speed proved to be highly reliable, providing consistent estimates of people's finger-tapping abilities. The test of intelligence proved to be only moderately reliable, providing only somewhat consistent estimates of people's measured intelligence.

  b. The highly reliable test of finger-tapping speed proved to be invalid as a predictor of school achievement. The moderately reliable intelligence test proved to be moderately valid as a predictor of school achievement. In this case, the more reliable test was less valid for a specific purpose to which it was poorly suited. Although reliability places an upper bound on validity, it is no guarantee of validity.

> **Experience Is the Best Teacher**
>
> There are many different kinds of reliability and validity. Therefore, it is incumbent on authors to state what kind of reliability or validity they are referring to. For example, validity could refer to the extent to which experts believe that the content of a test is measuring what it is supposed to measure, or it could refer to a correlation coefficient between a predictor measure (e.g., an aptitude test) and a criterion measure (e.g., school grades).

61. **repression, suppression.** Repression is a defense mechanism whereby a thought or feeling is removed from consciousness. Suppression is a defense mechanism whereby a thought or feeling remains in consciousness but is not overtly expressed. People are aware of suppressed but not repressed material.
    a. The patient had long ago repressed all memories of his brutal grandfather. At the therapy sessions, he honestly denied ever even having known his grandfather.
    b. The psychologist's therapy sessions with the student were getting nowhere, because the student suppressed any information that she thought might embarrass her in the psychologist's eyes.

62. **significant.** A statistically significant result is one that enables an investigator to reject a null hypothesis (see item 47). Statistical significance is sometimes contrasted with practical significance. A result can be statistically significant but not practically significant. Whenever the term *significant* is used by itself, it should be used only to refer to the technical meaning of *statistical significance*. Do not use the word to refer to any result that you think is important.

    The large difference between means in the two groups was statistically significant, enabling the psychologist to reject the null hypothesis of no difference between the groups.

> **What's Wrong Here?**
>
> "Our results are significant for showing that an asymmetrical smile rarely indicates happiness."

> **Answer:** It is not clear in this statement whether significance here is statistical or practical. It appears to be practical, but one cannot be certain.

63. **simulation.** See (5).
64. **state, trait.** A state is a temporary mood or frame of mind. A trait is a permanent disposition.
    a. Anxiety as a state refers to a temporary frame of mind in which the individual feels uneasy or apprehensive for no clear reason.
    b. Anxiety as a trait refers to a permanent disposition of an individual to feel uneasy or apprehensive for no clear reason.
65. **subject.** See (51).
66. **suppression.** See (61).
67. **trait.** See (64).
68. **unconscious.** See (55).
69. **validity.** See (60).
70. **variability, variance.** The variability of a set of observations refers to the amount of dispersion or spread in the observations. The variance of a set of observations refers to a specific measure of the amount of dispersion: $\sum(x^2)/N$, where x is the deviation of each score from the mean and N the number of cases. The term *variance* should be used only to refer to this specific measure, not to refer loosely to the amount of dispersion in the observations.
    a. The scores in the sample showed very little variability.
    b. The variance of the scores in the sample was only 4 points.
71. **variance.** See (70).
72. **white noise.** White noise is noise composed of sounds of all frequencies. It is called white noise as an analogy to white color, which is composed of colors of all wavelengths. It otherwise has no relation to white or any other color.
    White noise was piped into the testing room in order to distract subjects from the difficult memory task.

9 American Psychological Association Guidelines for Psychology Papers

This chapter summarizes the guidelines for preparing a psychology paper presented in the *Publication Manual of the American Psychological Association*, 6th edition (2009). You should consult this manual for a complete list of guidelines. If you intend to submit a paper for publication, then you cannot afford to be without this manual. It can be obtained from any bookstore or online book retailer, or directly from the American Psychological Association at www.apastyle.org.

Journals of the British Psychological Society (BPS) adopted the APA style as of October 2001. Publications other than journal articles of the BPS follow the *Style Guide* that can be found online by entering the search words "BPS style" in a search engine. Many other non-APA journals will accept articles prepared in accordance with APA guidelines as well, even though there are minor differences in style. You should always consult the guidelines of the journal to which you plan to submit to make sure you are adhering to its style regulations.

All examples used to illustrate principles in this chapter are fictitious. Note that the formatting of this book, as printed, does not always follow the conventions described in this chapter. The conventions in the chapter are for preparing manuscripts, not for printed versions of books and articles.

9.1 FORMATTING THE PAPER

■ Margins

Set your margins to leave 1 inch at the top, bottom, and both sides of each page. Each line should be no longer than 6 1/2 inches. Use flush-left style. In other words, the right margin should be "ragged." Do not use your word processor's automatic hyphenation option, and do not hyphenate words at the ends of lines yourself.

■ Vertical spacing

Double space between all lines, without exception. There may be times when you are tempted to single space – in writing references, footnotes, block quotations, and the like. Do not succumb to the temptation. Your paper should be double spaced throughout with the exception of tables and figures.

■ Horizontal spacing

Begin each new paragraph by indenting a half inch, or using a tab key, which you should set to default at a half inch. Type all other lines starting from a uniform left margin: (a) the abstract, (b) block quotations, (c) titles and headings, (d) table titles and notes, and (e) figure captions. Furthermore, leave no space after internal periods in abbreviations (e.g., a.m., i.e.) and in ratios. Leave one space after commas, colons, semicolons, and periods ending sentences, as well as after internal periods in first and middle initials (e.g., H. B. Hinkelmeyer).

■ Numbering pages

Number pages consecutively, starting with the title page. Use Arabic numerals. If pages are accidentally separated from the manuscript, the page numbers together with the running head help identify where they belong.

■ Font

For the text, use a 12-point font size with an easily readable font such as Times New Roman, Arial, or Courier (but the preferred font for APA publications is Times New Roman). For figures, use a sans-serif typeface.

9.2 GRAMMAR

9.2.1 Punctuation

9.2.1.1 Comma

A comma should be used

   1. before *and* and *or* in a series of three or more items:

> The participant, confederate, and experimenter all entered the room together.

2. before and after a nonrestrictive clause (i.e., a clause that is nonessential to the sentence):

The empty box, which had been rigged to look like a lie detector, was placed on a table next to the participant.

The empty box that had been rigged to look like a lie detector was placed on a table next to the participant.

3. to separate two coordinate clauses joined by a conjunction:

The experimenter pretended to activate the lie detector, and the confederate disappeared into an adjoining room with a one-way mirror.

A comma should not be used

1. before or after a restrictive clause (i.e., a clause that limits or further defines the word it modifies):

The button that the experimenter pushed served only to impress the participant.

2. between two parts of a compound predicate:

The experimenter attached two fake electrodes to the participant's wrists and told the participant that the machine would record the truth or falsity of each response.

3. to separate two independent clauses not joined by a conjunction:

First, the participant was asked to answer each question; then he was told that he would receive double pay at the end of the experiment if he succeeded in fooling the "lie detector."

4. to separate parts of measurement:

The participant was exposed to the white noise for exactly 5 min 15 s.

9.2.1.2 Semicolon

A semicolon should be used to

1. separate two independent clauses that are not joined by a conjunction:

The experimenter then proceeded to ask the participant a series of embarrassing questions; she pretended to be surprised at the participant's responses.

2. separate items that already contain commas:

The sets of questions asked by the experimenter dealt with sex, swearing, and bathroom habits; masculinity, undressing habits, and thumbsucking; or private fantasies, nightmares, and academic failures.

9.2.1.3 Colon

A colon should be used

1. before a final phrase or clause that amplifies the material that comes before it:

Most participants initially hesitated to answer the questions: They stared at the experimenter in disbelief.

2. in ratios and proportions:

The proportions of participants answering the questions honestly were 15:25, 13:37, and 18:26 in the three groups receiving the different sets of questions.

9.2.1.4 Hyphen

A hyphen should be used in

1. a compound with a participle if the compound precedes a noun it modifies:

The truth-telling participants showed less fidgeting than the lie-telling ones.

2. a phrase used as an adjective if the phrase precedes a noun it modifies:

A subject-by-subject analysis of the results showed strong differences in the honesty with which various individuals answered the questions.

3. a compound adjective comprising an adjective and a noun that precedes and modifies another noun:

High-anxiety participants were less honest in their answers than were low-anxiety participants.

4. all compounds involving the prefix *self:*

Self-report data indicated that high-anxiety subjects were more worried than low-anxiety participants that honest answers would later be used against them.

5. fractions that are used as adjectives:

To get approval for his high-risk study, he needs a two-thirds majority from the institutional review board.

A hyphen should not be used in

1. a compound with an adverb ending in *-ly:*

A widely expressed fear was that the participants' responses would not really be kept confidential.

2. a compound involving a comparative or superlative:

A less common fear was that the experimenter would know from the "lie detector" which responses were truthful and which were not.

3. a modifier with a letter or numeral as the second term:

The Session 2 data seem to have been affected less by these fears than were the Session 1 data.

4. foreign phrases used as adjectives/adverbs:

The a posteriori test revealed that the means for all three groups differed significantly.

5. fractions that are used as nouns:

Participants missed about one fourth of the stimuli.

There are several symbols that can be confused with a hyphen but are used in different circumstances. These symbols are as follows:

■ em dash

The em dash is longer than an en dash or hyphen – it is the width of the letter *M*, the widest letter in a font set. As with the hyphen, do not use a space before or after the em dash. If you do not have an em dash on your keyboard, you may use two hyphens instead (again, with no space before or after them). The em dash is used to delimit elements from the main clause that are used to amplify or digress. For example:

The subjects who lied in answering every question–all of them members of the high-anxiety group–confessed that they thought the "lie detector" was nothing more than an empty box.

▦ en dash

An en dash is longer is longer and not as thick as a hyphen – it is the width of the letter *N* in a font set. If you do not have an en dash on your keyboard, use a hyphen with no space before or after. En dashes are used between words of equal weight in a compound adjective:

The Freud–Einstein exchange of letters is still of highest significance today.

▦ minus sign

The minus sign is the same length as the en dash but somewhat thicker and higher. Should you not have a minus sign, you can use hyphen with spaces on both sides. Note, however, that negative values should be typed using a hyphen rather than a minus sign, with a space before but not after the hyphen, for example, -7.23.

9.2.1.5 Double Quotation Marks

Double quotation marks should be used

1. to introduce a word or phrase used in a special or unusual way (use quotation marks only the first time a word is used):

   The experimenter divided the participants into two groups: the "con artists" and the "apple polishers."

2. to reproduce material that is quoted verbatim:

   The con artists had taken to heart the experimental instruction, "You should lie whenever you think you can get away with it." The apple polishers seem to have ignored or disbelieved this instruction and almost always told the truth.

3. for names of articles:

   The experimenter planned to name the article "An Experimental Investigation of Con Artistry."

Double quotation marks should not be used

1. to qualify statements or to hedge bets:

   The apple polishers were relieved when the experiment was over; the con artists begged for more (not "begged" for more).

2. for quotations of 40 words or more; instead, use block format:

   The experimenter debriefed the participants at the end of the experiment:
   > The purpose of this experiment was to provide a source of examples for *The Psychologist's Companion*. The experiment itself made no sense and had no purpose other than to provide the examples. We hope you enjoyed this meaningful activity.

3. to cite linguistic examples up to the length of a sentence; instead, use italics:

   The use of *which* for *that* is common in psychological writing but is inadvisable.

4. to introduce an important technical term; instead, use italics:

   Schnallkraker's syndrome is a serious disease (or would be were there such a thing).

Observe the following rules in using quotations:

1. Omission of material within a sentence of a quotation is indicated by the use of three ellipsis points (...). Omission of material between sentences of a quotation is indicated by four ellipsis points. Ellipsis points should not be used at the beginning or end of a quotation:
   a. According to McGoof (2009), "The difference between groups ... was statistically but not practically significant" (p. 303).
   b. As he left the room, the participant said to the experimenter, "I hope I wasn't really supposed to write down the words in the order in which they were read... I know the instructions said to, but I didn't see the point."
2. Insertion of material within a sentence of a quotation is indicated by brackets. Such insertions are usually used to clarify the quotation for the reader or to make the grammar of the quotation

consistent with the sentence or paragraph in which it is embedded:

According to the instructions, "this test [should be] timed for 30 minutes."

3. Three kinds of changes are permissible in quotations without any indication to the reader: (a) The first letter of the first quoted word may be changed from a capital to a small letter, or vice versa; (b) the punctuation mark at the end of the quotation may be changed to fit the syntax of the sentence in which you have embedded the quotation; and (c) single quotation marks may be changed to double quotation marks, and vice versa. All other changes must be indicated by ellipses or brackets.

The sentence, "She ate the cheese," may be cited as, "she ate the cheese."

4. The source of a direct quotation should always be cited. Include in the citation the author(s), year, and page number(s) of the quotation. If the quotation is in the middle of a sentence, cite the source of the quotation in parentheses immediately after the quotation. If the quotation is at the end of a sentence, cite the page number in parentheses after the end of the quotation but before the final punctuation mark. If the quotation is in block format, cite the page number in parentheses after the end of the quotation and after the final punctuation mark:
   a. According to the author, "None of the mice ate the cheese until they had finished the task" (Rattsky, 2008, p. 108), so they were hungry.
   b. Rattsky (2008) found that "none of the mice ate the cheese until they had finished the task" (p. 108).
   c. According to Rattsky (2008),
      None of the mice ate the cheese until they had finished the task. After they ate the cheese, six mice proceeded to redo the task, while the other nine mice marched back to their cages. (p. 108)
5. In general, commas and periods are placed inside quotation marks and other marks of punctuation are placed outside, unless they are part of the quoted material, in which case they are placed inside:

"Eat the banana," he screamed at the monkey. Did he scream at the monkey, "Eat the banana"?

6. Long quotations may require permission from the owner of the copyright on the material. APA policy permits use of up to 400 words in single text extracts and up to 800 words for a series of text extracts without permission. Copyright owners vary in the number of words permitted, however, so for quotations of 100 or more words it is wise to check the policy of the copyright owner. Even if the copyright owner is a journal or book company, it is a common courtesy to request permission from the author as well as the company. If multiple authors are involved, request permission only of the lead author.

9.2.1.6 Single Quotation Marks

Single quotation marks should be used for quotations within quotations:

The experimenter, as if to emphasize the pointlessness of the experiment, said to the participants, "Remember the well-known proverb: `All's well that ends well.'"

9.2.1.7 Parentheses

Parentheses should be used to

1. set off items that are structurally independent from the rest of the sentence:

   After debriefing, participants were given a questionnaire in which they were asked their reactions to the experiment (see Table 1).

2. enclose the date of references cited in the text or references:

   The questionnaire was adopted with minor modifications from one used by Bozo (2007).

   Bozo, B. B. (2007). A questionnaire for measuring slapstick tendencies. *Humor, 3,* 26–31.

3. enclose abbreviations:

   Subjects were also given the Toliver Test of Tolerance for Trauma (TTTT).

4. enclose letters or numbers enumerating items in a series:

Finally, participants were given three ability tests: (a) the Penultimate Test of Pencil-Pushing Power, (b) the Scofield Scale of Hand–Foot Coordination, and (c) the Williams Test of Willpower.

5. enclose the page number of a cited quotation:

The Williams test seemed particularly appropriate for this experiment, because it is described in the manual as "an invalid test of practically anything an investigator might want to measure" (p. 26).

6. group terms in mathematical expressions:

On the Williams test, there is a correction for guessing, so that overall score is a function of both right and wrong answers:

$$R - (W/4).$$

7. enclose enumeration of equations:

The overall score on the Williams test can be converted to a standard score

$$z = (\mathrm{X} - \overline{\mathrm{X}})/\mathrm{SD}. \qquad (1)$$

In this notation, z is the standard score, X the overall score, X the mean of the scores, and SD the standard deviation of the scores.

8. to enclose statistical values:

The means of the two different experimental groups did not differ significantly ($p = .12$).

9. to enclose degrees of freedom:

$$F(3, 87) = 2.57$$

9.2.1.8 Brackets

Brackets should be used to

1. enclose material inserted in a quotation by someone other than the quoted writer or speaker:

A participant remarked as he left the experiment, "This is the most pointless [experiment] I've ever been in."

2. enclose parenthetical material within parentheses:

(The confederate [see "Method" section] was inclined to agree.)

9.2.2 Capitalization

9.2.2.1 Titles and Headings

1. Capitalize major words in titles of books and journal articles mentioned in the text of a psychology paper:

   The article reporting the experiment was to be titled "A Factor Analysis of Pencil-Pushing Power."

2. In references, capitalize the first word in titles of books and articles cited:

   Muddlehead, M. M. (2008). A factor analysis of pencil-pushing power. *Journal of Junky Experiments, 5*, 406–409.

3. In references, capitalize all major words of journal names:

   Muddlehead, M. M. (2008). A factor analysis of pencil-pushing power. *Journal of Junky Experiments, 5*, 406–409.

4. Capitalize major words of table titles and figure legends:

   Table 1.
   Loadings of Ability Tests on Pencil-Pushing Speed Factor

5. Capitalize the first letter of first words and proper nouns of figure captions and table column headings:

   Figure 1.
   A typical sample of copied material.

9.2.2.2 Proper Nouns and Trade Names

1. Capitalize trade and brand names:

   Subjects used a Pengo Permapencil to do their copying.

2. Capitalize names of university departments referring to specific departments in specific universities:

   The experiment was conducted under the auspices of the Department of Psychology, Zingo University.

3. Do not capitalize names of general laws, theories, and hypotheses:

The experimenter used a unifactor theory of pencil pushing to explain her results.

9.2.2.3 Titles of Tests

1. Capitalize exact, complete titles of tests:

Three tests of pencil pushing were administered: (a) the Penultimate Test of Pencil-Pushing Power, (b) the Staley Push-a-Pencil Test, and (c) the Pennsylvania Pencil Inventory.

2. Do not capitalize shortened or inexact titles of tests or titles of unpublished tests:

Scores on the Staley test showed no practice effect.

9.2.2.4 Nouns Followed by Numerals or Letters

1. Capitalize nouns followed by numerals or letters indicating membership in an enumerated series (except for enumeration of pages, chapters, rows, and columns):

In Session 1 of a new experiment on pencil pushing, participants were asked to copy on page 1 of their booklets a paragraph of printed material.

2. Nouns preceding a variable are not capitalized:

Scores in session n were no higher on average than were scores in session $n - 1$.

9.2.2.5 Names of Factors, Variables, and Effects

1. Capitalize names of factors from a factor analysis:

A factor analysis of the tests revealed just one reliable factor, which the experimenter called Pencil-Pushing Speed.

2. Do not capitalize names of effects taken from analyses of variance, unless they refer to an interaction (with $\times$):

An analysis of variance revealed no difference in school achievement as a function of pencil-pushing speed (but the Sex $\times$ Speed interaction was statistically significant).

9.2.2.6 Names of Conditions or Groups in Experiments

Do **not** capitalize names of conditions or groups in an experiment:

Participants in the experiment were divided into two groups, fast pencil pushers and slow pencil pushers.

9.2.3 Italics

Italics should be used for

1. titles of books, periodicals, and microfilms:
   a. The article relating bumps on the head to claustrophobia was published in the journal *Phrenology Today*.
   b. The author didn't think a book titled *Bump It or Lump It* would sell enough copies to make writing the book worthwhile.

2. introducing new, technical, or important terms:

   All participants in the experiment were told the meaning of *sociopathy*.

3. letters, words, phrases, or sentences cited as linguistic examples:

   Some participants did not even realize that *phrenology* was a noun.

4. letters used as statistical symbols or algebraic variables:
   a. The difference in number of bumps on the head between claustrophobic and nonclaustrophobic subjects was not significant, $t(32) = 0.26$, $p > .05$.
   b. The phrenologist still argued that the relation between degree of claustrophobia (y) and number of bumps on the head (x) could be expressed by the equation $y = 7x + 2$.

5. volume numbers in reference lists:

   Bumpo, B. P. (2003). The relation between bumps on the head and claustrophobia. *Phrenology Today, 13*, 402–406.

6. anchors of a scale:

   A 5-point scale was used ranging from 1 (*do not agree at all*) to 5 (*completely agree*).

Italics should not be used for

1. common foreign words and abbreviations:
   a. The a priori likelihood of a relation between number of bumps on the head and degree of claustrophobia seemed remote.
   b. The remarks of Zootz et al. (2006) vis-à-vis errors in counting number of bumps are still relevant today.
2. names of Greek letters:

   Zootz and his colleagues noted that there are two kinds of bumps, alpha (α) bumps and beta (β) bumps, and that only alpha bumps should be counted.

3. emphasis, unless the emphasis would be lost without italics:

   Zootz and his colleagues emphasized that there was no known relation between number of beta bumps and claustrophobia.

4. abbreviations:

   The National Phrenological Society (NPS) dissociated itself from the work of both Bumpo and Zootz.

9.2.4 Spelling

The standard reference used by American Psychological Association journals for spelling is *Merriam-Webster's Collegiate Dictionary*, 11th edition (2005). *Webster's Third New International Dictionary* (2002) should be consulted for spellings of words not in the collegiate volume. In cases where two or more spellings are acceptable, use the first, preferred spelling. You can also consult www.apastyle.org for the latest information on certain spellings not found in the dictionary.

9.2.5 Abbreviations

Use abbreviations sparingly. Explain each abbreviation the first time it is used (except in Example 1 here). Here are some general rules:

1. Abbreviations do not need to be explained if they are listed as word entries (i.e., are not labeled *abbr*) in *Merriam-Webster's Collegiate Dictionary* (2005):

   The participant scored 108 on the IQ test.

2. Abbreviations need to be explained when they are used for the first time:

The participant's average response time (RT) in responding to test items was 6.52 s.

3. Latin abbreviations should be used only in parenthetical material; their English translation should be used in non-parenthetical material. However, the abbreviation *et al.* should be used both in parenthetical and non-parenthetical text:

The procedure required the subjects to complete a variety of different assessments (e.g., a questionnaire to assess their state anxiety and an IQ test).

4. Metric and nonmetric units should be abbreviated when appearing together with a numerical value:

To give readers an idea of the length of the test, the authors noted that the test booklet was 2 cm thick.

5. Units of time that should not be abbreviated are *year, month, week,* and *day.* Abbreviations can be used for *hour* (hr), *minute* (min), *second* (s), *millisecond* (ms), and *nanosecond* (ns):

The participant's average response time in responding to test items was 6.52 s.

Abbreviations should not be used

1. if you use nonstandard abbreviations that you have made up, and
2. to abbreviate the words *subject* (S), *experimenter* (E), or *observer* (O). Although these abbreviations were once standard, they are no longer used.

Periods in abbreviations
Periods should be used with

1. initials of names:

A. C. Acney discovered the little known Acney effect.

2. Latin abbreviations:

The discovery was made at exactly 8:00 a.m.

3. reference abbreviations:

The effect is described in the autobiography of A. C. Acney (Vol. 3).

Periods should not be used with

1. capital-letter abbreviations, including acronyms:

The now discredited Acney effect relates IQ to facial complexion. Acney was unsuccessful in getting the report of his findings into any APA journal.

2. abbreviations of metric units:

Expressed in metric units, the weight of Vol. 3 of Acney's autobiography is 1.4 kg, 1.4 kg more than the book is worth.

3. abbreviations of nonmetric measurement:

This lengthy book weighs 3 lb and can be used to press leaves.

4. abbreviations of state and territory names:

He discovered the effect in his little lab in Washington, DC.

9.3 HEADINGS

APA editorial guidelines provide for five levels of headings:

1. a centered, boldface heading typed in uppercase and lowercase letters;
2. a flush left, boldface heading typed in uppercase and lowercase letters;
3. an indented, boldface heading typed in lowercase letters with a period at the end;
4. an indented, boldface, italicized heading typed in lowercase letters with a period at the end;
5. an indented, italicized heading typed in lowercase letters with a period at the end.

The complete set of five headings is usually needed only in very long articles, for example, reports of multiple experiments. Always start with the highest level of heading and work your way down to whatever number of levels you may need. This book does not follow this sequence of headings.

An example using all five levels of headings is the following:

Experiment I

Collection of Responses

   Method.

   Design.

   Independent variables.

9.4 QUANTITATIVE ISSUES

9.4.1 Units of Measurement

The American Psychological Association has adopted the metric system in all APA journals, and other journals have generally followed suit. Authors therefore should express measurements in metric units wherever possible. If measurements are expressed in other kinds of units, metric equivalents should be given. When a metric unit appears with a numeric value, use the metric symbol (without a period after the symbol); when it appears without a numerical value, spell it out in lowercase letters.

9.4.2 Statistics

Statistics can be presented in the text, tables, or figures. Authors must choose the means that most effectively communicate their data. Frequently used statistics (e.g., the mean, t, F) can be used without explanation. Infrequently used statistics (e.g., c_p) should be explained, and a reference for the statistic cited. A reference should also be given for use of a statistic in a controversial way (e.g., the F statistic when sample variances are widely discrepant).

The standard format for presentation of inferential statistics in text calls for inclusion of the name of the statistic, the degrees of freedom for the statistic (if relevant), the value of the statistic, and the probability level associated with the statistic. This information is presented in the following way:

a. Participants informed of the relation between lists recalled significantly more words than participants not informed of this relation, $t(68) = 2.93$, $p = .014$.

b. The personality scale did not differentiate among compulsive, hysterical, and normal participants, $F(2, 28) = 1.18, p > .05$.

Report exact p values unless the value is less than .001, in which case it is preferable to report as $p < .001$.

9.4.3 Equations

9.4.3.1 General Principles

Several general principles apply to the presentation of equations:

1. Space mathematical expressions as you would space words, keeping in mind that the primary consideration is legibility:

$$y = a/(b + c)$$

2. Align mathematical expressions carefully. Subscripts generally precede superscripts, but primes occur immediately following the primed letter or symbol:

$$y = x_p^3 + x_q'^2$$

3. Punctuate all equations, however presented, as you would any expression, mathematical or not:

The standard formula was used for computing IQ:

$$IQ = MA/CA.$$

4. Parentheses (), brackets [], and braces {} should be used in that order to avoid ambiguity:

$$y = a/(b + c)$$
$$y = a/[(b + c).(d - -e)]$$
$$y = \{a/[(b + c).(d - -e)]\} + f$$

5. Use the percentage symbol (%) only when a number precedes it. Otherwise, use the word *percentage:*
   a. Only 18% of the sample responded to the questionnaire.
   b. The percentage of respondents was disappointing.

9.4.3.2 Equations Merged with Text

Short and simple equations that will not have to be referred to later in the text can be placed in the midst of a line of text. Follow these rules:

1. Fractions presented in the midst of a line of text should be indicated by use of a slash:

   The data indicated that for any values of a and b, $y = a/b$.

2. The equation should not project above or below the line. If it does, use the format for equations described below.

9.4.3.3 Equations Separated from Text

Equations should be separated from the text if (a) they are referred to later, (b) they are complex, or (c) they project above or below a single line of text. Equations separated from the text should be numbered consecutively, with the number enclosed in parentheses and near the right margin of the page:

$$RT = 5x^2 + \frac{y+8}{2n} + \frac{z^3+5}{y} \tag{1}$$

9.4.4 Numbers

9.4.4.1 General Principles

Several general principles apply to the use of numbers in text:

1. Rules for cardinal numbers (e.g., *two*) and ordinal numbers (e.g., *second*) are the same (see below), except for percentiles and quartiles. Percentiles and quartiles should always be expressed in figures:

   The boy's score placed him in the 5th percentile.

2. Use Arabic rather than Roman numerals wherever possible. Use Roman numerals, however, where convention calls for their use:

   The probability of a Type I error was less than 5%.

3. For numbers greater than or equal to 1,000, use commas between every group of three digits:

   Her response was timed at 1,185 ms.

4. In writing decimals, place a 0 before the decimal point if the number is less than 1, unless the number *must* be less than one:
   a. The average score on the test was a pitiful 0.73.
   b. The proportion of participants finishing the task was .86.
5. Use decimal notation instead of mixed fractions wherever possible. Do not use decimals, though, if their use is awkward:
   a. The maximum score on the test was 8.5 out of 10.
   b. The oldest child in the experimental group was 5 1/2 years old.
6. Round numbers, in most cases, to two decimal digits, not more (e.g., a correlation of .53, not .5297).

9.4.4.2 Numbers Expressed in Words

Numbers should be expressed in words if

1. they are between zero and nine inclusive (with exceptions described in the next section):

   There were only six children in the sample.

2. they begin a sentence, regardless of whether or not they are less than 10:

   Eleven children were tested.

3. they are common fractions:

   One sixth of the participants failed to complete the given tasks in under 1 hour.

9.4.4.3 Numbers Expressed in Figures

Numbers should be expressed in figures if they satisfy any of the following conditions. Notice that all conditions except the first are exceptions to Rule 1 above for expressing numbers in words. Express numbers in figures if they are

1. greater than or equal to 10:

   There were 18 adults in the sample.

2. ages:

   All of the adults were older than 21 years of age.

3. times and dates:

The experiment took place between the hours of 8 a.m. and 10 a.m. on October 6, 2009.

4. percentages:

More than 90% of the participants finished the task.

5. ratios:

This was a ratio of 9:1.

6. fractions or decimals:

The corresponding fraction was 9/10, and the corresponding decimal, .9.

7. exact sums of money:

Participants were each paid $3 for participating in the experiment.

8. scores and points on scales:

The student received a score of 8.32 on a scale ranging from 0 to 9.

9. references to numerals as numerals:

The numeral 0 was placed next to each true item; the numeral 1 was placed next to each false item.

10. page numbers:

The students were told to write their identification numbers on page 1.

11. series of four or more items:

Students were assigned consecutive identification numbers: The first four students, for example, were assigned the numbers 1, 2, 3, and 4, respectively.

12. numbers grouped for comparison either between or within sentences if any of the numbers is 10 or greater:

There were 11 participants in the first group, but only 9 participants in the second group.

13. sample or population sizes:

The experiment involved 8 participants, half of them male and half of them female.

9.5 SERIATION

9.5.1 Seriation within a Paragraph

Seriation within a paragraph is indicated by lowercase letters written in parentheses. Do not italicize the letters.

The five categories of words to be recalled were (a) fruits, (b) animals, (c) nuts, (d) countries, and (e) oceans.

If the elements within the seriation have commas, the elements are separated by semicolons.

The four categories of words to be recalled contained (a) fruits, vegetables, and nuts; (b) mammals, insects, and birds; (c) lakes, rivers, and oceans; and (d) countries and continents.

9.5.2 Seriation of Paragraphs

Seriation of paragraphs is indicated by Arabic numerals followed by periods. Do not enclose the numbers in parentheses.

The experimenter used a three-step procedure:

1. The experimenter greeted the subject as the subject entered the room.

2. A confederate entered the room and asked for the time of day. He appeared to be in a state of great confusion.

3. The confederate noticed the subject, and struck up a conversation with him.

9.6 REFERENCES

9.6.1 Citations in Text

9.6.1.1 Standard Formats

References that are generally available may be cited either directly or indirectly.

1. If the author is cited directly, the date follows the author citation in parentheses:

Nimbus (2008) found that cloud formations can be used to predict persons' moods.

2. If the author is cited indirectly, both the author's name and the date are placed in parentheses:

It has been found that cloud formations can be used to predict persons' moods (Nimbus, 2008). This result has since been replicated (Nimbus, 2009; Stratus, 2009).

3. If the date is mentioned in the text, it need not be repeated in parentheses:

In 2008, Nimbus found that cloud formations can be used to predict people's moods.

4. If a work is cited more than once within the same paragraph, the date need not be repeated if there is no resulting ambiguity:

Nimbus's (2008) work on cloud formations and mood has received little attention. The lack of attention may be due to Nimbus's opening sentence: "Only a fool would take the work reported here seriously" (p. 1).

5. Multiple references to work of the same author published in the same year are assigned lowercase letters to distinguish them when they are cited. The letters should be assigned alphabetically, by title name:

Snow (2005a) has concluded that precipitation can dampen people's spirits. Snow (2005b) has argued that frozen precipitation is most demoralizing.

9.6.1.2 Multiple Authors

Follow these rules in citing work of multiple authors:

1. If a work has just two authors, cite both names and the date every time you make a citation:
   a. McLeod and O'Dowd (2007) found an artifact in Nimbus's (2008) study. (First citation)
   b. McLeod and O'Dowd (2007) corrected the artifact. (Later citation)
2. If a work has up to five authors, cite all names and the date the first time you make the citation – in later citations, you need only cite the first author, followed by "et al." and the date. If a work has six or more authors, only cite the surname of the first author followed by the "et al." statement, regardless of how many there

are. If two different pieces of work shorten to the same form, then always cite as many surnames as needed to distinguish the two different sources:

   a. McLeod, O'Dowd, and Giroud (2007) found no relation between cloud formations and mood. (First citation)

   b. McLeod et al. (2007) did not investigate cloud formations during tornadoes or hurricanes, however. (Later citations)

3. If citations with multiple authors are made directly, the names of the authors are connected by *and*. If citations are made indirectly (i.e., parenthetically), the names of the authors are connected by an ampersand (&):

   a. McLeod and O'Dowd (2008) found the artifact.

   b. An artifact was discovered (McLeod & O'Dowd, 2008).

9.6.1.3 No Author

If you cite a reference with no author, use the first two or three words of the entry as described in the references. In this case, the entry will usually be cited by title.

The pamphlet suggests ways of improving one's memory ("Tips on Memory," 2001).

9.6.1.4 Corporate Author

A corporate author may be cited instead of a personal one. Lengthy corporate names should be abbreviated only if they are readily identifiable in the reference list:

The book presented 15 ways to make friends (Golden Friendship Society, 2008).

9.6.1.5 Authors with the Same Surname

If you refer to more than one author with the same surname, include each author's initials each time you cite the author:

S. Jones (2009) disagreed with the interpretations of E. Jones (2007).

9.6.1.6 Electronic Sources

If available, provide the digital object identifier (DOI) number as an article identifier for electronic version of works you are citing. The

DOI is an alphanumeric string that starts with a 10. If no DOI exists, cite the home page URL of the journal or publisher:

Firestone, N. Z. (2007). You can prevent pyromania. *Journal of Exotic Ailments, 15,* 63–68. doi:10.1023/4587-6667.22.3.345

Lazynik, C. C. (August 15, 2009). How to make every day a Sunday. *The Lazy Times.* Retrieved from www.lazytimes.com

9.6.2 The Reference List

The References section of a paper contains an alphabetical list of the references cited in the text of the paper. References to more than one work by the same author are arranged by order of date of publication, with earlier works listed first. Each reference should include the author(s), title, and facts of publication. Details regarding format are given in Chapter 4 of this book: The format for the references is the same as the format for the author notes described in that chapter. There are so many different kinds of reference formats that it is not possible to include them all in this book. Please consult the *APA Manual* (2009) for a complete list of formats.

Note the use of the hanging indent in reference entries, whereby the first line of each reference is flush with the left margin and other lines are indented. Here are some examples of different kinds of references:

REFERENCES

Balderdash, H. Q. (2008). *Writing for meaning.* Los Angeles: Perfection Press.

Crumpet, C. D., & Donut, D. C. (2009). *Sugar tastes good and is good for you* (Vol. 1). Honolulu: Sugar Promotion Press.

Finn, D., Jr. (2008). Breathing in fish. In G. Trout & H. Bass (Eds.), *The physiology of fish.* San Francisco: Fisherman's Press.

Firestone, N. Z. (2007). You can prevent pyromania. *Journal of Exotic Ailments, 15,* 63–68.

Gambling for fun and profit. (2009). Las Vegas, NV: American Gambling Institute.

Lemon, B. J. (2002). *Vitamin C in your diet* (2nd ed.). Miami: Citrus Press.

Lohne, E. Z., & Sharke, P. P. (in press). Should usury be a crime? *Money Minder's Digest.*

Pompus, V. Q. (Ed.). (2004). *Encyclopedia of knowledge* (16 vols.). San Francisco: Worldwide.

9.7 AUTHOR NOTES

The author note (a) provides information about the author's complete departmental affiliation, (b) notes a change of an author's affiliation, (c) acknowledges financial support for a study, (d) acknowledges assistance in preparing, conducting, analyzing, or reporting a study, (e) explains special agreements with regard to authorship, (f) reports on any special circumstances (e.g., the data used as a basis for the paper have been used for a prior publication, or a conflict of interest), and (g) provides an address for correspondence. All of the above functions can be combined in a single author note; the order of statements should be as listed above. Author identification notes are not numbered. They are placed on the title page below the title, byline, and affiliation.

Phineas Phlom, Department of Psychology, Lazy State University at Slow River. The author is now at Rocky Ridge State College. The research was supported by grant G1O7H5 to the author from the National Institute of Rodent Research. I thank Whyte Meise for assistance in conducting the study. Correspondence regarding this article should be sent to Phineas Phlom, Department of Psychology, Rocky Ridge State College, Small Town, Vermont. E-mail: pphlom@rrsc.edu

9.8 FOOTNOTES

9.8.1 Kinds of Footnotes

9.8.1.1 Content Footnotes

Content footnotes are used for material that elaborates on the text but is not directly relevant to it. When citing a footnote in the text, place the note citation after all punctuation (except dashes).

Because footnotes can distract the reader, they should be used sparingly. Before using a footnote, you should decide whether the material might be better incorporated into the text or deleted.

[1] The only ill effect on the subject resulting from the treatment was a deep fear of furry animals, a fear we hope eventually to eradicate.

9.8.1.2 Reference Footnotes

Reference footnotes are used only rarely in psychological reporting. Almost all citations should be made through references. Reference footnotes may be used, however, for legal citations and copyright permissions.

[1]From *Writing for Meaning* (p. 113), by H. Q. Balderdash, 2009, Los Angeles: Perfection Press. Copyright by Perfection Press. Reprinted with permission.

9.8.1.3 Table Footnotes

Table footnotes amplify information contained in tables. These footnotes are of three kinds.

1. General notes

A general note provides further information about the table as a whole and explains any abbreviations and symbols.

2. Specific notes

A specific note provides further information about one or more entries in the table. Such notes are indicated by letter superscripts attached to the appropriate entries. If there is more than one note, the notes are ordered horizontally by rows.

3. Probability levels

Probability levels are used to ascertain the significance of statistical tests. A single asterisk should be used for the highest probability level, and an additional asterisk should be used for each lower probability level.

The number of asterisks used for a given probability level should be consistent across tables. The most common use of asterisks is for one to represent $p < .05$, two to represent $p < .01$, and three to represent $p < .001$. When possible, authors should report exact p values (e.g., $p = .03$) rather than ranges (e.g., $p < .05$).

When more than one kind of footnote appears in a single table, general footnotes precede specific ones, and specific ones precede probability levels. The footnotes to a single table might look like this:

Note. All subjects were veterans.

[a] Two subjects were caught copying from each other, and were eliminated from this group. [b] One subject in this group refused to finish the task and was eliminated.

$^*p < .05, ^{**}p < .01, ^{***}p < .001$

Observe that multiple footnotes of a given kind follow each other on a single line, where possible.

9.8.2 Numbering of Footnotes

Content and reference footnotes are numbered consecutively throughout a paper. Footnotes are indicated by Arabic numeral superscripts. If a footnote is referred to more than once, subsequent references should use a parenthetical statement rather than a super-script. Footnotes to a table should be lettered consecutively within each table.

Jones (2008) found that subjects suffered from few ill aftereffects.[1] Critics have lambasted Jones's (2008) alleged insensitivity to subjects (see Footnote 1).

9.8.3 Placement of Footnotes

In papers to be submitted for publication, footnotes are placed on a separate page after the references. In student papers, however, it is often more convenient for the reader if the footnotes are placed at the bottom of the page on which each footnote is cited.

9.9 CREDITING SOURCES AND PERMISSIONS

All direct quotations need to be accompanied by a reference citation, regardless of the length of those quotations. If you quote, you must supply an exact citation, including page numbers, even for short quotes. You also need permission from the rights holder for longer quotes. The length of the quote for which you need to express per-mission varies by copyright holder. Hence, you may need to check whether written permission is needed. The same rules apply to use of electronic material and for use of material in an electronic medium. The APA requires permission for quotes of more than 400 words in length for single text extracts and more than 800 words for series of text extracts.

9.10 CONFLICT OF INTEREST

When you go to publish an article, you may be asked to sign a form either stating that no conflicts of interest are involved in the research or else stating what they are or may be. For example, if a drug company has funded you to test the psychological effects of a drug that the company produces, you are in a potential conflict-of-interest situation. You must report all such conflicts or potential conflicts fully and accurately.

9.11 A FINAL WORD

You should adhere to these rules diligently, whether you submit your paper to a course instructor or to a journal editor. In the former case, your instructor will appreciate your concern for correct format, even if he or she has not explicitly requested it. In the latter case, a journal editor will expect strict adherence to the rules and may send back a paper that does not conform to them. The *APA Manual* (2009) provides a very useful checklist on pages 241–243 that helps you determine whether you have conformed to all the formal requirements.

10 | Guidelines for Data Presentation

The goal of this chapter is to help you understand how optimally to present data. The chapter draws heavily on three sources to which we refer readers for more details. For the presentation of data in the form of tables, Andrew Ehrenberg's *A Primer in Data Reduction* (2007) contains much good sound advice. For the use of figures, William Cleveland's *The Elements of Graphing Data* (1994) is a style guide that is required reading for anyone considering using a graph, from the most junior undergraduate to the most experienced researcher. Good advice is also available in the works of Tufte (2001) as well as in the sixth edition of the *APA Manual* (American Psychological Association, 2009).

Tables and figures allow large amounts of material to be presented concisely. Well presented, they often enable readers to understand at a glance patterns of data and exceptions that would be obscured if presented in the text. Tables and figures are more expensive for journals to produce than text, however, so if you plan to submit a paper for publication, you should present in this form only your most important sets of data. Do not duplicate data from one table or figure to another unless it is essential for comprehension. Extensive sets of data should be reported in appendices rather than in the body of the paper, or should be made available online with an appropriate note in the paper indicating the web address at which the data can be obtained.

The same principles that apply to the effective presentation of tables and figures also apply to effective scientific writing. The basic rule is to aim for a simple, direct presentation, without clutter.

Parts of this chapter have been prepared by Chris Leach.

Stylistic excesses like the moiré pattern graphics that appear on many histograms hinder rather than help, because they often direct attention away from the data. Edward Tufte (2001) uses the term *chartjunk* to refer to such unnecessary elements of graphs and has good advice on how to avoid it.

Care in preparing tables and figures helps you to understand your data. As you produce better versions, you explore your data and tease out meanings as well as choose how best to communicate the data. For this reason, tables and figures should be constructed first. Together with their captions, they should be able to communicate much of the information in the paper, without one's even having to read the text.

10.1 RELATION BETWEEN TABLES OR FIGURES AND TEXT

Three common mistakes in the use of tables and figures are the following:

1. Duplication in the text of material presented in tables and figures;
2. Presentation of tables and figures that are unintelligible without reference to the text; and
3. Presentation of tables and figures with no or minimal discussion.

First, data presented in tables and figures should be discussed in the text, and not just re-presented. Give brief verbal summaries to lead readers to the main patterns and exceptions, but do not repeat values that they easily can read from tables or figures. Second, construct each table and figure and the caption accompanying it so that readers are able to understand it without reference to the text. Third, remember that, even if readers are able to understand the table or figure by itself, they may not see the conclusions you want to draw. If data are important enough to present in tabular or graphical form, they are important enough to discuss.

What's Wrong Here?

"As shown in Table 3, the mean for the men was 8.19 with a standard deviation of 3.11 and the mean for women was 9.73 with a standard deviation of 2.98."

Answer: The data in the text exactly repeat data in the table.

10.2 SOME GENERAL TIPS FOR DESIGNING YOUR DATA DISPLAYS

No matter what kinds of data displays you are planning to use in your paper, there are a few guidelines that are always worth considering when you start designing your displays to ensure that your displays are as reader-friendly as possible (see also American Psychological Association, 2009):

- If your readers are supposed to compare different numbers or columns, place the items that need to be compared right beside each other.
- Be sure that all text in your display is legible without the use of a magnifying glass.
- Include all information in your display that is necessary to understand it – that is, make use of table notes, explain uncommon abbreviations, and so on.
- Keep the look of your display factual, and avoid using elements just for decorative purposes.

10.3 TABLES

10.3.1 When to Use Tables

Tables are preferable to figures for many small data sets. For larger, more complex data sets, a good choice of graph may do a better job of showing the patterns and exceptions. Tables also may be preferable if it is important to show precise values.

10.3.2 Four Rules for Constructing Tables

Compare Tables 10.1 and 10.2, which show the same crime figures for 15 states over a 3-year period. Table 10.2 was produced using four guiding principles suggested by Andrew Ehrenberg that make it much easier to understand than Table 10.1. (See Ehrenberg, 2007, for a more comprehensive account of this example.)

1. Order rows and columns by size.

Table 10.2 has the rows ordered by the three-year average for each state. In Table 10.1, they are ordered alphabetically. The only

Table 10.1. The number of murders and non-negligent manslaughters by states, 2005–2007 (first 15 states alphabetically)

| | Murder and non-negligent manslaughter | | |
| | Number | | |
	2007	2006	2005
Alabama	412	382	374
Alaska	44	36	32
Arizona	468	465	445
Arkansas	191	205	186
California	2,260	2,485	2,503
Colorado	153	158	173
Connecticut	106	108	102
Delaware	37	42	37
District of Columbia	181	169	195
Florida	1,201	1,129	883
Georgia	718	600	564
Hawaii	22	21	24
Idaho	49	36	35
Illinois	752	780	766
Indiana	356	369	356

Source: Federal Bureau of Investigation (2005, 2006, 2007).

advantage of alphabetical ordering is that it is easier to find a given state. The columns have not been reordered because the yearly averages do not differ much, and there is some interest in year-to-year fluctuation. It is clear from Table 10.2 that the ordering of the crime figures is similar to the ordering of the states' population sizes. Although it may seem obvious that the larger states would have higher crime rates, this fact is not obvious from Table 10.1. Rather than using the row averages to order the table, we could have used population size.

Using such an external criterion is helpful if a number of tables are to be compared, because the same fixed order can be used for each table. Of course, the external criterion should be one that is likely to be of help in making sense of the data, as population size is here.

Table 10.2. Murder and non-negligent manslaughter: states ordered by 3-year averages[a]

| | Murder and non-negligent manslaughter | | | |
	2007	2006	2005	Average
California	2,260	2,485	2,503	2,416
Florida	1,201	1,129	883	1,071
Illinois	752	780	766	766
Georgia	718	600	564	627
Arizona	468	465	445	459
Alabama	412	382	374	389
Indiana	356	369	356	360
Arkansas	191	205	186	194
DC	181	169	195	182
Colorado	153	158	173	161
Connecticut	106	108	102	105
Idaho	49	36	35	40
Delaware	37	42	37	39
Alaska	44	36	32	37
Hawaii	22	21	24	22
Average	463	466	445	458

Source: Federal Bureau of Investigation (2005, 2006, 2007).
[a] Reordered data from Table 10.1.

2. Use averages to summarize or provide a focus.

Table 10.2 has both row and column averages. Where the individual numbers do not differ much, the average provides a good summary. For example, the average of 360 murders and non-negligent manslaughters per year summarizes the numbers for Indiana in this period quite well. Where the numbers differ, the average provides a focus for comparison, as with the column averages. In Table 10.2, we can see that crime was fairly stable over this period, and that this stability applies equally to states with low and high crime rates. We can also see exceptions clearly. The numbers are, on average, higher in 2006 than in 2005, although Hawaii, Colorado, the District of Columbia, and California had lower crime rates in 2006 than in 2005.

3. Round numbers to two effective digits.

Rounding numbers sensibly is practically always helpful, because it saves on memory load, thus making it easier to do quick calculations. For example, we can quickly see that 740 is about three times 250, but comparing 737 and 245 takes longer. We also rarely need the greater accuracy. Rounding to two effective digits gives sufficient accuracy for most purposes. Effective digits are digits that vary in that sort of number. Numbers like percentages vary in tens and units, so 18.3 and 35.8 are rounded to 18 and 36. With numbers like 1,836.7, 1,639.3, 1,234.2, and 1,122.8, the decimal numbers are not effective in distinguishing the numbers. The rounded versions are 1,837, 1,639, 1,234, and 1,123.

4. Table layout should make it easy to compare relevant numbers.

The main principle of table layout is that numbers to be compared should be close together. In Table 10.2, it is easier to compare the numbers in any column than in any row. This is because the leading digits are close to each other, allowing for quicker calculations. The larger numbers have also been put at the top, as we are more used to doing subtractions that way. Other aspects of table layout are also important. Widely spaced rows prevent easy comparison, as does irregular spacing of rows and columns. However, occasional regular gaps help emphasize the patterns, as in Table 10.2. If tables need to be compared to each other, put them next to each other.

Experience Is the Best Teacher

Always make sure that any table can be read without reference to the text. That is, make sure the table is self-explanatory. Some people may see only the table and so if it is not self-explanatory, they simply will not understand it.

10.3.3 Placement of Tables

In articles submitted for publication, tables are placed after footnotes (see Chapter 5). In the text, refer to table numbers but do not say "table above" or "table below" as you do not know exactly where the typesetter will place the tables. In student papers, it is often more convenient to insert the tables at the appropriate places in the text for easier reading.

10.3.4 Table Numbers

Tables are numbered consecutively with Arabic numerals, starting with Table 1. Suffixes (e.g., Tables 5 and 5a) should not be used. Tables should have numbers only, so Tables 5 and 5a should be numbered Table 5 and Table 6. If you present tables in an appendix, identify them with a combination of capital letters and Arabic numerals. The second table of Appendix A is Table A2, for example, and the fifth table of Appendix C is Table C5. The table number is written at the top of the table. It is typed flush against the left side of the page.

10.3.5 Table Title

The title of a table should describe concisely what the table is supposed to show and should be understandable without reference to the text. In addition, it should be as brief as possible. Type it below the table number, flush against the left side of the page.

10.3.6 Ruling of Tables

Table 10.1 has both vertical and horizontal rules, whereas Table 10.2 has only horizontal rules. Most journals have standard formats. For example, vertical rules are almost never used in APA or British Psychology Society (BPS) journals. The variable spacing in Table 10.2 achieves the same effect without reducing the clarity of the table.

10.3.7 Formatting of Tables

Some tables have standard forms for data presentation. The *APA Manual* (American Psychological Association, 2009) lists and exemplifies those different tables. There are standards for regression tables, descriptive statistics, and word tables, among others. It will facilitate the design of your tables significantly if you comply with the APA guidelines. In addition, it is hardly possible to forget to report an important variable in a series of numbers when using a template. There are also some general guidelines that should always be followed:

- Table headings should be as short as possible and not be much wider than the longest entry
- You can use standard abbreviations without explaining them (e.g., *M* for mean or *N* for number). Nonstandard abbreviations should be explained in the table heading or table notes.
- Only the first letter of the first word in each heading should be capitalized.
- When a cell of the table is empty because data were not measured, insert a dash in the cell. If the data are not applicable to that cell, however, leave the cell blank.
- A dash in the main diagonal of a correlation matrix indicates the correlation of a variable with itself, which is 1.
- Tables can be submitted in either single- or double-spaced format.

10.4 FIGURES

10.4.1 When to Use Figures

A figure is any type of illustration other than a table. Figures include stem-and-leaf displays, graphs, charts, photographs, and drawings.

Before making a figure, consider which type of figure will present your information most effectively.

Figures, like tables, allow large amounts of data to be presented concisely. Their advantage over tables is that they often enable the reader to see at a glance trends that otherwise would not be readily apparent. With the exception of stem-and-leaf displays, figures have the disadvantage, however, that they do not convey precise values of data.

Use figures when they augment rather than duplicate the text, and then only to convey essential facts. Omit visually distracting details. Make sure your figures are easy to read and understand, and use a consistent style for presenting figures throughout the paper.

> **Give It Some More Thought**
>
> Many data sets can be shown visually either by a table or by a figure. How do you decide which to use? For example, you

might decide to use a table if you believe readers need precise numerical values and a figure if you believe that readers are more interested in general trends than in exact data points.

10.4.2 Stem-and-Leaf Displays

Table 10.3 shows the scores on a Sensation-Seeking Questionnaire (SSQ) of 32 hobby parachutists who have completed at least 15 jumps.

The distribution is skewed to the left. This skewness makes it misleading to report just means and standard deviations as summary statistics. Both will be heavily influenced by the two or three unusually high scores (or outliers). In this case, the outliers are particularly interesting, raising questions about why a person who is not high in sensation seeking would engage in such thrill-providing activities as parachuting. Reporting robust estimates of location and spread (e.g., median and interquartile range instead of mean and standard deviation) will reduce the impact of the outliers. However, a more comprehensive report of the data, rather than just summary statistics, would be more informative, particularly if outliers are considered potentially interesting cases rather than just nuisance values that mess up the calculation of summary statistics.

The frequency distribution given in Table 10.3 is one compact way of presenting all the data. A better way is to use a stem-and-leaf display, which combines the advantages of tables and graphs by retaining all the numerical information as well as showing clearly the shape of the distribution of numbers. Stem-and-leaf displays were developed by John Tukey (1977). The simplest type is produced by first rounding the numbers to two effective digits. The 32 scores in Table 10.3 are already in this form. Each score is now broken into two

Table 10.3. Sensation-seeking scores for 32 parachutists

SSQ	1	4	6	8	9	11	12	13	14	15	16	17	18	19	20
Frequency	1	1	2	2	1	2	3	2	3	4	3	3	2	2	1

parts, the part up to and including the first effective digit (the tens in this case) forming the stem and the second effective digit (the units) forming the leaf. So 18 has 1 as stem and 8 as leaf.

The stems determine which row of the display the score appears in and the leaves are written alongside the appropriate stem to identify the individual scores, as shown in Figure 10.1a. This display makes clear the skewness of the distribution, but it is too short and fat to give a clear view of the bulk of the distribution. In this case, it helps to have narrower stems to spread out the display. Figure 10.1b uses stem widths of 5 SSQ points, with the *s containing leaves between 5 and 9 and the ·s containing leaves between 0 and 4. The 14 is therefore placed alongside the 1·stem, whereas the 8 goes with the 1* stem.

Figure 10.1c gives an even more spread-out display, drawing attention to the outliers more effectively than do the other displays. Here the stem widths are 2 GHQ points, with the stems identified by • (for leaves 0 and 1), t (for two and three), f (for four and five), s (for six and seven), and * (for 8 and 9). So 4 and 8 now go in stems 1f and 1*. These displays are helpful for exploring data and also give a compact

(a)		2	0
		1	11222334444555556667778899
		.	1466889

(b)		2	0
		1*	55556667778899
		1.	1122233444
		*	66889
		.	14

(c)	1	2	0
	5	1*	8899
	11	1s	666777
	7	1f	4445555
	14	1t	22233
	9	1.	11
	7	*	889
	4	s	66
	2	f	4
		t	
	1	.	1

Figure 10.1. Stem-and-leaf displays of SSQ scores
Notes: (a) Stem widths of 10 SSQ points; (b) stem widths of 5 SSQ points; (c) stem widths of 2 SSQ points, with a cumulative count from either end to the middle.

way of communicating complete data sets when summary statistics are not sufficient.

10.4.3 Box Plots and Quartile Plots

For cases in which the data are too extensive to report the full stem-and-leaf display, Tukey's (1977) box plot is a convenient way of reporting summary statistics. Tufte's (2001) quartile plot is a more compact version of a box plot. The quartile and box plots both plot a five-number summary of the data, including the two extremes (highest and lowest scores), the first and third quartiles (called lower and upper hinges by Tukey), and the median. For the SSQ data, the extremes are 1 and 20, the hinges are 11 and 16.5, and the median is 14.

These five values can be obtained easily from the stem-and-leaf display. First, it helps to add a cumulative count from either end in toward the middle of the display, as has been done in Figure 10.1c. From this panel, we can see that there are 11 scores of 16 or higher, 14 of 12 or lower, and seven in the middle stem with values of 14 or 15. The lowest and highest scores, 1 and 20, can be read off immediately.

The median is the unique score in the middle if there is an odd number of scores, or the average of the two middle scores if there is an even number of scores. To see how deep we have to count in from either end to hit the median, the general rule is depth of median = (1 + number of scores)/2.

Here, there are 32 scores, so the median depth is (1 + 32)/2 = 16.5. The half shows that there is no unique middle score, so the median is the average of the 16th and 17th scores in from either end. Counting from low to high, the cumulative count tells us that there are 14 scores of 12 or less and seven in the middle stem, so the 16th and 17th scores will be the second and third entries in the middle stem. Both those scores are 14, so the median is 14.

The hinges are the scores in the middle of the two halves of the data from the median to the extremes. The middle half of the data lies between the two hinges, so the hinges give a good indication of the spread of the bulk of the data. The simplest general rule for the depth of the two hinges is depth of hinges = (1 + depth of median)/2. For an even number of scores, the half that crops up on the end of the median depth should be removed before calculating the hinge depth.

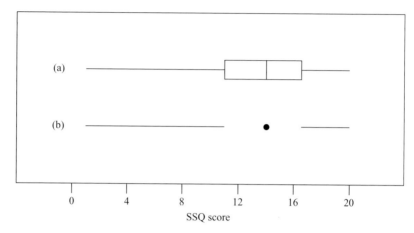

Figure 10.2. (a) Box plot; (b) quartile plot of SSQ scores

For this case, with a median depth of 16.5, the hinge depth will be (1 + 16)/2 = 8.5. So the hinges can be computed by taking the eighth and ninth values in from either end and dividing them by two [(11 + 11)/2 = 11, and (16 + 17)/2 = 16.5].

Figure 10.2a shows the box plot of this five-number summary. The two hinges form the outer edges of a box, with a line inside the box where the median is. Outside the box, whiskers are extended to the extremes. (Tukey's [1977] original term was *box-and-whisker plot*, now contracted to *box plot*.) From this plot, it can quickly be seen that the middle half of the data lies between scores 11 and 16.5 – the two hinges – with a median score of 14. The fact that the left whisker is longer than the right one suggests the skewness that is actually present in the data.

Figure 10.2b gives the more compact quartile-plot version, with a filled circle for the median and the boxes omitted, but the whiskers the same. This version is the preferred one, particularly when several plots are to be compared.

10.4.3.1 Outliers

Information about outliers can be added to these plots very straightforwardly. Tukey (1977) suggests a simple general procedure for detecting outliers. Calculate the midspread (or interquartile range), which is just the difference between the hinges. Outliers are those scores more than 1.5 midspreads beyond the hinges. Extreme outliers

Figure 10.3. Quartile plot of SSQ scores with outlier marked

are scores more than 3 midspreads beyond the hinges. In this example, the midspread is 16.5 – 11 = 5.5, so scores less than 2.75 [= 11 – (1.5 × 5.5)] or greater than 24.75 [= 16.5 + (1.5 × 5.5)] are outliers, whereas scores lower than –5.5 or higher than 33 are extreme outliers. The low score of 1 noted earlier now counts as an outlier. There are no extreme outliers. On this criterion, none of the high scores is high enough to count as an outlier.

What's Wrong Here?

"In analyzing our data, we removed all outliers. This procedure resulted in a loss of only 1.8% of the data."

Answer: The author did not state the criteria used for removing outliers so there is no way of knowing whether these criteria were reasonable. Suspicious people may suspect that data were removed that were inconvenient for the researcher but that really should have remained in the data set to be analyzed.

The outliers can be marked on the quartile plot or box plot, using ×s to represent outliers, $$ to represent extreme outliers, and extending the whiskers only to the highest (or lowest) scores not counted as outliers. The quartile plot in Figure 10.3 shows the three high outliers, with the whisker extending to 4, the lowest score in Figure 10.1c that is not an outlier.

There are many other methods of detecting outliers. The method given here is a general-purpose rough-and-ready approach that works well in many cases.

10.4.3.2 Comparing Data Sets

Stem-and-leaf displays and quartile plots are also helpful in comparing two or more sets of data.

Figure 10.4 shows the depression scores for 20 patients who demonstrated mood improvement after four weeks of cognitive therapy, back-to-back with scores from 13 patients who showed improvement after eight weeks. Figure 10.5 shows the two quartile plots of the data. From each display, it can be seen that the scores for the four-week group are lower, on average, and less spread out than the scores of the eight-week group. Although there are no outliers here, these displays are much more informative than a table of means and standard deviations.

10.4.4 Graphs

To the extent possible, always show your data in a clear and compelling way. William Cleveland's rules, listed in the next section, are

Improvement after four weeks		Improvement after eight weeks
	2.	0123
9876	1*	79
33311100	1.	2334
98765	*	68
332	.	0

Figure 10.4. Back-to-back stem-and-leaf display of depression scores for 20 patients showing improvement after four weeks of cognitive therapy and 13 showing improvement after eight weeks

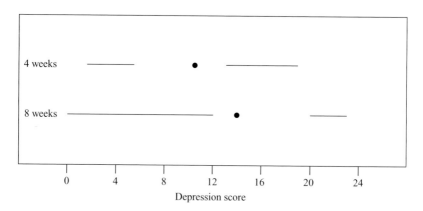

Figure 10.5. Quartile plots of depression scores for patients showing mood improvement after four or eight weeks of cognitive therapy

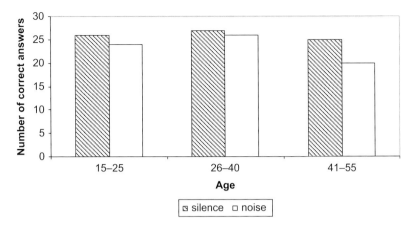

Figure 10.6. Bar chart of mean number of correct answers in an intelligence test by three age groups under conditions of silence or noise

good ways of following this advice, aiding both your own understanding and your ability to communicate the data. Before looking at these rules, two graphs will illustrate some of the main points. We have chosen two graphs that already do a reasonable job of communicating the data and suggest some improvements. Most published graphs could be improved; many have worse problems than these two; and many are quite dreadful.

Figure 10.6 shows a grouped bar chart that depicts the mean number of correct answers in an intelligence test under conditions of noise and silence by three age groups. The main point being communicated is that, whereas the three age groups did not significantly differ in their performance when working under conditions of silence, the age group of 41- to 55-year-olds had much more trouble keeping up their performance with noise than did the younger participants.

The first thing to note is that the figure communicates only eight numbers, so a table is likely to do a better job than a graph. If you write a paper that contains many tables, though, you may decide to choose a figure to highlight those data.

How can you do worse in presenting the data than in Figure 10.6? A common choice is to use a divided bar chart, as in Figure 10.7. This chart makes it difficult to compare the mid-periphery values, because nonaligned length judgments are involved. The only thing worse than a divided bar chart is a pie chart, because such a chart involves

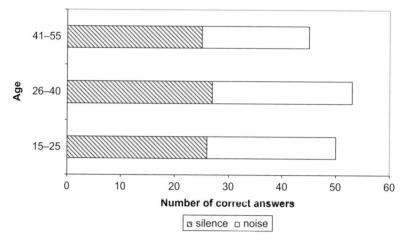

Figure 10.7. Divided bar chart version of the data in Figure 10.6

judging areas, which people find hard to do accurately. And the only thing worse than a pie chart is several pie charts.

Cleveland (1994) reported the results of a number of studies in graphical perception, examining the performance of people at the elementary tasks required for understanding graphs. He reported the following ordering of elementary tasks, from most to least accurate:

1. Position along a common scale;
2. Position along identical, nonaligned scales;
3. Length;
4. Angle or slope;
5. Area;
6. Volume; and
7. Color hue, color saturation, and density.

When choosing which type of graph to use, it helps to choose one involving judgments as high up in this ordering as possible. Divided bar charts and pie charts involve judgments low down in the ordering. They can always be replaced by a dot chart of the type shown in Figure 10.8, which involves judgments of position along a common scale. For this reason, divided bar charts and pie charts should never be used.

How can you improve on Figure 10.6? There is no need to use boxes to represent the numbers. If anything, the boxes might be

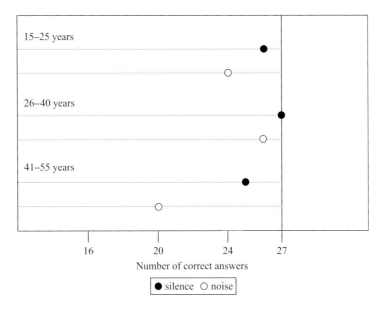

Figure 10.8. Dot chart for the data in Figure 10.6

misleading, as they invite viewers to make area judgments and the areas contain no information about the numbers, particularly as the scale does not start at zero.

Figure 10.8 shows a dot chart for these data. Here the eight dots are visually prominent, with light dotted lines extended across the display up to the maximum value of 27 for easier comparison. Because the scale does not start at zero, it would be misleading to stop the dotted lines at the data points; this procedure would invite viewers to compare lengths rather than positions. The data region is enclosed in a rectangle, with a pair of scale lines marked in, again for easier comparison.

Figure 10.9 gives a comparison of four treatments for obsessive-compulsive behavior. The data are the mean number of obsessive-compulsive acts averaged over the time period from one treatment session to the next. Means and standard deviations for each group on each of nine occasions are presented. The main problem with this graph is that it is incredibly cluttered. With some effort, it is possible to see what is going on. The group receiving Treatment 4 shows a rapid reduction in obsessive-compulsive behaviors, which is not maintained. Treatment Group 3 stays basically the same, whereas

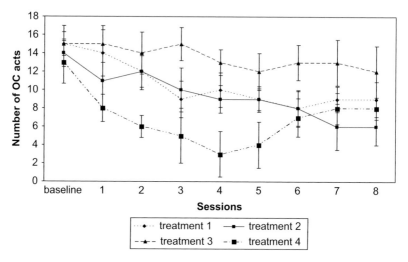

Figure 10.9. Cluttered graph of mean number of obsessive-compulsive (OC) acts and standard deviations by treatment sessions

the other two groups show a gradual reduction in obsessive-compulsive acts, with a slight advantage to Treatment 2.

The error bars show a fair bit of variation. It is likely, but not absolutely clear, that sample standard deviations rather than standard deviations of the mean (or standard errors) are reported – standard errors would be shorter. Many published graphs that incorporate error bars give less information than in this case, making it difficult to decide whether sample standard deviations, standard errors, or confidence intervals are shown. It is important to state which is being used, because which is used will affect judgments of group differences.

Figure 10.10 shows one way of reducing the clutter. At the top, only the group means are plotted for easier comparisons between groups. The means and error bars for each group are then shown in four separate aligned displays. As in Figure 10.8, the data region is enclosed in a rectangle, with two scale lines for each variable. The light reference line highlighting the baseline measures is optional.

10.4.5 Rules for Constructing Graphs

The rules given here are the main principles offered by William Cleveland (1994), with minor modifications. We have divided them into two parts, one with general information on the planning of your

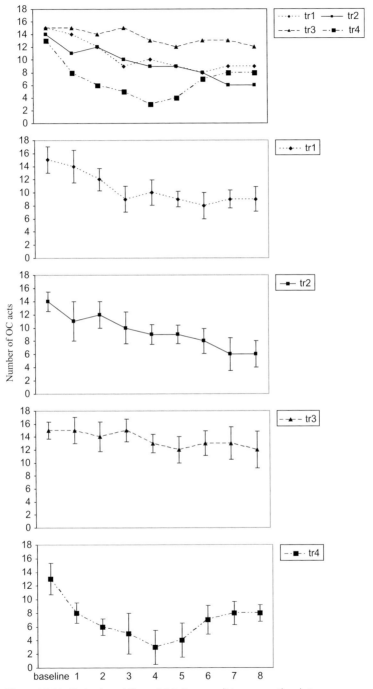

Figure 10.10. Redrawing of Figure 10.9 (top panel) to remove the clutter

chart and one with more specific information on the graphic details of charts. The following sections present some tips for planning the design or your graph.

1. Make the data stand out.

The data in Figure 10.9 do not stand out well. Figure 10.10 improves on this situation, although the baseline points are not well discriminated. Using different plotting symbols for the four groups may help a little.

2. Avoid superfluity.

Getting rid of unnecessary elements would improve many graphs. The boxes in Figure 10.6 do not hinder communication, but serve no useful purpose beyond what is provided by the dots in Figure 10.8. For the same reason, quartile plots (Figure 10.2b) are often better than box plots (Figure 10.2a).

3. A large amount of data can be packed into a small region.

Although clutter and superfluous elements should be avoided, there are many examples of clear graphs with large amounts of data. Computer graphics allow clear graphics to be produced more easily. See Cleveland (1994) and Tufte (2001) for examples.

4. Graphing data should be an iterative, experimental process.

Graphing data in several different ways is a good method for exploring the data.

5. Graph data two or more times when necessary.

If the error bars in Figure 10.9 are worth having, it is better to present them in separate graphs, as in Figure 10.10, rather than cluttering up the display.

6. Many useful graphs require careful, detailed study.

The messages in the graphs presented here are all straightforward and fairly easy to see. Straightforwardness is not the most important criterion for a good graph. A more important one is whether we can see something using a graph that would have been difficult or impossible to see without a graph. Some of the graphs in Cleveland (1994) or Tufte (2001) deserve careful study.

10.4.6 Practical Tips for Designing Graphs

1. Use visually prominent graphical elements to show the data.

   Many published graphs have the data points obscured by lines connecting the data or background grids, or in other ways, simply because the plotting symbols are not prominent enough.

2. Use a pair of scale lines for each variable.

   Make the data region the interior of the rectangle formed by the scale lines. Put tick marks outside the data region. Using two scale lines, as in Figures 10.8 and 10.10, makes it easier to compare points. All the figures here have the tick marks outside the data region, which helps prevent them from obscuring data points.

3. Do not clutter the data region.

   Figure 10.9 is too cluttered. Readers should be able to read figures without effort, which is not the case here.

4. Avoid using too many tick marks.

   Figure 10.9 has overdone the number of tick marks. Using half as many, as in Figure 10.10, still allows data values to be judged well. Between 3 and 10 tick marks usually suffices to give a broad sense of the measurement scale.

5. Use a reference line when necessary.

   Use a reference line when there is an important value that must be seen across the entire graph, but do not let the line interfere with the data.

6. Do not allow data labels in the data region to interfere with the data or to clutter the graph.

   The labels in Figure 10.10 do not get in the way of the data. Added to Figure 10.9, they would have increased the clutter. Make sure labels do not decrease the comprehensibility of the graph.

7. Avoid putting notes and keys in the data region.

   Put keys to symbols just outside the data region, and put notes in the figure caption or the text.

8. Overlapping plotting symbols must be visually distinguishable.

   In Figure 10.10, the baseline measures overlap a little but are distinguishable. Using different symbols for the four groups would help in worse cases.

9. Superimposed data sets must be readily visually discriminated.

   The four groups are clearly discriminable in Figure 10.10, although there is a slight problem with the scores of Treatment Groups 1 and 3 in Session 1. Use different plotting symbols where there is poor discrimination.

10. Put major conclusions in graphical form.

    Make captions comprehensive and informative. Readers often look first at the tables and figures. The captions should communicate most of the major points. Captions should briefly describe what is in the display and bring attention to the important features and the main conclusions you wish to draw.

11. Error bars should be clearly explained.

    Error bars are useful ways of indicating variability in the data, but only if they are described unambiguously. Say clearly whether you are using (a) sample standard deviations of the data, (b) standard errors of the statistic graphed, or (c) confidence intervals for the statistic graphed.

12. Choose the scales wisely.

    Choose the scales so that the data fill up as much of the data region as possible.

13. Choose appropriate scales when graphs are to be compared.

    The graphs in Figure 10.10 are all on the same scale, making it easy to compare them. In some cases, though, using the same scale results in poor resolution.

14. Do not insist on zero always being included on a scale showing magnitude.

    Including zero often helps comparisons, but it is not absolutely necessary to include it if doing so results in poor resolution of the data. Clearly labeled tick marks are essential, though.

15. Use a logarithmic scale when it is important to understand percentage change or multiplicative factors.

    When magnitudes are converted to logarithms, percentage change and multiplicative factors are easy to understand because equal percentage or multiplicative factors have equal distances on a logarithmic scale. (For explanation and examples, see Cleveland, 1994.)

16. Showing data on a logarithmic scale can improve resolution.

    Many data sets in psychology are skewed to the right. Plotting the data on the original scale will often result in graphs with most of the data bunched together at the low end and just a few points at the high end. This bunching can cause poor resolution. Using logarithms reduces the skewness and improves resolution.

17. Use a scale break only when necessary.

    If a break cannot be avoided, use a full-scale break. Do not connect numerical values on two sides of a break. In some cases, scale breaks are needed to improve resolution, although transforming the data (logarithms, again, for data skewed to the right) often removes the need for a break.

10.4.7 Placement of Figures

In articles submitted for publication, figures are placed at the end of the article (see Chapter 5). Refer to figures by number. Do not refer to them as "above" or "below" as you cannot be sure where the typesetter will place them in the text.

Figure captions, along with the figure numbers, are typed double-spaced on a separate page, which is placed before the figures. In student papers, it is often more convenient to insert the figures at the appropriate places in the text, with the figure captions directly underneath each figure.

10.4.8 Figure Legends

Many figures require a legend or key to symbols. The legend appears within the figure itself and is photographed as part of the figure. The legend should thus be consistent in style and proportion with the rest of the figure. Put the legend just outside the data region so as not to interfere with the data.

10.4.9 Figure Numbers

Figures are numbered consecutively with Arabic numerals, starting with Figure 1.

10.4.10 Figure Captions

A figure caption should describe concisely what the figure is supposed to show. It should be understandable without reference to the text. If you need to include any further information, add it in parentheses after the figure caption. If you use a figure that is not original, obtain written permission to reprint the figure, and cite the source in the figure caption.

10.4.11 Preparing Figures for Publication

If you plan to submit your paper for publication, remember that figures may be reduced in size so that detail becomes harder to see. Be sure, then, to make your figures especially sharp and legible. Follow the particular journal or book publisher's instructions regarding the submission format for electronically prepared figures. If you draw your figures by hand, use black India ink on bright white drawing paper. Most figures these days are computer generated, but it is still important to make sure that their quality meets the standards of the journal:

■ **Graphs**
When plotting values of a dependent variable against values of an independent variable, place the independent variable on the horizontal axis and the dependent variable on the vertical axis. It is usually helpful for the vertical axis to be about two thirds as long as the horizontal (see Tufte, 2001).

> ## Experience Is the Best Teacher
>
> When drawing a graph, try to include a 0 point on the ordinate (Y-axis). Otherwise, it is hard for the reader of the graph to gain a perspective on the data set as a whole. Also, do not draw the graph so as to exaggerate differences. Novices may be fooled but experts may think less of you for trying to distort your data.

■ Drawings

Drawings are most effective when kept simple. Drawings with shades of gray, like photos, require halftone processing, which is more expensive than regular processing. Avoid the added expense, when possible, by using patterns of lines or dots to create a shaded effect.

■ Photographs

Submit professional-quality black-and-white photographs with high contrast. If necessary, crop the photograph to remove unwanted material. If it is a photograph of a person, obtain written permission to use it.

10.4.12 Submitting Figures

For journals, figures should be submitted as electronic files (for those journals that use electronic submissions), as hardcopy laser-printer printouts (not dot matrix), or as 20 × 25 cm glossy photographs. Glossy prints smaller than 20 × 25 cm should be mounted on 22 × 28 cm paper. For other journals, follow the publisher's instructions. On the back of each figure write "TOP" to show which side is the top of the figure, and write the figure number and the article's short title. On a photograph, write lightly in pencil so as not to damage it. Do not use staples or paper clips. Protect prints by covering them with tissue paper and separating them with cardboard if necessary. Before submitting figures, carefully proofread them. You want to make sure that you, not readers, spot the errors!

CHECKLIST FOR TABLES

☐ Have you assigned Arabic numerals to all tables?
☐ Does every table have a clear title that explains the content?

☐ Have you chosen the design with the reader in mind?
☐ Is the content of the table limited to the essential information?
☐ Are items that need to be compared placed beside each other?
☐ Are the tables discussed in your paper?
☐ Is the table supplementing the text and not duplicating it? Are no data duplicated in more than one table or figure?
☐ Can fonts be read without magnification?

CHECKLIST FOR FIGURES

☐ Have you assigned Arabic numerals to all figures?
☐ Does every figure have a clear title that explains the content?
☐ Have you chosen the design with the reader in mind?
☐ Is the content of the figure limited to the essential information?
☐ Are figures that need to be compared placed beside each other?
☐ Are the figures discussed in your paper?
☐ Is the figure supplementing the text and not duplicating it?
☐ Are no data duplicated in more than one figure?
☐ Did you exclude any design detail that does not contribute to the understanding of the figure?
☐ Is your figure consistent in style with other figures in your paper?
☐ Did you explain all elements of your figure?
☐ Are the symbols used easy to differentiate?
☐ Can fonts be read without magnification?

Experience Is the Best Teacher

There are few visuals more annoying than cluttered figures. Sometimes authors put so much data into their figures that the reader needs to look at the figure and puzzle over it for a long time to figure out what it is saying. In a good figure, the data leap out at the viewer. The viewer can figure out the message quickly without having to piece together all the disparate bits in a complicated figure.

PART III

Writing and Preparing Articles for Journal Submission

11 | Article Writing 101

This chapter summarizes 50 tips from experts on writing articles. We're first presenting the tips to you in list format so you can gain a quick overview. We then elaborate on each of the tips.

1. Ask yourself whether your ideas are interesting to you, and why they would be interesting to other people.

2. Realize that new ideas are often difficult to get accepted.

3. Write the article that emerges from your research rather than the article you planned to write.

4. Explore the data to find out what they have to say and not just what you expected them to say.

5. A good article tells a story.

6. Write the story the data tell rather than the story of your discovery of the data's story.

7. Write at a level that students will understand.

8. Make clear what is new in your article.

9. Write with your reviewers in mind.

10. Write in the manner of an hourglass: Start broadly, become more specific, and then end broadly.

11. Make clear how your study tests your hypotheses.

12. Polish and proofread.

This chapter is adapted from R. J. Sternberg (2000). Article writing 101: A crib sheet of 50 tips for the final exam. In R. J. Sternberg (ed.), *Guide to publishing in psychology journals* (pp. 199–206). New York: Cambridge University Press. Reprinted with permission.

13. Do not use synonyms, especially for technical terms, just to avoid redundancy.

14. Make length proportional to contribution.

15. Use a title that clearly expresses what the article is about and that also, if possible, captures attention.

16. Write an abstract that contains the information readers would want to know most.

17. Accept feedback non-defensively but critically.

18. A good literature review (whether as a general article or as part of an article) defines and clarifies a problem; summarizes previous research to inform readers of existing research; identifies relations, contradictions, gaps, and inconsistencies; and suggests next steps.

19. Good authors write with their readers in mind.

20. A good article has a take-home message.

21. Write for a class of journals.

22. Choose carefully the journal to which you submit your article.

23. Do not take reviews personally.

24. When you resubmit an article, be clear as to how you handled each of the points made in the reviews.

25. Relate what you are writing about to people's everyday experiences.

26. Use interesting rhetorical questions.

27. Say clearly why what you are studying should matter to your readers.

28. Review relevant literature in a way that relates it to the argument you want to make.

29. Use direct quotes only when necessary.

30. State your research question(s) clearly.

31. Treat differences of opinion with respect.

32. Keep in perspective the importance of your own work.

33. Be generous in your citations of others.

34. Be current in your citations of others.

35. Avoid secondary sources.

36. Actively solicit feedback.

37. Make sure your article includes a description of the main elements of your design.

38. Make clear why the design you chose is appropriate to the problem you have studied.

39. Make clear the strengths and limitations of your design.

40. Provide top-down structure.

41. Let the story of your data rather than an arbitrary order based on statistical tests guide your explanation of the results.

42. Justify your choices of statistical tests.

43. Be thorough in your reporting of results without being overwhelming.

44. If you cleaned up your data, be clear as to how you did it.

45. Be sure your conclusions follow from your data.

46. The "Discussion" should make clear what you have contributed, how your study helped resolve the original problem, and what conclusions and theoretical implications can be drawn from your study.

47. The "Discussion" should be viewed as argumentation, not just as explanation.

48. Decide what is worth emphasizing in your "Discussion" and what is not.

49. Use the "Discussion" to make clear the limitations of your work.

50. Never end an article with an expression like "Further research is needed."

1. Ask yourself whether your ideas are interesting to you, and why they would be interesting to other people (Tesser, 2000).

All of us read articles that leave us gasping for breath: How could anyone find the work interesting other than the author? You are more likely to avoid the embarrassment of proposing boring ideas if you ask yourself why others and not just you should be interested in the ideas you have to offer.

2. Realize that new ideas are often difficult to get accepted (Sternberg, 2000; Tesser, 2000).

The more your ideas depart from mainstream ways of thinking, the harder it probably will be to get your ideas accepted. Thus, the more the ideas depart from the mainstream, the more effort you have to devote in your article to convincing people that what you have to say is worth listening to.

> ### Give It Some More Thought
>
> Why are people so reluctant to accept new ideas? For example, new ideas may interfere with the way they have been doing things or might, in the extreme, even cost them their jobs (as in the case of some kinds of automation).

3. Write the article that emerges from your research rather than the article you planned to write (Bem, 2000).

It is rare that the research you do leads you to the particular outcomes you expected. Write up the article that best takes into account what you found rather than the one that takes into account what you had hoped to find but never did.

4. Explore the data to find out what they have to say and not just what you expected them to say (Bem, 2000; Grigorenko, 2000).

Data often are perverse: They come out in a way you did not expect or perhaps never even considered. You should analyze your data to find out what they really tell you rather than only analyzing them for what you thought they might tell you.

5. A good article tells a story (Eisenberg, 2000; Salovey, 2000).

You may view story writing as different from professional writing in psychology. In fact, in many ways they are the same. A good psychological article has a story to tell and develops that story from the beginning to the end, or at least the end as the author knows it.

6. Write the story the data tell rather than the story of your discovery of the data's story (Bem, 2000).

Readers usually do not want an autobiographical account of how you got to where you are. They just want to know where you are and why. Sometimes, editors of book chapters will allow you substantially more latitude to tell the story of how you personally got to where you are. But journal space is so tight that journal editors typically do not allow long autobiographical accounts.

7. Write at a level that students will understand (Bem, 2000).

Many writers grossly overestimate the background knowledge of their readers. Write an article that any bright introductory-psychology student could understand. Be accurate, clear, well organized, and direct. Write linearly. Stick to material that elaborates on your main story and avoid subplots. Avoid jargon where possible, but if you need it, be sure to define it.

8. Make clear what is new in your article (Sternberg, 2000).

It often is not clear what is new in an article. Make sure you state it directly rather than hoping readers will see it.

9. Write with your reviewers in mind (Sternberg, 2000).

Think of the people who are likely to review your article and the kinds of objections they are likely to raise. They represent many other readers who may see things differently from you and who need to be convinced of the validity of what you say.

10. Write in the manner of an hourglass: Start broadly, become more specific, and then end broadly (Bem, 2000).

Start your article dealing with the broad questions you will address. Then get specific in terms of what you did. Finally, you should discuss broadly the implications of your work.

11. Make clear how your study tests your hypotheses (Kendall et al., 2000).

Sometimes authors present a set of hypotheses and research, but it is not at all obvious how the research actually tests the hypotheses. Make clear how it does.

12. Polish and proofread (Bem, 2000; Eisenberg, 2000; Sternberg, 2000).

Do not expect referees or editors to do your rewriting for you or to tolerate loose, sloppy, or error-laden writing. Polishing and proof-reading are your responsibilities.

13. Do not use synonyms, especially for technical terms, just to avoid redundancy (Bem, 2000).

Readers may believe you are varying the words you use because you are referring to different concepts.

14. Make length proportional to contribution (Kendall et al., 2000).

Journals have limited space. Longer articles therefore consume valuable resources. Hence you need to be confident that the longer your article, the greater its contribution.

15. Use a title that clearly expresses what the article is about and that also, if possible, captures attention (Sternberg, 2000).

An irrelevant title tricks people into scanning (but rarely reading) something they do not want to read. A boring title may lead them to avoid reading the article altogether.

16. Write an abstract that contains the information readers would want to know most (Sternberg, 2000).

Some people never will see anything more than the abstract. The better the abstract captures the key ideas and findings of your article, the better disseminated your work will be.

17. Accept feedback non-defensively but critically (Wagner, 2000; Warren, 2000).

Most of the comments you get from referees will help you produce a better article. Some will not. In revising an article, make the changes that will improve the article. Consider making the changes that, at least, will not hurt the article. But do not make the changes that will hurt it. In your letter to the editor, you can explain why you did not make certain changes. Editors, of course, are free to accept or not accept your explanation, as they wish.

18. A good literature review (whether as a general article or as part of an article) defines and clarifies a problem; summarizes previous research to inform readers of existing research; identifies relations, contradictions, gaps, and inconsistencies; and suggests next steps (Eisenberg, 2000).

The literature review thus informs readers of where things have been, where they are, and where they need to go.

19. Good authors write with their readers in mind (Eisenberg, 2000; Reis, 2000).

Write with your readers in mind. Ask yourself how well they will be able to understand what you write. For example, readers often become confused by pronouns without clear antecedents and imprecise language.

20. A good article has a take-home message (Eisenberg, 2000).

Often, readers finish an article without any clear idea of what the main point of the article was supposed to be. A good article has a clear take-home message so that readers briefly can summarize what the article was about.

21. Write for a class of journals (Eisenberg, 2000).

You should have a journal or class of journals in mind when you write an article. You can then target the article to the readership and requirements of that journal or class of journals.

22. Choose carefully the journal to which you submit your article (Warren, 2000).

You can save yourself a lot of time by choosing a journal that is appropriate in terms of what it publishes and that is likely to accept an article of the quality of yours. Moreover, make sure your way of reporting your article fits the journal to which you are submitting. Different journals have different requirements. For example, *Psychological Science*, a journal of the Association for Psychological Science, now recommends reporting results in terms of new ideas in statistics, which emphasize confidence intervals rather than conventional statistical hypothesis testing. Moreover, the journal gives badges of merit to contributors who make their materials and/or data available to others. It also gives a badge of merit to contributors who preregister their designs with the journal. The point is that different journals have different practices, so you need to make sure that you are choosing a journal that fits the way you want to conduct and report your research.

23. Do not take reviews personally (Warren, 2000).

Reviews are of work, not of you. Some reviewers get personal. Ignore such remarks. Read the reviews in the spirit of using them to improve your article.

Experience Is the Best Teacher

Often, when authors get reviews back on their article, their first reaction is to be either furious or discouraged. They may feel that the reviewers have a personal grudge against them. That is why you need to be non-defensive in the face of feedback. Take comments seriously, ignoring the sometimes aggressive tone of the comments. If you can use them to revise your article, do so. If not, explain to the editor why the comments miss the mark.

---

24. When you resubmit an article, be clear as to how you handled each of the points made in the reviews.

Reviewers and editors get annoyed when they are ignored. You should follow most of their suggestions and indicate how you did so in a resubmission letter. Those suggestions you cannot accept should be highlighted in the letter, and you should explain why you did not follow them.

25. Relate what you are writing about to people's everyday experiences (Kendall et al., 2000).

You capture people's attention and interest when you draw them in by relating what you are studying to experiences they have faced or expect to face in their lives.

26. Use interesting rhetorical questions (Kendall et al., 2000).

People often find themselves wanting to answer rhetorical questions, thus drawing themselves into the article they are reading.

27. Say clearly why what you are studying should matter to your readers (Kendall et al., 2000).

Do not expect readers to see on their own the importance of your work. Make clear why the work should matter to them.

28. Review relevant literature in a way that relates it to the argument you want to make (Kendall et al., 2000).

No one likes to read an unfocused, rambling literature review. Organize your literature review around the ideas that you wish to communicate in your article.

29. Use direct quotes only when necessary (Kendall et al., 2000).

Use direct quotes only if they are needed to convey the flavor or exact message of an original text. Otherwise, they just clutter up and often obscure your message.

30. State your research question(s) clearly (Kendall et al., 2000; Sternberg, 2000).

You need to be very clear as to just what questions will be addressed in your article. Often, you also need to make clear what questions readers may expect to be addressed that are not, in fact, addressed.

31. Treat differences of opinion with respect (Kendall et al., 2000).

Treat others the way you would want them to treat you – with respect – even if you disagree with what they say and are convinced that anyone in his or her right mind would see things as you do.

32. Keep in perspective the importance of your own work (Kendall et al., 2000).

Readers tend to be turned off by authors who glorify the importance of their own work beyond reasonable bounds or who fail to make clear the ways in which their own work builds on the work of others.

33. Be generous in your citations of others (Smith, 2000; Sternberg, 2000; Tesser, 2000; Wagner, 2000).

No one likes to be ignored, especially referees of articles. It therefore is important to cite relevant past work, especially if someone is likely to be a referee of your article. It further is important to cite work that is not consistent with your point of view in addition to the work that is consistent.

34. Be current in your citations of others (Smith, 2000).

No one likes to read an article whose author obviously stopped keeping up with the field a decade ago. Make sure your citations are current.

35. Avoid secondary sources (Smith, 2000).

Extensive use of secondary sources suggests laziness on the part of the author. Cite primary sources. In this way, you not only show better scholarship skills but also greatly increase the likelihood that what you say people said will correspond to what they actually did say.

36. Actively solicit feedback (Sternberg, 2000; Wagner, 2000; Warren, 2000).

You can avoid a lot of headaches and heartaches if you anticipate the comments referees are likely to make before they get a chance to make them. Ask colleagues to read your work and comment on it before you submit the work to a journal.

37. Make sure your article includes a description of the main elements of your design (Reis, 2000).

The main elements of design are type of design, how participants were assigned to groups, independent variables, and dependent variables.

38. Make clear why the design you chose is appropriate to the problem you have studied (Reis, 2000).

Do not expect readers to figure out why you designed your study as you did.

39. Make clear the strengths and limitations of your design (Grigorenko, 2000; Reis, 2000).

Claim only what you can on the basis of the design you used, and show readers that you know what appropriate claims are.

40. Provide top-down structure (Salovey, 2000).

It often is difficult for readers to follow the line of argument in an article. By providing top-down structure and making transparent how you will organize, you facilitate your readers' understanding of what you have to say.

41. Let the story of your data rather than an arbitrary order based on statistical tests guide your explanation of the results (Salovey, 2000).

Do not write your "Results" section merely to conform to the order of output in a bundle of computer outputs. Write in the order that best conveys the message you wish to convey.

42. Justify your choices of statistical tests (Grigorenko, 2000; Salovey, 2000).

Do not assume that readers will know why you did the tests you did. Explain why you did them.

43. Be thorough in your reporting of results without being overwhelming (Grigorenko, 2000; Salovey, 2000; Sternberg, 2000).

Often, referees will ask for just those data analyses you chose to omit, so include the full set of data analyses you need to tell your story completely. But omit analyses that are irrelevant to the story you have to tell.

44. If you cleaned up your data, be clear as to how you did it (Grigorenko, 2000).

Say how you handled missing data, outliers, or any other peculiarities in the data, such as non-normality.

45. Be sure your conclusions follow from your data (Grigorenko, 2000; Sternberg, 2000).

It is often tempting for authors to go beyond the data in establishing conclusions, saying what they want to conclude rather than what the data allow them to conclude. Draw only the proper conclusions, and properly label anything else as speculation.

46. The "Discussion" should make clear what you have contributed, how your study helped resolve the original problem, and what conclusions and theoretical implications can be drawn from your study (Calfee, 2000).

A good "Discussion" goes well beyond summarizing the results: It relates your results back to why you originally did the study and makes clear the meaning of what you found out.

47. The "Discussion" should be viewed as argumentation, not just as explanation (Calfee, 2000).

Good writing in articles is not merely expository, but also persuasive. You are trying to convince readers of the validity of your position and, often, of the lack of validity of alternative positions. However, be realistic in terms of what alternative positions you can rule out.

48. Decide what is worth emphasizing in your "Discussion" and what is not (Calfee, 2000).

Good writing is hierarchical: It clearly distinguishes between the important points and the supporting points.

49. Use the "Discussion" to make clear the limitations of your work (Sternberg, 2000).

Reviewers will notice them. You take some of the wind out of their sails when you anticipate what they are likely to say in objection to your work.

50. Never end an article with an expression like "Further research is needed" (Sternberg, 2000).

What a bore! Of course further research is needed.

12 How to Make Your Article even Better: Proofreading, Revising, and Editing

12.1 BEFORE SUBMISSION: PROOFREADING AND REVISING

It is a common misperception that once you have written your first draft, you are done. Good writers do not submit their first draft. Indeed, a good part of the work on your manuscript starts only once the first draft has been written. Don't get into the bad habit of thinking that the draft is the final version. Advisers, editors, reviewers, and others are likely to make you do at least one and probably more revisions before your paper ever sees the light of day.

Here are some general tips for successful proofreading and revising:

- Get some distance.
- Rethink.
- Don't fix what you think is good.
- Revisit the checklists in this book and use them for proofreading.
- Make structural changes first.
- Check for typos and orthographic errors.
- Write for your likely referees and readers.
- Try to think of your work in terms of explaining it to a layperson.
- Check for fit to journal guidelines and subject matter.
- Read your paper at least once while imagining yourself to be a critical reviewer, or even better, ask a colleague to do the same.
- Cite likely referees (who conceivably merit citation).
- Make sure the references cited are up to date.
- Make sure all cited works are in your references.

Part of the material in this chapter was previously published in R. J. Sternberg (1992). How to win acceptances by psychology journals: Twenty-one tips for better writing. *APS Observer*, 5, 12–13; and in R. J. Sternberg (2001). Writing for your referees. In R. J. Sternberg (ed.), *Guide to publishing in psychology journals* (pp. 161–168). New York: Cambridge University Press. Reprinted with permission of the American Psychological Society and Cambridge University Press, respectively.

■ **Get some distance.**

When you have worked on your paper for a long time, you become so involved in it that it is hardly possible to see it in an objective way. You don't read sentences carefully anymore because you have read them so many times that you feel like you know already what comes next. You might even be bored when you read your paper for the tenth time. Just put it away for a while. Ideally, let it rest for a few days or weeks, or if you are in a rush, try not to look at it for at least a day or so. A fresh perspective will be very helpful in revising your paper by aiding you in finding incongruities and passages that are difficult to comprehend and in seeing other shortcomings that might have eluded you.

Experience Is the Best Teacher

Have you ever listened to your recorded voice? It probably does not sound all that much like your voice as you hear it. We hear ourselves differently from the way others hear us. We read our papers differently from how others read them. The longer the gap between when you write a paper and when you read it, the more objective you will be able to be about the paper. So putting some time between when you write a paper and when you review it is essential.

■ **Rethink.**

When you look at a paragraph, think about its intention. And then try to think about what you are saying in a different way. Are there other ways to put it? Are there parts of the picture that have been left out so far, or have you taken sides without being justified? Once you have reconsidered what you have written, you are ready to reformulate problematic sentences or paragraphs and to add or delete information that you have reevaluated.

■ **Don't fix what you think is good.**

In the heat of the battle, it is easy to keep revising and making changes until your paper looks very different from your first draft. Be cautious and selective in revision. Don't revise things just for the sake of revising them – have a reason for changing them.

■ **Revisit the checklists in this book and use them for proofreading.**
This book contains several checklists you can use to assess and evaluate your manuscript. Go back to these checklists and use them to revise the content, style, and language of your manuscript.

■ **Make structural changes first.**
Before you start working on the details, reconsider the big picture. What is the message of your paper? Does it come across clearly? Does your paper contain a lot of redundancy that you could eliminate? Does the organization of your paper follow logical principles? Evaluate these aspects of your paper first, and make those changes before concentrating on details.

■ **Check for typos and orthographic errors.**
When Bob was the editor of the journal *Psychological Bulletin*, he found that the single most annoying flaw in a submitted article is a slew of typographical errors. Why? Because they're the easiest thing for the author to correct. It's neither the editor's nor the reviewers' job to do your proofreading for you. Always proofread. It's the one thing you most easily can do to improve the impression you make. If you don't proofread, some reviewers and editors will simply tell you to do it. But others won't be so congenial, and you may have problems changing that first impression. (No matter hwat, you loose.) Spell-check features associated with word processors help, but they are no substitute for proofreading, as shown in the preceding sentence. A spell-checker would pick up the first spelling error (*hwat*) because it is not an English word, but it would not detect the other spelling error (*loose*), which is an English word.

■ **Write for your likely referees and readers.**
Expert article writers do not just write articles. They write for an audience. They decide on likely journals before they put pen to paper (or fingers to computer keys).

You can get a good idea of the types of articles a given journal publishes simply by reading the journal's mission statement (usually near the front or back of the journal and often on the Web) and by looking at recent past issues. But there is a more informal kind of knowledge you need to acquire either through your own experience or by profiting from the experience of others.

Many characteristics of journals go beyond mission statements. Some journals seem to emphasize methodological rigor above all else. One reads them and has the feeling that the study could be infinitely trivial but nevertheless published as long as it was methodologically sound. Other journals seem to emphasize articles that are interesting but lacking in substance or rigorous methodology: The ideas are provocative but the evidence for them is slim. Still other journals seem more concerned about length than about anything else. Such journals will not publish relatively longer articles, no matter how good those articles may be. One journal to which we have submitted seems to care more about the article's being in standard APA journal-article format than about what is said in this or any other format. These kinds of characteristics tend to come and go as the editorships of journals change, but oftentimes, the culture of a given journal endures beyond any single editorial board.

It thus behooves you to find out as much as you can about the kinds of issues that are important to the editor and referees of a given journal. You can save yourself a lot of lost time by seeking out journals that publish the kind of article you have written and by avoiding journals that do not publish that kind of article.

Give It Some More Thought

What are some advantages of deciding where you want to submit an article before you actually start writing the article? For example, by having a target journal in mind, you can ensure that you are writing to the proper audience, using the proper formatting for the target journal, and following all the journal's submission guidelines, such as for references.

■ **Try to think of your work in terms of explaining it to a layperson.** If you feel stuck with the organization and formulation of your paper, try to think about ways to convey your message to a layperson. This rethinking will help you reflect on your subject in a different way. It will facilitate finding simpler words and ways to explain what you are talking about.

■ **Check for fit to journal guidelines and subject matter.**
One of the single most common causes of outright rejection is the submission of articles that even a casual review would reveal to be inappropriate for that journal. For example, many authors sent Bob, as editor, empirical studies of substantive psychological phenomena, despite the fact that *Psychological Bulletin* never accepts articles of this type. Those authors wasted their own time and the editor's. The editor also returned articles that departed substantially from APA writing guidelines (e.g., were single spaced or used notes in place of references). You can save yourself and others major headaches by checking the submission guidelines, usually printed in each issue of the journal, to make sure that your article fits its intended home. (You've probably guessed by now that this very article was rejected from *Physical Sciences Ideas of the Century*.)

■ **Read your paper at least once while imagining yourself to be a critical reviewer, or even better, ask a colleague to do the same.**
We tend to be enamored of our own work. We often don't see the flaws that would be obvious if the same paper had someone else's name on it. So try reading your paper with the same devastating analytical acuity you would use if you wished to demolish the work of your most loathsome enemy. Ask a colleague to do the same. In this way, you will be able to anticipate and perhaps eliminate some reviewer criticisms – use of faulty logic, for example. If your logic is faulty, your paper suffers; of course, that also means that if your logic is perfect, so is your paper.

■ **Cite likely referees (who conceivably merit citation).**
Suppose Karin considers herself one of the world's greatest experts on the effects of high-fat, sugary foods on amorous behavior. (She doesn't, really!) And suppose she views herself as one of the few people who really knows what happens subsequently when romantically involved couples go out on a date and share a large piece of cheesecake. She gets an article to review on the topic and looks forward to reading it. First, of course, she checks the references to see which of her superlative articles on this topic have been cited. She discovers that none of them are cited. She cannot believe it. How could anyone write about this topic without citing her work? She now

starts reading the article, but she already knows it is a pretty poor piece with awful scholarship. All she needs to do is find some reason to reject it, and she most likely will.

It is impossible to anticipate everyone who might referee an article. Nor can one cite every potential reviewer. But it is important to cite likely referees who have made a serious contribution to work in the field that the article covers. And if the editor has sent the article to a particular reviewer, the editor, at least, considers that individual to be one of the more active contributors to the field the article covers. Thus, this suggestion is not a cynical one: The likely referees are the same people who are likely to be the major contributors to the field.

■ **Make sure the references cited are up to date.**
As editor of *Perspectives on Psychological Science*, Bob reads many literature reviews. It is a real turn-off to read a literature review that is years, or in the worst case, decades out of date. If your references are out of date, reviewers are likely to infer that the research is out of date as well. Make sure, therefore, that you cite not only relevant references, but *recent* relevant references.

■ **Make sure all cited works are in your references.**
Always ensure that the works and sources you are citing in your paper are listed in the reference list.

12.2 AFTER SUBMISSION: MAKING THE BEST OF REVIEWS

Some time after you submit your article, you can expect to receive several reviews of your work. Here are some tips on how to deal with reviews and how to benefit most from them.

■ **Don't take reviewers' comments personally.**
Reviewers criticize work, not people (unless they do their job incorrectly). We have written fairly strong critiques of the work of some of our closest friends in the field, and they have done the same of our work. We know better than to take professional differences personally. If you do so, you will find yourself holding grudges against an awful lot of people. (Send us a self-addressed stamped envelope with $10 worth of postage if you'd like a copy of our own 300-page list of personal enemies!)

Experience Is the Best Teacher

Bob received two reviews of his first book. One was positive but brief; the other was 17 single-spaced pages of merciless criticism. The reviewer really went over the top. One option when you receive such a review and can figure out who wrote it is to hold a grudge, perhaps for an extended period of time. But who gains from holding grudges? Bob later became friends with the negative reviewer. The friendship was certainly not Bob's best. But he and the reviewer even collaborated on a later project, something that would not have been possible had Bob held a grudge.

■ **Take journal reviews seriously, but remember that reviewers are not gods (a fact that has escaped some reviewers).**

Many but not all criticisms by reviewers are credible. Sometimes, individual comments are downright asinine. But points gain force when they are repeated across reviews or by editors in their letter to you. You don't have to make every change suggested in every review. But should you be given the opportunity to revise, you are expected to write a letter accompanying your revision. This letter should explain to the editor how you dealt with each point of criticism or why you did not respond to selected points. You should realize that, although you usually don't have to address every point in every review, the editor's comments should not be ignored. Reviewers and editors do not expect perfection; they do expect, however, to be taken seriously. They put the time and effort into reviewing the article and want to see something for it.

One final note about reviewers: People often whine and moan about how nasty reviewers are. Some of them are. But remember: We have met the enemy, and we are it. Reviewers are drawn roughly from the same pool of people as those who write articles. If we all do our part, there will be fewer nasty reviews. (And if you don't agree with us, you must be stupid and utterly worthless!)

■ **Perseverance pays, to a point.**

While Bob was editor of *Psychological Bulletin* and today as editor of *Perspectives on Psychological Science,* no article submitted to either journal has been accepted outright with no changes whatsoever.

In other journals, the rate of outright acceptance may be slightly higher, but not by much. It can easily take two, three, or even more revisions before an article receives final acceptance. Journal editors differ in terms of how many rounds are typical. Moreover, even if one journal flatly rejects your article, another may love it. We're not alone in having been brutally rejected by one journal only to be welcomed with open arms by another. But if your article is being rejected across the board, you need at least to consider the possibility that you don't need to go to the supermarket for your next turkey.

Finally, remember that the journal reviewing process and science as a whole are basically conservative. Articles are often rejected because they're just not very good, but we believe that some of the best work in psychology and in other sciences is rejected because people are not yet ready to hear the message (see Sternberg & Lubart, 1992). We're not personally impressed by people who tell us they've never had an article turned down.

To do creative work, you must take risks, and to take risks, you must occasionally fail. Much more important than whether you fail (and everyone does sometimes) is how you handle the failure and learn from your mistakes. Should you ever reach the point at which you never fail to get your articles accepted and no one ever disagrees with you, beware: You are probably not doing your best and most creative work. And if you really want to avoid rejections, then don't take chances. Never submit. You'll be completely safe from criticism and from making a scientific contribution, as well.

Give It Some More Thought

Why is it not necessarily a good thing never to have had an article rejected? For example, it may mean that the author is afraid to take risks or is simply not very productive.

12.3   AFTER ACCEPTANCE: EDITING FOR PUBLICATION

Once your manuscript has been accepted for publication, you will most likely receive proofs at some point from the publisher that need to be proofread before they go to press. Proofs are very time sensitive, so you are well advised to look at them in time. Although nowadays, with the use of computers, errors are less common in preparing the typesetting, they still do occur. Look over your proofs carefully, and make sure there are no typos and that the numbers are all correct.

Generally, editing is done electronically these days. There are some publishers, however, that still work with paper-based page proofs. If this is the case with your publisher, you may want to familiarize yourself with the standard proofreader's marks that indicate unambiguously what changes you want to be made. You can find lists of proofreader's marks online, such as at webster.commnet .edu/writing/symbols.htm.

13 | Critical Checklist before Submitting an Article for Publication

There are certain issues you always should consider before you submit an article for publication. Here is a checklist that may be helpful to you.

■ **Are all authorship issues resolved?**
There are many situations in academia you do not want to be in. Certainly one is a public authorship dispute. You need to make sure, before you submit an article for publication, that all authorship issues are taken care of. Who will be an author and in what order will the authors be placed? If you have a dispute you cannot resolve yourselves, often the chair of a department, the office of the vice president for research, or the office of the appropriate dean can be helpful in mediating the authorship dispute.

■ **Is the paper appropriate for the journal?**
The easiest thing you can do to increase your chances of an article's being accepted is to ensure that the journal to which you send the article is appropriate. Bob is currently editor of a psychological journal and has edited other journals in the past. He is amazed by the number of submissions that are downright inappropriate for the journal. He does not even send these submissions out for external review. He "desk-rejects" them. By submitting to the wrong journal, the author has wasted his or her own time and the time of the editor, as well as, potentially, external referees. If a journal only accepts empirical articles, don't send a theoretical article with no data. Or if the journal only accepts articles in the field of cognition, don't send an article in the field of clinical psychology. Simply reading the journal's

mission statement, as well as looking at articles recently published, can give you an idea of what kinds of articles a particular journal publishes.

■ Did you proofread?

The second easiest thing you can do to increase the chances of an article's being accepted by a journal is to proofread the article. Referees get annoyed when they receive to review articles that have not been proofread. After all, referees typically are not paid anything to review, and they often feel, rightfully, that authors who submit articles with multiple typographical or other easily correctible errors are not respectful of the referees' time. Therefore, proofread before you send out your article. Don't expect referees to do your proofreading for you. That's not their job, and typographical errors distract the referees from being able to pay attention to the kinds of bigger issues they are supposed to address.

■ Is the length of the article within the journal's word or page limit?

Many journals have word or page limits. These limits are usually expressed quite clearly in the instructions to authors. If you submit an article that is over the limit, you are advertising to the journal editor (and referees) that you don't care enough about them to respect the limits imposed by the journal. Take word and page restrictions seriously and don't go outside them.

■ Are all needed permissions in place?

If you are using figures from other sources, or long quotes, or reproducing tables, or whatever, you need permission, usually from both the publisher and the author(s) of the article. Have permissions in place before you submit. That way, if you do not get the permissions, you won't have to change the article after it is reviewed or even accepted, possibly necessitating re-review.

■ Is the article readable?

We all can understand our own articles. What matters is whether the audience for whom the articles are written can understand them. One of the most frequent mistakes we see in reviewing and editing articles is writing that is way over the heads of readers. Moreover, referees typically are not all specialists in the area in which you are writing. Few things annoy them more than having to slog through an article that is difficult to understand. They are busy people and don't want to spend their time piecing together what you say. Make sure, therefore, that your writing is readable and easily manageable for nonexperts who may choose to read your article.

■ **Have you avoided passive voice where possible?**
Passive voice is harder to understand than active voice, and also takes up more time to read. Write in the active voice whenever possible.

■ **Have you shown why the article is interesting?**
You of course know that your article is interesting. But does the reader? What have you done to make the article interesting? Why should the reader want to start your article, and having started, keep reading? Be sure to show why any reader in his or her right mind will want to read your article.

■ **Does the article make clear what is new?**
Journal space is precious. As a result, journals only publish articles that have something new to say. If you don't have something new to say, don't try to publish. If you do have something new to say, make clear what it is. Don't expect it to be obvious to the reader and don't leave it to the reader to figure out what the news in the article is.

■ **Does the article emphasize what is important and deemphasize what is not?**
When writing an article, it is easy to get bogged down in every little detail. Although you may have to include some details, the little details are generally not what interest readers. Be sure, therefore, to emphasize what is important and deemphasize what is not.

■ **Does the introduction catch people's attention?**
People often decide whether to continue reading an article after they read just the first paragraph. You need therefore to capture readers' attention in that first paragraph. Beginnings like "Many psychologists have studied...," "There are many views on...," and "Smith (2000) found..." are really boring. Engage readers by starting with some questions and/or some concrete examples that bring to life the problem you are studying.

■ **Is the sample size large enough?**
Journals are not interested in underpowered studies: studies that, even if the sought-after effects existed, would not be able to find the

effects because the sample sizes are too small. Make sure either that you have done a formal power analysis or otherwise ensured that, if there were effects, you could find them.

Experience Is the Best Teacher

Experimenters often pay a lot of attention to sample size without paying attention to how representative the sample is of the population from which it is supposed to be drawn. For example, if you have a large sample of students from a prestigious private university in the Northeast, you may have a lot of power to draw conclusions, but for a very limited population of individuals. You need to be clear somewhere in the "Discussion" that the conclusions may be limited to a relatively narrow sliver of any population in which large numbers of readers would be interested.

■ **Are the materials adequate to test the hypothesis?**
Check that whatever materials you used in the study are wide-ranging enough that they will be viewed by referees as adequate for testing the hypotheses of the study. A large sample is of no help if the materials are too narrow in scope adequately to test the proposed hypotheses.

Experience Is the Best Teacher

Experimenters often pay even less attention to the representativeness of their study materials than they do to the representativeness of their samples of subjects. If, for example, you want to draw conclusions about words, how representative of words in general are the words you have used in your study? If you want to draw conclusions about pictures, how representative are your pictures of the universe of pictures? Do not assume that your selection of stimuli is representative. Show that it is.

■ **Are subjects, materials, and procedure clearly described?**
Make sure that you clearly describe your methods. Who were the subjects? Have you broken them down in relevant ways, such as by gender and age? Have you provided a clear description of the

materials and, if appropriate, given sample items? Sample items particularly help readers figure out what subjects were expected to do in the study or studies.

■ Are the statistical tests appropriate?

Have you made sure that the statistical tests you used were appropriate for the questions you asked? Have you ensured that the data met the requirements of the statistical tests, for example, homogeneity of variances? Frequently we have seen articles rejected not because the studies themselves were bad, but because the data were misanalyzed so that they could not address the questions that were asked.

What's Wrong Here?

"As stated earlier, because of past inconsistencies in the literature, we were unable to predict whether Group A or Group B would perform at a higher level. However, the results were clear: A one-tailed t-test revealed that Group A indeed performed better than Group B ($t(48) = 3.01$), $p < .001$."

Answer: A one-tailed t-test is generally inappropriate when there is no prior hypothesis. The author would be obliged to explain why she used a one-tailed test without such a hypothesis. In all likelihood here, the choice of statistical test was incorrect.

■ Are the conclusions those implied by the data?

Ensure that whatever you conclude is what the data actually show, not what you wish they showed. And make sure the conclusions do not go beyond the data. It is entirely common for authors to draw conclusions stronger than those the data warrant. You may or may not notice. Referees will notice, however.

■ Is there a take-home message?

No one wants to finish reading an article, especially a long one, and then sit there trying to figure out what the author or authors were trying to say. Your article should have a clear take-home message – what you want readers to remember long after they have forgotten the details of your study.

Give It Some More Thought

How often do you read an article and finish reading it with a very clear sense of what you have learned that you didn't know before? If it is not very often, ask yourself why that's the case and what you could do differently.

◼ Does the article cite critical references?

Most referees are experts in the field carved out by your study. Have you cited their work? We have seen numerous referees check the references even before they read the article, usually to look at whether they are cited. If they believe they have done important work in the area of the article, but that they have not been cited or have not been appropriately cited, their mood goes downhill quickly. Ensure that you have cited everyone who might reasonably review your article!

◼ Would you be able to send out your data to someone who wanted to reanalyze your data? Would you be able to describe your methods precisely enough for precise replication?

If someone requests your data, as sometimes happens, are you ready to send them? Are you pretty confident that reanalyses of your data will yield essentially the same results you got? Are your methods adequately enough described so that someone could replicate your study with no problem?

◼ Have you acknowledged weaknesses?

No study is without weaknesses. Referees are always happy to pick apart those weaknesses. Anticipate what they are going to say and acknowledge explicitly what you believe to be the weaknesses of the study – before the referees do it for you.

14 Deciding on a Journal and Submitting an Article to a Journal

If you write a paper that you believe makes a substantial contribution to psychological knowledge, you may want to consider submitting it for publication. This chapter will give you some information to help you decide on a journal. We will give you an overview of what you need to do to submit your paper and what goes on behind the scenes in an editor's office.

14.1 DECIDING ON A JOURNAL

If you decide to submit a paper for publication, the first step you must take is to decide on a journal to which you want to submit the paper. Ten considerations should enter into your decision:

1. Quality

Journals vary widely in quality. Some journals publish papers that do little more than fill up journal space; other journals publish only outstanding contributions to the literature. Better journals generally have higher rejection rates for submitted papers, so the probability of a paper's being accepted in such journals is lower.

One way to evaluate quality is to look at the impact factor of the journal. In Point 10, we describe how you can determine the journal's impact factor, or the extent to which papers in the journal are cited by authors in the field.

2. Content

All journals limit by content the kinds of papers they accept. Journal editors use either or both of two criteria in deciding on the appropriateness of a paper's content. The first criterion is substantive focus. What is the topic of research? The journal may accept, for example, only developmental, or cognitive, or applied papers. The second criterion is methodological focus. How was the research done? The journal may accept, for example, only experimental or theoretical or review papers. The journal lists we provide later in this chapter describe the content restrictions of many psychological journals.

3. Readership

Journals vary in (a) who reads them and in (b) how many people read them. Readership depends in turn on the quality and content of each journal and, to a lesser extent, on the cost of the journal. Journals publish annual statements of their circulation, so the extent of the readership can be determined by looking through recent back issues of a journal for the annual statement. The composition of the readership can be inferred by assessing quality and content, and by examining the kinds of papers in which articles from the journal are cited.

4. Length restrictions

Most journals have implicit restrictions on length of submitted papers, and some journals have explicit restrictions. If the journal's editorial statement (carried in every issue of most journals) does not make any statement about length, an examination of several recent issues of the journal will indicate the range in length acceptable to the journal editor.

5. Publication lag

The length of time between acceptance of an article and publication of the article is the publication lag. Journals vary in publication lags from as little as 1 month to as much as 18 months or more. In submitting an article, authors should decide how long they are willing to wait for the article to be published, keeping in mind that there will be an additional lag from the time the article is submitted to the time it is accepted or rejected.

6. **Cost of submission**

   Most journals do not charge authors for publication. Some journals do charge, however, so that publication of even a short article can cost an author several hundred dollars. The journal's editorial statement will indicate what costs, if any, are involved. Authors must decide before submitting an article to such a journal whether they are willing and able to meet the costs of publication.

7. **Authorship restrictions**

   A small number of journals restrict in some way their potential contributors. Submission may be by invitation only, or limited to individuals belonging to or sponsored by members of some organization. The journal's editorial statement will indicate whether any such restrictions apply.

8. **Editorial failings**

   Although some things should not happen in theory, they do happen in practice. One of those is editorial biases. Editors sometimes gain reputations for preferring articles that represent a certain point of view, or favor a certain kind of paradigm, or outright rejecting papers that are contrary to the editors' own beliefs. You learn about such shortcomings through the grapevine, not through any formal source. But you may want to make inquiries. Another failing of editors is taking a long time in the review process. The editors send material out for review and then take an excessively long time to get back to authors. Publication of your article can be held up for long periods of time simply by being stuck in a lengthy review process. A third failing is letting authors revise articles endlessly in the hope that the authors will just stop resubmitting. Especially in the case of senior colleagues who are well known in the field, it sometimes is hard for an editor to reject an article. He or she may then keep asking for revisions until the author tires of resubmitting. You should learn what you can from colleagues about any possible editorial failings associated with a particular editor of a journal.

9. **Open versus closed access**

   Some journals are "open access," meaning that anyone can read the journals. Instead of the readers (or their institutions) paying a fee to read articles, the authors of articles pay a fee to publish the articles. These fees can be substantial, in some cases, several thousand dollars. So you need to balance the advantages of open access (more people can read your article) against the costs (you typically have to pay for publication). Another factor to consider is that some granting agencies now require that articles be made available for open access, if not right away, within a certain period of time. If you have a grant requiring open access, you need to choose a journal to which to submit your work that will meet your funding agency's requirements for open access.

10. Journal citation reports

A good way to compare and evaluate journals is to have a look at the *Journal Citation Reports* published by Thomson Reuters. Of particular importance to social scientists is the *Social Sciences Citation Index* (*SSCI*), which contains statistics about hundreds of journals. You can access this information through your university library. To get to the *SSCI*, choose *Thomson Reuters Web of Science* (wokinfo.com) as a database. You'll have to select a database again; choose *Journal Citation Reports* (*JCR*). Once you have chosen the database, you can select the Social Sciences Edition and view a list of all journals, get lists for groups of journals, or search for a specific journal.

▪ Total cites
This number indicates the total number of citations to a particular journal in a given year.

▪ Impact factor
The impact factor is the average number of citations to articles of a given journal published during the two previous years. That means that the impact factor for the year 2015 of the *Journal for Psychology in the Vegetable Garden* gives you the average number of citations in 2015 to articles that were published in 2013 and 2014 in that journal. Note that *all* citations count in journals that Thomson Reuters monitors, including ones in different journals. However, Thomson Reuters does not monitor all journals, so citations in some journals do not count simply because they are not included in the database.

▪ Five-year journal impact factor
The five-year impact factor does essentially the same thing as the impact factor; however, it indicates the average number of times in

the particular *JCR* year that articles published by the journal in the last five years were cited.

■ Immediacy index
The immediacy index indicates how often an article is cited in the year it is published. Note that articles published earlier in the year will have an advantage in the immediacy index, as they will have had more opportunity to be cited. Also, articles from journals that publish more frequently during the year will have an advantage, as there is more opportunity for articles in frequently publishing journals to appear earlier in the year.

■ Number of articles
The number of articles refers to the total number of articles that were published in a given year by the journal.

When you look at the *Journal Citation Reports* for different journals, remember that prestigious, high-impact journals are not always the best choice for your article. The previous seven points made above, about content and readership, play a role as well. A journal that is highly rated in *JCR* but that does not publish on the topic of your study will, in all likelihood, not publish your article. You should also consider that the more prestigious a journal, the higher are the rejection rates. Some journals have rejection rates of 90 percent or more, so you may end up wasting valuable time trying to get your article published before it becomes out of date.

In general, then, you need to weigh many factors in deciding to what journal to submit an article. The decision is important but can be extremely difficult. For example, if you are trying to get a job or receive tenure, articles will count little on your curriculum vitae (CV) if they are not at least in press. Articles "in preparation" or "in progress" or "under editorial consideration" often count little, if at all. If you aim too high in submitting an article to a journal, you may find that it does not have a publisher when you need it to count on your CV. If you aim too low, you may find that the article has an acceptance or even is published, but it is weighed less because it has not been published in a first-rate journal. Thus, an important part of the process in writing is targeting a journal at the right level – aiming neither too high nor too low. You might want to seek advice from people with more experience in the field as to what they believe is a reasonable journal to which to submit your article.

The journal descriptions are citations from the journal's website unless otherwise noted by a*.

Foreign language publications that do not at least partially publish in English have been excluded from this list.

Although publication statistics are used primarily for journals, they also can be used for individuals. Up to now, we have been focusing on statistics for journals. It is also possible to focus on statistics for individual investigators. The Web of Science gives one set of figures; Google Scholar gives another. Google Scholar is much more comprehensive because it includes *all* published work, not just published work from a particular set of journals that a particular index monitors. At the same time, that means that some of the citations will be in journals considered to be of lesser merit. Here is an example of a Google Scholar report (for Bob – keep in mind it is not typical because Bob has been in the field for a long time and has published a lot):

Citation indices	All	Since 2011
Citations	112,899	42,177
h-index	161	96
i10-index	809	549

The citation report (from Mid-July, 2016) shows several things. First, it shows total number of citations available on the Web to an author's work. Second, it provides an h-index. The h-index is the number of publications that have been cited at least h times. Third, it provides an i10-index. The i10-index is the number of publications that have been cited at least 10 times. Note that Google provides total statistics as well as statistics based on citations in the past five years. The idea of the latter statistics is to show whether the citations are recent. For example, someone whose work was cited a lot for a while but then stopped being cited might have a relatively large number of total citations, but a relatively small number of recent citations.

The citation report also shows in graphic form the number of citations over a period of years. In this way it is possible to see the trends in how much a person has been cited over recent years. For example, Bob was cited 778 times in 1990, 2,275 times in 2000, 6,904 times in 2010, and 7,936 times in 2014, the last year for which full data are available. The graphs show the trend in citations – whether a person is tending to be cited more – or less – over time.

The report further shows citations to individual publications. In this way, the investigator can determine which publications have been most influential. For example, Bob's most influential publication, according to citation statistics, has been a book he wrote, *Beyond IQ*, which has been cited 4,520 times. Highly successful publications can be cited much more often. For example, Professor Susan Fiske of Princeton University's most highly cited article has been cited 13,101 times!

14.2 SUBMITTING THE ARTICLE

Once you have decided on a journal, you should make certain that your article meets the editorial requirements of the journal. In most cases, this means that the article conforms to the APA guidelines outlined in Chapter 9. If your article conforms to these (or other) guidelines, you are ready to send it out. Most (but certainly not all) journals nowadays have an electronic submission portal where you can submit your manuscript. If you submit a paper version, you will generally be required to submit several copies of the article, with the exact number depending on the journal.

You may not submit what is essentially the same article to two different journals, even if the articles differ in minor respects. You should therefore send the article initially to your first-choice journal, keeping in mind a second and possibly a third choice in case your article is rejected.

When you send the manuscript, include a cover letter indicating

- your intention to submit the manuscript;
- the title of the manuscript;
- the length of the manuscript and the number of tables and figures in the manuscript;
- requests for masked review (i.e., review that does not identify you to reviewers), if you wish it and the journal offers this option;
- information regarding any previous presentations of the data (such as in scientific talks);
- information regarding any closely related manuscripts, such as ones that report portions of the data;
- suggestions for potential reviewers or persons who should not review the manuscript (optional);
- notice of any possible conflicts of interest;

- verification that human or animal subjects have been treated in accordance with APA guidelines; and any permissions that may be needed for reproduction of copyrighted material.

Experience Is the Best Teacher

If you have suggestions for possible individuals to review your manuscript, make them! Journal editors often have difficulty in finding reviewers so they usually welcome your suggestions. Just make sure that the suggestions do not include advisers or former advisers, research collaborators, or colleagues in the same institution. You have to be more careful about indicating people you do *not* want to review your article. Some journal editors will honor your wishes. But others purposely will send the article to these reviewers to get a different point of view. They will take into account that the review may well be adversarial, but they may seek the review nevertheless. In Bob's experience as a journal editor, reviewers' reactions are often unpredictable. He has had suggested reviewers who utterly panned the papers for which they were suggested and also reviewers whom he expected to be adversarial who welcomed the publication of the paper. If you are going to suggest individuals who should not review your article, list at most only a couple of names. If you list a large number of names of people whom you do not want to see the paper, you may inadvertently make the editor suspicious of its quality.

Be sure to indicate in the notes to the paper sources of financial support you received for the research described in the article and for preparation of the article. *Listing sources of support is extremely important*, as granting or other agencies may "count" publications as emanating from a grant only if they are actually listed in the acknowledgments.

Here is a sample of a cover letter to your editor:

Dear Dr. Knowitall,

Attached please find my submission entitled "Do I Like It or Do I Not: The Impact of Personal Tastes on Personal Preferences." The manuscript is 27 pages long and includes 1 table.

I wish to request masked review, and I have deleted all references in the manuscript that contain my name.

Parts of the data in this paper have been previously presented at the Annual Convention of Preferential Psychology in Adversity, OH, in May 2010.

When conducting the research, I followed informed consent procedures as well as APA ethical standards. The article is original and not submitted elsewhere. Thank you very much in advance for considering my paper.

Sincerely,
Like A. Roni

Department of Psychology
University of Likeridge
144 Chooseitall Way
Favortown, MN 11222
222-333-4444 (voice)
222-333-5555 (fax)

LikeARoni@likeridge.edu

14.3 A LOOK BEHIND THE SCENES: IN THE EDITOR'S OFFICE

14.3.1 What Happens after Submission to the Editor

Once you submit your manuscript to the editor, it will be assigned a manuscript number. With the help of this number, your manuscript can be tracked throughout the whole process until it is published or rejected. You will receive a confirmation e-mail or snail-mail letter that your manuscript has been received that also contains your manuscript number.

Next, the editor chooses external reviewers – typically two or three but sometimes more – who will be sent your manuscript for review. Some journals have a policy of "blind reviewing." All identifying information is removed from the manuscript, and reviewers are not informed of authors' identities. Almost all journals keep the identity of the reviewer(s) a secret from the author. Some reviewers choose to reveal their identities, and it is then the editor's decision whether to reveal their identities to authors.

External reviewers do their work on a voluntary basis and in their free time. Therefore, it is not uncommon for it to take several weeks or even, sometimes, several months for the editor to receive all requested reviews. The speed of the review process also depends on the journal. Some journals pride themselves for having a speedy publication process. This fact may influence your decision to submit to a particular journal. Once a journal gets a reputation for a slow review process, some authors are reluctant to submit to the journal because they do not want to delay publication of their article inordinately.

If you would like to learn more about the review process, you may be interested in the book *Reviewing Scientific Works in Psychology* (Sternberg, 2006b), which discusses how to review literature reviews, experimental papers, and book chapters, as well as book and grant proposals.

14.3.2 The Editorial Decision

Once journal editors have received reviews, they typically make any one of five decisions:

1. Acceptance without revision

The article is accepted as is and is immediately placed into the publication queue. Such acceptances are relatively rare.

2. Acceptance with revision

The article is accepted contingent on revisions, usually minor ones. The editor sends back the article and review(s), informing the author of the changes that need to be made. Typically, the article is not sent out for re-review.

3. Rejection with suggestions for revisions

The article is rejected, but the editor suggests ways in which the article might be made suitable for publication in the journal. Because the article is rejected, however, the editor does not commit to publication of the article, even if the author makes the specified changes. This decision is sometimes called "revise – resubmit" or "rejection without prejudice." In this case, the article is typically sent out for re-review.

4. Rejection

The article is rejected outright. The editor makes clear in a letter to the author that the article is not suitable for the journal.

5. No decision

The editor decides not to decide on the article. The editor indicates to the author that a decision is being withheld pending either additional information or the incorporation of suggestions for revision.

Although most articles that are rejected are rejected after external review, this is not always the case. Sometimes an editor or associate editor may read an article and decide that it is not appropriate for the journal. In this case, the article may be rejected without being sent to external referees.

What are the major reasons that editors reject articles? We asked this question of Professor Allan Wagner, former editor of the *Journal of Experimental Psychology: Animal Behavior Processes*. He indicated that, by far, the most common reason papers are rejected is lack of substance: The paper represents too little work; the findings do not present a sufficient advance over what is already known; or the findings are insufficient to establish a real, reproducible phenomenon. Other reasons for rejection include omission of necessary experimental procedures and controls, inappropriate or inadequate data analyses, shoddy scholarship, and a failure to place the work in a proper perspective. But Wagner indicated that the primary consideration in his decisions is the substance of the work. If the work represents a genuine contribution, then he (and other editors) would often bend over backward to help the author make the paper acceptable for publication.

Give It Some More Thought

Would you rather submit an article to a highly prestigious and competitive journal for which rejection of your article is likely, or to a journal that is more likely to accept your article but that is less prestigious? You might want to consider how urgently you need publications and just how much of a challenge it would be to be published in the more prestigious journal.

14.3.3 The Aftermath

If an article is rejected, the author can either give up on the article or restart the editorial process by submitting the article elsewhere. If the article is accepted, it goes into press. The author may be asked to sign over the copyright to the publisher of the journal. The author may also be sent back a copy-edited version of the article. This version includes instructions to the printer and may include queries to the author. The copy-editor may want to know, for example, whether a certain symbol is meant to be a particular Greek letter or whether an editorial revision is acceptable to the author. Authors almost always receive page proofs of their articles. Proofs are the preliminary version of the printed article as it will appear in the journal. The author checks the proofs for typographical and other errors. If an author makes what the publisher deems to be excessive changes in the article at this point, the author may be charged for a portion of the cost of the changes to the printer. Finally, the article is published. Most journals are willing to supply reprints to the author. Some journals charge for any reprints the author orders; others supply a certain number of free reprints, and charge for additional ones. Increasingly, reprints are handled electronically rather than by mail: The author is sent by e-mail a PDF of the article, which lets the author keep a copy of the article as it was published.

When an article is rejected, you can either submit to another journal or give up on it. If you choose to submit to another journal, it is a good idea first to read the reviews carefully and to make revisions to the new journal before resubmission so you do not receive from the new journal the same comments you got from the old journal. If your article is rejected several times, you may wish either to give up on it, or, as we do, put it away for a while and then look at it again a few months later in the hope of being able to evaluate more objectively its chances of getting published.

Bob once wrote an article. He submitted it to three journals and all of them rejected it. He put it away in a file drawer and pretty much forgot about it. Ten years later, he was cleaning out the file drawer and discovered the article. He brazenly submitted it to another journal, not changing a thing. The journal was comparable in quality to those that rejected the article. He got back reviews that were glowing except for one point: They noted that the references appeared to be ten years out of date. He updated the references and the article was published. So sometimes you just have to put an article aside and wait, and then maybe reconsider at a later time!

What's Wrong Here?

"Dear Dr. Jones: I have received your rejection of my article and I'm writing to let you know why I think you have made a serious

(*cont.*)

mistake. Under the circumstances, it would behoove you to reconsider my article immediately..."

Answer: The tone of this letter is misguided. Although an author may appeal a negative decision, telling an editor that he or she has made a serious mistake and that it would behoove the editor to reconsider the article is not the way to get reconsideration of the article. It is the way to offend the editor and little more. A better strategy would be to thank the editor for considering the article, state that you understand the decision, but note any extenuating circumstances you can find that might lead the editor to reconsider the article, such as a review by someone who appeared, at least to you, to have a personal bias.

PART IV
Presenting Yourself to Others

15 | Preparing a Poster Presentation

At some time or other, you may find yourself having to prepare a poster presentation. Posters are an excellent way of conveying a lot of information in a concise, efficient, and compelling form. They are especially useful for early-career scientists – including psychological scientists – to learn how to communicate effectively and also to meet colleagues from other institutions.

A poster generally should include the following elements:

■ Title

You want a title to be descriptive of what you have done but also compelling. Which poster would you rather read: "Effects of Professors' Level of Interestingness on Students' Attention During Class" or "Boring Professors Really Do Put Students to Sleep"? Try to formulate a title that conveys your main message and at the same time will capture people's attention.

■ Authors and institutional affiliations

List all authors and their institutional affiliations. Make sure not to omit anyone who has done substantial scientific work on the project that gave rise to the poster.

■ Abstract

In the abstract, you should state the big question, how you addressed it, what you found, and what it means. Abstracts, especially in posters, need to be concise and to the point.

■ **Background/literature review**

In a poster, you do not have a lot of space for literature review. Therefore limit the review to previous research directly relevant to your own research. Make sure you do not omit any citations that are crucial to the theory and/or hypotheses underlying your research.

■ **Research question(s)**

State directly the question (or questions) you are asking in your research. Beyond that, say something about why the research question is important both to science and to the person reading your poster. Why should the person attending a poster presentation read your poster when there are so many other posters to read?

■ **Methods**

Specify who your subjects were, what materials you used, what the design of your study was, and what your procedure was. It often helps to give an example of any materials that were central to your study.

■ **Results**

What were your main findings? Give the statistics on which the findings are based, either as numbers or, better, in a figure. You cannot, in a poster, give lots of results, so limit your presentation to the most important ones.

■ **Discussion**

What do the results mean? How do they tie in with past studies? What are their broader implications? Where are you going with the research?

■ **Acknowledgments**

Is there any assistance you want to acknowledge, such as that of an adviser, a funding organization, a partner who put up with you while you were working on the research and the resulting poster?

■ **Contact information**

How can people get in touch with you if they want more information or if they just want to stay in touch on other matters? Make sure that you do not give out any information that you later might regret having divulged, such as a home address or phone number.

Now, here are some tips for your poster presentation:

■ **Tell a story.**
Presentations are more compelling if they tell a story. You may think of story-telling as something that is only done in fiction; but that's not the case. The story begins with the question you are asking. It continues with past attempts to answer this or similar questions. It then describes how you have sought to answer the question. Then it states what you found. Finally, it tells what it all means.

Experience Is the Best Teacher

A good poster tells a compelling story just with a quick look. That is, a viewer can look at your poster and, within seconds, figure out what it is about, what its main message is, and why it is important. When people go to poster sessions, they often have a relatively short amount of time to view a large number of posters. You therefore need to "sell" your poster by having a catchy title, a compelling visual presentation, but most of all, a story to tell. Because many people will just glance at your poster, you will get the most mileage out of your poster if even that glance tells them, in a summary way, the story you want to tell.

■ **Keep it simple.**
No matter how complicated your work is, a poster needs to communicate it in a simple way. A poster is not the place to go into complicated details regarding your work. Present only what you need to in order to communicate what you did, why you did it, what you found, and what it means.

■ **Avoid jargon and be sure to define acronyms.**
Many viewers of your poster will be only vaguely familiar with your area of research. You want viewers to understand the poster as quickly and easily as possible. Therefore, avoid jargon and, to the extent possible, complicated terms. If you use acronyms, make sure you say what they mean.

■ **Make clear what the purpose of your study was (or studies were).**
Perhaps the most important thing you can do is to make sure viewers know why you did your study. Don't leave it to viewers to figure out. Make it explicit right up front. And be sure to say why the purpose was important to the field and to the viewer.

■ **Be well organized.**

Organize the poster and your presentation on it in a logical, clear, and coherent fashion. Viewers and listeners should not have to try to figure out what you are trying to say. Organize in a way so that your presentation is easy to follow.

■ **Proofread.**

Typographical errors seriously damage posters. They are a way of saying that you did not care enough about the poster or its contents to bother to proofread it. They send a negative message about your conscientiousness. And if you cannot even spell words right, how can viewers know that you can analyze data correctly? Don't undermine your poster with typos and other kinds of errors.

What's Wrong Here?

"Whereas 60 patients in the experimental group showed an improvement after their treatment, only 30 patients in the control group did after their treatment. The experimental treatment thus was 100 percent as effective in the treatment group as in the control group."

Answer: The treatment in the experimental group was 100 percent *more* effective. The author failed to proofread carefully.

■ **Use large text lettering.**

People will be reading posters from a distance. No one wants to incur eye strain by looking at posters.

Therefore make sure they can easily see what you have written. If letters or numbers cannot easily be read at a distance, they are too small. If the text is important enough to include, it is important enough to be easily readable.

■ **Don't use a lot of different fonts or styles. Limit yourself to 2–3 simple fonts.**

Some poster creators are tempted to use lots of different fonts for different purposes – perhaps one for the title, one for main text, one for figure captions, maybe another for acknowledgments. Having a lot of fonts is confusing to viewers and also creates visual distraction rather than clarification. So keep in check your temptation to have lots of fonts.

■ **Double-justify text if possible.**
In a poster, it is usually easier to read the text if it is justified at both the left and right margins. But at the very least, justify the left margin. Don't have ragged, jagged text edges all over the place.

■ **Use color judiciously.**
A nice feature of a poster is that you can use color to highlight your points. You might, for example, use one color for the introduction box, another for the methods box, another for the results box, and yet another for the discussion box. But don't let colors run riot. You want colors to correspond in a sensible way to the organization of your poster. Use color to organize your poster and to help viewers better understand what you are saying. Don't use color just to dress up the poster.

■ **Balance text with white space.**
You probably feel that you have a lot to say. That's good. But don't succumb to the temptation to cram as many words and figures as you can into the poster. Posters with very little white space are off-putting. People feel besieged and perhaps assaulted by them! Balance text with white space in a way that lets the poster flow easily.

■ **Keep figures and tables simple. Figures are generally preferable in place of tables.**
A poster is no place for complicated figures and tables. You want visuals that leap out at viewers, not ones that the viewers need to stand in place for a long period of time trying to figure out. The visuals should help simplify your story, not make it more complicated.

■ **Give appropriate citations.**
Make sure you have all necessary references but don't include extraneous ones. References take up room so you don't want a lot of them. But you also don't want viewers asking you why you didn't include So-and-So in your reference citations.

■ **Have an elevator speech.**

You need to have an elevator speech that explains in a few minutes (preferably 2–3 and no more than 5) what you did and what you found. Make the elevator speech engaging, impactful, and memorable.

Experience Is the Best Teacher

Your elevator speech is often as important as, or even more important than, the poster. Senior scholars often identify promising junior scholars by gazing through poster sessions. They zero in on the posters that seem intriguing and then talk to the junior scholar to see whether the individual is "as good" as his or her poster. A strong elevator speech can land you an invitation to a future collaboration, a colloquium, or, in the best of cases, a job offer. So do not feel that your work is done once you have created your poster. Work hard on your elevator speech because that speech may pay even higher dividends than the poster.

■ **You are on display as well as the poster.**

Remember that you and not just your poster are on display. You will be there to present the poster. Make sure you not only present the poster well, but also yourself. Dress appropriately, smile at viewers, and always show good manners. Never get into an argument with a viewer. Poster presentations are not the place for arguments or loud debates.

Give It Some More Thought

What is the potential cost of dressing in a flashy, eye-catching way for your poster session? You might mention, for example, that people may spend more time looking at you than they do at your poster or paying attention to what you say; a poster session probably is not the right forum to show off your most eye-catching apparel.

■ **Don't spend too much time with any one person.**

Sometimes a viewer/listener may seek to monopolize you. If you succumb, other viewers will never get the chance to chat with you or ask whatever questions they might have. Make sure you divide your attention among the people interested in your poster.

■ **Be on time in putting up and taking down your poster.**

It makes a bad impression when people enter a poster session to see your poster and find you are not there. This is not the way to build a fan club. Be at the poster session when it starts, stay for the whole thing, and then take down your poster and disappear when the session ends.

■ **Don't take criticism personally.**

Some viewers use a poster session as an opportunity to be informed. Others use it as an opportunity to continue their fun days from their high school debating club. Don't let debaters bother you and don't get involved in debates during a poster session. Your goal should be to inform viewers of what you did and what you found. If someone wants to debate with you, suggest that you continue the conversation after the poster session ends or else by e-mail.

■ **Engage with viewers.**

Some viewers will want to view your poster but not get into a conversation. Other viewers enjoy looking at the poster and also hearing what you have to say about it. Prepare to engage with viewers. The impression you and your work make may be determined as much by your interpersonal engagement with viewers as by the poster itself.

■ **Have a handout.**

Always have a handout that people can take with them. The handout could be a paper version of the poster or it could be a summary of what is on the poster. Encourage but do not push people to take your handout. People are more likely later to cite the poster if they have a handout to which to refer.

■ **Stay with the poster.**

It sometimes is tempting to walk away from your poster, especially if no one is looking at your poster at the moment, or if there are other posters in the session you would like to view. But you should stay with your poster. You never know who will come by when and you don't want to miss the opportunity to present your data – and yourself – to interested parties. It seems to us that the most interesting people show up just when the poster author vanishes. If you have multiple authors, you of course can alternate who stays with the poster.

16 Writing a Grant or Contract Proposal

Bob's first grant proposal was a horror story: It was long, verbose, and poorly organized. Fortunately for him, in 1975, one could write a grant proposal that had all of these flaws and more and still get funded. He did. But in 2015, he probably wouldn't have had a prayer and would have had to rewrite the whole thing. In 1975, the competition for grants was stiff; in the 2000s, it is close to ridiculous. Only the very best proposals even have a chance of success, and many that meet all of the scientific criteria for funding are not funded, simply because of a lack of money. Therefore, it is important to know how to write a grant proposal to maximize your chances of getting funded. In this chapter, we describe some basics of proposals, some keys to writing good proposals, and some things that agencies look for in making funding decisions.

Different funding organizations have different guidelines for writing proposals. There would be no sense to consume space in this book describing the requirements of various organizations; there are too many organizations and requirements, and the requirements are constantly changing. Rather, we here describe 18 keys to writing a good proposal. Paying attention to these keys does not ensure that you will be funded, but they will surely help!

16.1 SOME BASIC CONCEPTS ABOUT GRANTS AND CONTRACTS

Before describing the keys, we briefly summarize some basic concepts, beginning with a proposal. A proposal is a description of what you will carry out – usually research – if you receive funding. The proposal may request money for salaries, equipment, supplies, travel, reproduction, communication costs, experimental subjects, or whatever. Some proposals request funding for educational programs rather than for research. Typically, a proposal contains a statement of what is being requested, a description of why the research or program is important, a review of relevant literature, pilot data showing that your hypotheses are plausible, a description of just what will be done with the money, a budget, human-subjects approval from the review board of your institution (if necessary), and the proposer's CV. A proposal can be for a grant or a contract.

When you receive a grant, you receive support to accomplish some end, usually research and almost always research that you have described in the grant proposal. Although grants can be given for other things, we concentrate in this chapter on research grants. The agencies that give out grants almost always do some monitoring of how their money is spent, but the monitoring is generally flexible. If you want to add some experiments that were not in the original proposal or modify ones that were in the proposal to capitalize on what you have already discovered, doing so usually is not a problem if your money was given to you in the form of a grant and if you get permission for the change. Major changes in the research or budget almost always require approval, however. In other words, if you request funds for paying personnel, and you want to switch some of those funds to travel, you probably have to ask permission of the granting organization for the switch. However, if you want to switch funds from one category of personnel to another category of personnel (e.g., graduate to postdoctoral students), you are less likely to need to request permission for the switch. Organizations differ widely in their flexibility with respect to reallocation of funds. If you are not sure about a switch, always ask permission.

Contracts generally allow less flexibility than grants. All but the most minor deviations from the original plan generally require permission. Moreover, with contracts, usually you must generate specific producibles at agreed-on times. These producibles can take various forms, such as progress reports, budget statements, technical reports, products, and the like. With a contract, you are generally held fairly strictly to the deadlines that are given for the producibles. The fundamental difference between a contract and a grant is that, with a contract, you are being contracted to produce specific pieces of work, whereas with a grant, you receive money to do more or less what you described in your proposal. Some funding organizations give only grants, others give only contracts, and still others give both. Should you be awarded a grant or a contract, it is essential that you be clear on the reporting requirements before you begin, as failure to render required financial or progress reports could result in termination of the funding.

Should you receive funding, it is also imperative that you make sure that you or a financial officer of your institution keeps careful track of spending and how money is allocated. Virtually all organizations require regular and fairly detailed reports of expenses. These reports are carefully scrutinized. If you are not keeping careful records, you may find yourself in some very hot water.

A warning: Never spend money from one project on another grant-receiving project. It is illegal to do so. If and when you are audited, switching money between grants can cause great hardship both for you and for your institution. Funds awarded for a grant can support research only for that grant.

You should also realize that unless the grant is made directly to you personally – an unusual arrangement – the institution for which you work will most likely take out overhead on most or all expenses, as well as benefits on personnel expenses. *Overhead* refers to an amount charged by your institution for administering a grant. It goes to pay for the people who keep records, the space you use for doing the research, library facilities, custodial services, heating, air-conditioning, and all other expenses the institution believes might conceivably be charged against your funding. Overhead rates are negotiated between your institution and the source of funding. Overhead ranges from zero (some foundations do not allow any overhead to be taken out of the grants they give) to roughly 70 percent in some private universities. In non-university organizations, the overhead may be even higher. The percentage refers to the amount of money the institution takes out for every $1 you spend on research. For example, if you spend $1 on research at No Name University, the university may take out from the grant or contract another $0.64 as overhead. You can see that the charging of overhead results in your not having available to you for research all of the money that the granting institution provides. Different funding organizations have different arrangements both for requesting and for paying out overhead. In general, private universities charge more in overhead than do public ones, although there are many exceptions to this generalization.

Benefits refer to amounts of money taken out by the institution to pay for extra expenses that are associated with the hiring and maintenance of personnel. For example, if a research assistant is hired on a grant, the university generally contributes some percentage of the assistant's salary toward retirement pension, health benefits, insurance benefits, Social Security, and the like. These charges are figured into benefits costs. Benefits have generally been going up and can reach as high as 40 percent of personnel costs or even more. In other words, for every $1 you pay an employee on a grant, the university may take out as much as $0.40 for benefits that the employee receives. When you combine overhead and benefits, you begin to realize just how limited is the amount of a grant that you will be able to use for research or other intended purposes.

There is one general exception to the taking out of overhead, and that is a grant received directly from a university or other institution for which you work. In other words, if you receive a direct grant from your university or other institution to do research, it will almost certainly not take out overhead on the money that it directly provides you. Rather, those costs will have already been figured in by the organization providing the money.

It is hard to overestimate the value of having a grant or contract. Most institutions have little or no money available for research, and almost all institutions smile on their faculty and students who receive outside support. If you are a faculty member, having a grant almost inevitably helps you when it comes to promotion or tenure time and enables you to do the research that will get you that promotion or tenure. Moreover, even if you are able to do research without a grant, you will often find that you are better able to do the research you really want to do with more funds available. You can use the grant to pay for summer salary, among other things. Summer salary is money that you pay yourself over the summer to work on research related to the grant. You can pay yourself summer salary off a grant only if the salary your institution pays you is for fewer than 12 months. Many institutions pay on a 9-, 10-, or 11-month schedule, and so summer salary is an issue. Typically you can pay yourself for no more than 12 months, and some institutions have rules that enable you to pay yourself only up to 11 or fewer months. In typical situations, grantees receive 9 months of salary from the institution and pay themselves 2 months of summer support off a grant if money in the grant is available to pay for it. Remember that overhead and benefits will be taken out of your own salary, just as they would be taken out of salary paid to others.

In general, you need to be careful about payments to yourself or to anyone else, as it is common these days for grants to be audited at some time during their duration. Questionable expenses may be disallowed, and auditors who see any such expenses are likely to start digging further. Therefore, it is to your advantage to make sure that you spend money carefully and that you monitor your expenses.

What's Wrong Here?

Vanessa received a grant for which a substantial amount of money was allocated to salaries. She found that she did not need as much money to pay salaries as she had expected to so she spent the money on equipment.

Answer: With most granting authorities, although you may be able to switch around money within a category (e.g., paying one person instead of another), you generally are not allowed to switch categories for the money without written approval in advance. Before moving around money, make sure that you are within the spending guidelines for the grant.

16.2 EIGHTEEN TIPS FOR WRITING PROPOSALS

Having reviewed the major concepts behind proposals, we now consider 18 tips for writing proposals.

1. Clearly state the big question you hope to address.

2. Show why the big question is important.

3. State how your work both builds on and departs from work that has been done before.

4. State your theory and how it relates to the theories of others.

5. Show why your theory is better than its competitors.

6. Present pilot data.

7. Make sure that the research you propose fits the amount of time for which you are requesting funding.

8. Clearly state the proposed research and leave no holes.

9. Be concise.

10. Be very organized.

11. If your proposal involves empirical research, make sure that you clearly describe how you will analyze the data.

12. State clearly what the producibles of the work will be, especially for contracts.

13. Make clear what kinds of results you expect, and why they will be interesting.

14. State your qualifications for doing the proposed research.

15. Request all the funds you need to do the proposed work, but not more.

16. Show that you have the facilities you need to do the research.

17. Write a clear and compelling abstract.

18. Make sure that you have observed all formal requirements in writing the proposal.

1. Clearly state the big question you hope to address.

You should state right up front what the big question is that you hope to address in your grant proposal. Do not leave it as a puzzle for readers to figure out. If you are not sure about what the big question is, do not expect that your readers somehow will be able to fill in what you are unable to supply.

Evaluators generally prefer proposals that address some larger question and that address it in a fairly deep way. They look less favorably on proposals that are scattered and that seem to address a lot of smaller questions superficially, none of them very well. Therefore, you should be able to describe in a sentence or two the issue that you are dealing with and how you hope to address it.

2. Show why the big question is important.

After stating clearly what the big question is that you hope to address, you need to say why it is important and for whom. Again, do not assume that just because you think the question is important, others will as well. You need to build a case for why the granting or contracting agency should fund research on this question over research on other questions that other investigators might address. Even if the competition is restricted to proposals that all address the same issue, you need to say how you are framing the issue and why it makes sense to frame it that way. For example, all proposals in a given competition may be on memory, but why is your approach to memory a significant one? In sum, justify up front why the work you propose is important.

Experience Is the Best Teacher

You may know why you think your big question is important but you need to remember that each granting agency reads a grant proposal through its own lenses. Read the granting agency's mission statement carefully as well as any relevant request or call for proposals. Make sure you say why funding the grant should be important, not just in terms of what you think is important, but also in terms of what the granting agency is likely to think is important.

---

3. **State how your work both builds on and departs from work that has been done before.**

Virtually all grant proposals contain some amount of literature review. The amount will depend in part on the requirements of the agency that is providing the funds and in part on how much relevant past work there is. In your review, concentrate on past work that is clearly relevant; do not try to show that you know all literature that is remotely related to what you are going to study. But be sure that you cite work that is directly relevant. Outside reviewers see many proposals, and they tend not to be favorably impressed if their own work is not cited. Reviewers are likely to perceive their own work as highly relevant, even if you do not. It is therefore important in the literature review to show both how your work builds on what others have done and how it is different from past work. If you do not show how your work builds on that of others, you are likely to be perceived as grandiose – as someone who does not appreciate the value to your own endeavors of what others have done. But if you do not make clear how your work goes beyond past work, you may be perceived as uncreative and as not having anything new to propose.

What's Wrong Here?

"This grant proposal is unusual in that it is the first to study the question of humility from a truly scientific point of view. Thus, although there have been some previous studies, none of them really would quality as scientific in the true sense of the word."

Answer: Obviously, humility is not a characteristic of the authors of the grant proposal. Many proposers want to think that their research is the first to be truly scientific or that it is special and different from that of all other previous investigators. But a statement like the one above advertises a shallow understanding of the cumulative nature of science and is likely to offend reviewers.

4. State your theory and how it relates to the theories of others.

Funding agencies tend to look more favorably on work that has some motivating theory. The theory does not necessarily have to be your own. The important thing is that there is a set of ideas that motivates the work you propose. Merely proposing experiments or reviewing literature, or producing a product without any rationale or framework for what you are going to do, is usually considered unsatisfactory. Of course, agencies differ greatly in what counts as theory. The important thing is that you show both that a coherent set of ideas motivates the work you propose and that you are aware of how the set of ideas is similar to and different from that of others.

Experience Is the Best Teacher

Not every grant proposal has a single underlying theory. Some grant proposals are largely atheoretical. Nevertheless, it is essential to provide some kind of interpretive framework within which your results can be understood. Granting agencies expect more than a set of empirical findings with no framework in which to interpret them.

5. Show why your theory is better than its competitors.

Show why you chose or formulated the theory you did and why you chose it in comparison with other competing theories. Usually, there are a number of different accounts of the same phenomena. For example, there are a number of different theories of perceptual, learning, or attribution phenomena. In choosing one theoretical framework, you automatically exclude others. Justify your choice.

6. Present pilot data.

With funds so tight these days, agencies have become more and more concerned that the work they fund has a good chance of being successful. Probably the single best way to convince an agency that the work is likely to be successful is to present pilot (preliminary) or informal data showing that the paradigms you suggest or the results you expect are plausible. In other words, build the case for the new research by showing that there exists at least a preliminary demonstration of the phenomenon you hope to uncover. In some cases, investigators have already done more than they let on. It is unethical to request funding for work already completed. But it is not only ethical but also sensible to request funds for work that you have shown to a first approximation is likely to be successful. The pilot data need not have tremendous numbers of cases or even necessarily have been published. But they should be relevant to the phenomena you wish to study and useful in showing the likely success of your approach to these phenomena.

7. Make sure that the research you propose fits the amount of time for which you are requesting funding.

Grants may be funded for anywhere from one year (or even less) to five years. Funding for more than five years is unusual. With most agencies, typical funding is for three years. Agencies and reviewers check to make sure that the work you are proposing is reasonable, given the time frame you are suggesting. If you propose only one year of work, an agency is not likely to want to fund you for three years. But conversely, it will wonder about your sense of reality if you propose five years of work to be done in three years. The work should match the time frame.

8. Clearly state the proposed research and leave no holes.

Reviewers are overburdened, and agencies have many more proposals than they can handle. Reviewers do not have time to figure out what you meant to say or what you might have said had you remembered to say it. You need to write very clearly so that the reader can easily grasp your points and so that there are no holes in the descriptions. Do not expect readers to fill in what you have not provided, because they will probably assume that what is missing you do not know.

9. Be concise.

Many agencies have a page limit. Such page limits are strictly enforced. Some agencies will even return proposals that exceed the specified page limit. Therefore, it is to your advantage to write not only clearly but also concisely. Often, to cut out excess words, you can go through a proposal after you have written it and have someone else do so, too. Remember, also, that readers of grants often volunteer their time, so they want to read the maximum possible in as little time as possible. Therefore, reviewers and the agencies themselves appreciate concisely written proposals.

10. Be very organized.

Good organization is always important in writing, but there are times when it matters more and other times when it matters less. In grant proposals, it matters more. Often, agencies specify the organization for the proposal, and you are expected to use their guidelines. But even if they do so specify, organization within the sections of the proposal is important. You want to make the proposal as easy to read and as logical as possible. Readers almost never appreciate having to figure out where they are or where they are going in the proposal. Therefore, you should give some kind of advance organizer at the front of the proposal and in each section. This advance organizer specifies what will come when. A sentence or two of summary at the end of each section also helps. It is often useful to construct an outline before you write the proposal to make sure that you are maintaining a tight and logical organization. If you have not done an outline in advance, consider doing one at the end to check whether the proposal is tightly organized. Again, with such a premium on funds, every little edge you can get will help you in the competition, and a well-organized proposal is a definite edge.

11. **If your proposal involves empirical research, make sure that you clearly describe how you will analyze the data.**

In addition to describing clearly the proposed research, you are expected to show that you know how you will analyze the data. When data analysis is fairly straightforward, as with a simple two-way analysis of variance or even a set of *t* tests, the description of data analysis may be a short paragraph. If more complex forms of data analysis are involved, however, make sure you specify clearly what you are going to do and why. If the form of analysis is nonstandard (e.g., some nonparametric statistical tests), it is in your best interest to specify a reference that justifies your use of the chosen technique. Make sure that you are explicit in your description and that the form of analysis does fit the form of data you will collect.

12. **State clearly what the producibles of the work will be, especially for contracts.**

What will come out of the proposed research? Grant and contract monitors want to know. Do you expect to write articles, books, or particular chapters? Will there be any curriculum or other kind of product? Be as clear as possible in stating what you intend to produce. Also, you should clarify in advance whose property the producibles will be. Such clarification is especially important for contracts, with which typically the producibles become the property of the funding agency. You also want to know what credit (e.g., authorship, acknowledgment), if any, you will receive in the case of such producibles and whether your name will even be identified with them.

Experience Is the Best Teacher

As time goes on, you may start to forget exactly what you wrote in your grant proposal and what producibles you said you would deliver. The problem is that the grant monitor at the agency that funds your grant may remember quite well what you said you would do and what you said you would produce. Therefore check your original proposal periodically. If your research or the producibles resulting from it change from what you promised, make sure you get permission from the granting agency to make changes. Better to clear up these matters in advance than to have misunderstandings later.

13. Make clear what kinds of results you might expect and why they will be interesting.

Funding agencies are generally not interested in proposals that look like fishing expeditions. They want you to show that you know what the plausible alternative outcomes might be and, especially, what these outcomes might mean. It helps to show that the results will be interesting almost without regard to how they come out. Agencies know as well as you do that many experiments do not come out in the way experimenters intend, and hence they would like to see that even if the results do not come out in the intended way, the funding will still produce something of interest. The more clearly you can specify the alternative outcomes, their meanings, and their value, the more confidence a funder will have that it is getting something for the money you want it to provide.

14. State your qualifications for doing the proposed research.

When you submit a grant proposal, you nearly always submit along with it a curriculum vitae (CV), which contains the record of your accomplishments. The CV, at minimum, includes

(a) your name;

(b) your address;

(c) your phone number;

(d) your government identification (e.g., Social Security) number;

(e) your educational history (degrees, starting with a college degree, or institutions attended);

(f) your employment history (including all jobs, full-time or part-time, that are potentially relevant to the grant, but not those that have no relevance, such as being a waiter during the summer or a camp counselor);

(g) your special honors and achievements (such as Phi Beta Kappa, cum laude, honors, or any prizes you may have received);

(h) your publications, if any;

(i) past and current grant support;

(j) committee service, offices held, or special assignments;

(k) any consulting or other work you have done that might be potentially relevant to the grant; and

(l) anything else you can think of that helps build a case for your receiving the grant.

Granting agencies also typically ask if you are submitting the same proposal to any other agencies and for the percentage of your time that you plan to spend on the proposed grant. You may also include a brief statement outlining your main credentials in prose format. Again, the important thing is to emphasize that you have the needed background to do the proposed work successfully.

Obviously, a new investigator will have a thinner CV than will a more established investigator, but granting agencies take this fact into account. Often, they give a slight edge to younger investigators, realizing how difficult it is for them to get started. Whether or not an agency does so depends on the particular agency. Although you should be sure to include all relevant qualifications, avoid including things that are obviously irrelevant and may make a statement about you. Including irrelevant things (e.g., your summer experience as a waiter) makes it look as though you are padding the CV and that you have so few worthwhile things to say that you have been forced to say things that are irrelevant to the grant.

Give It Some More Thought

If you are an early-career investigator, how can you emphasize to a granting agency your competence to do the research you propose? For example, you might emphasize that you have done research directly relevant to the research proposed, or that your training as a graduate student or postdoc was highly relevant to the proposed research.

17 | How to Find a Book Publisher

Although good books differ from one another in a multitude of ways, good book proposals are surprisingly similar. All of them have a set of standard features. In this chapter, we will describe what these features are.

17.1 CHOOSING A PUBLISHER

One thing you should realize right away is that, whereas a scientific article generally may be submitted to only one scientific journal at a time, a book proposal typically may be submitted to several publishers simultaneously. It is to your advantage to submit the proposal to multiple publishers, because what greatly interests one publisher may be of limited or no interest to another. Each publisher has its own set of priorities and standards for judging proposals. Before sending a book proposal to a given publisher, look at some of that publisher's recent books to determine whether your book would be a good match. Or you may even want to write the publisher a letter of inquiry, briefly describing what you would like to do and asking whether the publisher would be interested in seeing a full-length proposal. In this way, you can save yourself and the publisher the bother of a submission if the proposal does not fit into its publishing program. Publishers vary in the level of prestige, the quality of the books they produce, the amount of royalties they pay, and many other respects. You may therefore want to talk to publishers' representatives (called acquisitions editors) as well as to other people who have worked with various publishers to get advice as to which houses are worth pursuing. Looking at a publishing house's publication list, however, is usually the best way of evaluating both the range and quality of the books it produces.

In our careers, we have worked with a large number of different publishers and have found that they vary greatly in almost every respect imaginable. Some are completely honest, and others less so. Some always pay royalties on time; others get around to it sooner or later, but often later. Some spare no expense to produce the finest-quality books; others produce books that start to come loose from the binding as soon as they are opened. Working with a publisher is like forming a close relationship. It is to your advantage to make sure that you carefully investigate the publisher with which you will enter into a relationship.

Three fundamental kinds of proposals are frequently found in psychology. Two of these are relatively infrequent, and we do not discuss them here: textbook proposals and trade-book proposals. Textbook proposals are, as their name implies, for texts, and they require certain special techniques that are beyond the scope of this book. Trade-book proposals are for books that will sell primarily in general bookstores. These proposals are even more specialized and difficult to write, and they often are submitted to publishers through literary agents. Again, they are beyond the scope of this book. In this chapter, we will concentrate on the features of scholarly book proposals, the kind that psychologists most often write.

One thing to keep in mind is that book publishers sometimes will provide a small grant, separate from any advance on royalties, prior to your starting on the book to help you defray the costs of doing research and preparation of the book. It makes sense to ask the publisher if it is willing to provide such a grant. The worst that can happen is that you are refused.

17.2 THE PROPOSAL

A book proposal contains several different parts. In the following, we describe those parts.

17.2.1 Opening

A book proposal opens with the title "Book Prospectus" or "Book Proposal" at the top and the proposed title and author or authors of the book below that.

17.2.2 Description of the Book

You start the main body of the proposal by describing what the book is about. What story do you want to tell? Why is it a story that bears telling, and what makes it interesting? Book publishers have to sell books, and so no matter what the scholarly value of the contribution, they have to care about whether you have interesting things to say. If you do not, they would most likely lose money if they published the book. Even university presses, which are willing to take more risks on scholarly work that has scholarly value even if it does not have great sales potential, still need their books to sell so they can remain financially solvent.

17.2.3 Audience of the Book

Next, you need to specify the intended audience or audiences for your book. What kinds of people are likely to read it? Will it be written in a language that can be understood only by people in the field, or by graduate students, or by undergraduates, or even by educated people in other fields? Publishers are interested not only in the level of the book but also in the breadth of audience to which it will appeal. Is your book written only for developmental psychologists, or will it be of interest to a broader range of psychologists? The broader the range of people who may be interested in the book, the better the potential sales are, and therefore the greater the potential interest of the publisher. However, if the appeal is very broad, then the publisher will check to make sure that the book makes a real contribution and is not written at such a general level that it has nothing new or interesting to say. Audiences can range across as well as within fields. For example, you might write your book to appeal to people in education as well as to those in psychology or to people in sociology or anthropology as well as psychology. Perhaps certain computer scientists or philosophers would also have an interest. Specify as thoroughly as you can who might be interested and why.

17.2.4 Outline of the Book

After specifying what the book is about, why it is important, and who the potential audience is, provide a general outline of the book. This outline should cover the chapters of the book and, if there are parts into which the chapters are organized, a description of what they will be. It should give the chapter names and a summary of what will go into each chapter. The book should show a logical organization and a sensible progression of ideas from beginning to end. Try to make the summaries as readable as possible, illustrating abstract points with concrete examples whenever such examples will help clarify the points you want to make. You need not cover every detail in every chapter, but you need to convey a sense of the flavor of the book. You also need to show in the sequencing how you will develop the main idea of the book that you stated at the beginning. Even scholarly books must tell a story, and you cannot expect readers to figure out what the story is. The proposal should make clear what the story will be.

Occasionally, people submit proposals for edited books. Such books consist of a sequence of chapters by different authors, all revolving around some general theme. In the case of edited books, it is particularly important to show how the chapters tie together. There are any number of edited books that seem to be a motley collection of unrelated essays, and such books generally do not sell well. With edited books, it is especially important to have an introductory chapter that sets the framework for the chapters to follow, and a concluding chapter that integrates the various contributions of the authors.

17.2.5 The Competition of the Book

After describing the main contents of the book, you need to describe the competition. This section is particularly important, because book publishers want to know what they are up against. When there are potential competitors for a new volume, the potential audience for that new volume is reduced, so it is particularly important that you assure the publisher that your book will make some kind of unique contribution that other books do not make. Therefore, it is important to state not only what the competition is but also why your book is better, or more nearly complete, or more up to date, or broader, or more representative of the field, or whatever. The same principle holds for both written and edited books. Pay a lot of attention to this section, because unless it is well done, your book may be rejected not because it is perceived as inadequate but because the competition is perceived as insurmountable.

> **Experience Is the Best Teacher**
>
> Your view of what is competitive and a publisher's may be rather different. If your book fails, you will get little in royalties; but the publisher will lose all the money it has invested. The publisher is thus likely to take a broader view of what is competitive than you are. Be sure to include books that are roughly competitive, even if you think your book is much better than the others or that the others are only somewhat relevant to your topic or focus.

17.2.6 Details

Typically, the next thing you will specify is nitty-gritty detail. What is the proposed length of your book in double-spaced, single-sided manuscript pages? How many tables, roughly, do you expect there to be? How many figures? Generally, you are expected to provide figures, but not tables, in camera-ready form, which means that the figures can be photographically reproduced and used as is. Some journals will accept figures in PowerPoint or similar form. If you need special kinds of reproduction, such as that required for color plates, you need to specify as much. Most important, you need to specify the expected completion date for the book. It is generally better to pick a date that is somewhat later but more realistic than one that is somewhat earlier but that you cannot meet. Publishers of scholarly books are usually willing to give reasonable extensions on due dates if it appears that you cannot meet the deadline that you set for yourself. (Publishers of textbooks and trade books tend to be less forgiving because such books often involve substantial advances, and the publisher loses money each day that the advance on royalties is not recovered. Moreover, the publisher may have made specific sales commitments for such books – commitments it will be unable to meet if books are delivered late.)

> **Experience is the Best Teacher**
>
> Academics tend not to be very careful about contract submission dates. But publishers need to take them more seriously,

> (*cont.*)
>
> especially textbook publishers. The reason is that they set a schedule for producing, marketing, and selling their books, and need to know how to fit your book into their schedule. With textbooks, schedules are crucial because the buying season for texts is restricted to narrow ranges of dates. If you miss that range of dates, you may lose most of your sales for the given sales year. And given that textbooks are usually revised every few years, you cannot afford to miss a sales season.

17.2.7 Your Qualifications

You need also to specify your qualifications for writing the book. It is common to include a CV and possibly a written summary of accomplishments. Publishers want to make sure that you are qualified to write the book. Moreover, with books, as with practically anything else, name recognition counts. It is generally easier for a well-established author to get a book proposal accepted than for a new author. However, publishers are always looking for new, potentially successful authors, and so if you can convince them that you have a product of quality that will sell, they may be quite interested in your book, even if you are new to the field or have not previously published widely or at all.

> ### What's Wrong Here?
>
> "Qualifications for Writing the Textbook: I have written over 50 scholarly articles and my scholarly work has been cited over 300 times. I have won an early career award and have just received tenure one year ahead of schedule. My PhD is from UC Berkeley and I currently hold two federal grants valued at over $500,000."
>
> **Answer:** The problem is that the proposal is apparently for a textbook but the proposer mentions only scholarly credentials. At least as relevant for a textbook would be previous experience in writing textbooks or parts of textbooks, experience teaching the course for which the textbook is being written, and publications in particular on the teaching of the subject matter relevant to the textbook.

17.2.8 Sample Chapter(s)

Some publishers require that you submit a sample chapter or several sample chapters of the book, especially if you are not a well-known author. Practices differ widely among publishers, and some publishers may agree to publish the book only if they have the complete item in front of them to evaluate. If you can write one or more sample chapters, it is to your advantage to send them, because publishers will then have a better idea of what the book will actually consist of. If you do send a sample chapter or chapters, it is important to make sure that the chapters represent the best effort you can make.

17.2.9 Summary

At the end of the proposal, you will want to summarize the main points of your proposal. Here, and possibly at the beginning, it does not hurt to pay attention to special features. What sets your book apart? What particular features does the book have that would make it particularly salable? For example, do you take a new approach to a problem that you think is bound to catch the eye of the reader? Do you have access to special information that no one else has reviewed? Do you have recent data that are likely to shed a new perspective on the field? Publishers are always interested in knowing special angles that may increase sales.

17.3 CONTRACT OFFERS

Up to now, we have discussed what you need to do to convince a house that it should contract your book. But if several publishers are interested, you will then be in a position to ask them what it is that makes them special. Why should you publish with one publisher as opposed to another that is interested in your book? There are a number of different things to look for in choosing among alternative publishers, or even deciding whether you should pursue more alternatives.

17.3.1 Royalties

Royalties are sums of money, based on a percentage of sales, paid to the author. Royalties can be paid either on gross receipts or on net receipts. These two quantities are quite different, and it is important to know on which quantity the publisher bases its royalties. Relatively few book contracts grant royalties paid on gross receipts. "Gross receipts" refer to the selling price of the book. For example, if your book costs $40, and your royalty rate is 10 percent of gross, you will receive $4 per book sold.

By far the more common way of writing contracts is in terms of net receipts. Net receipts are the publisher's actual receipts for the books it sells. For example, suppose that the publisher sells to a bookstore. Although the book may sell for $40, the publisher will receive considerably less than $40 from the bookstore, because bookstores receive a discount in buying books from a publisher so that they can make a profit when they sell the books to their customers. Your royalty would be based on the amount the publisher received from the bookstore (perhaps $30), rather than on the ultimate selling price of the book. If there are sales to book clubs, net receipts may be proportionately even less than they are for bookstores. Publishers frequently give away sample copies for promotional purposes, and no royalties are paid on sample copies. Moreover, royalties tend to be lower on foreign sales and on paperback sales (if there is a paperback version). Royalties are usually lower on foreign sales because of the added costs entailed in such sales, especially when they are done through a distributor or intermediary, who takes a portion of the receipts. Paperback books receive lower royalties because they generally have to be priced lower than hardcovers, and so publishers receive less profit per book.

In comparing royalties among publishers, make sure that you compare apples with apples. In other words, make sure that the royalties are on the same basis (e.g., net receipts) and involve the same exclusions (e.g., for sample copies that are given away free by publishers for promotional purposes).

It is sometimes possible to work out a sliding-royalty arrangement with a publisher. Such an arrangement more fairly shares risk between author and publisher. Publishers are often reluctant to give higher royalties because they want to make sure that they recover their own costs of producing and marketing the book. A sliding-scale arrangement results in a greater proportion of royalties being paid as more books are sold. For example, you might receive a royalty of 10 percent of net on the first 2,500 copies sold, 12 percent of net on the next 2,500 sold, and 15 percent of net on all copies sold thereafter. Sliding-scale royalties are usually negotiable (both in terms of thresholds for increases in royalties and for amounts of increase), especially if competing publishers are in the picture. However, not all publishers are willing to offer a sliding-scale arrangement. What level of royalties can you expect on a scholarly book? Typically, it seems to the authors, surprisingly little. Commonly, royalties are between 10 and 12 percent of net receipts. A high royalty rate is 15 percent, and rates greater than that are relatively rare. Although this level might not seem like much to you, you need to remember that the publishing house bears most of the expenses and is eager not only to recover those expenses but to make a profit as well. The more competitive offers you have, and the stronger they are, the greater the royalty rate you may be able to negotiate for yourself.

Royalties typically are paid out once or twice a year, depending on the publisher. If they are paid once a year, it is commonly in the spring. If they are paid twice a year, it is commonly in the fall and spring.

Experience Is the Best Teacher

If you are fortunate enough to receive contract offers from more than one publisher, you may be tempted to decide which offer to accept solely on the basis of royalty levels. Deciding solely on the basis of royalties is a mistake. If the publisher offering lower royalties produces a more attractive book, or has a more powerful sales force, or does better marketing of your book, you might actually end up getting more money working with the lower royalties than with the higher ones.

17.3.2 Advance on Royalties

An advance is money that a publisher pays up front in anticipation of future royalties. Once the book is published and begins selling, royalty payments to the author will be withheld until the publisher has recouped the advance. In the event that the book does not sell enough copies to earn back the advance given to the author, the publisher forfeits the money – the author does not have to pay back the advance. Usually, the only circumstances under which authors must pay back an unearned advance are those in which they don't finish the book or if they complete it but the publisher deems the manuscript unacceptable and declines to publish it. These eventualities are usually spelled out in the contract.

Some publishers are willing to give small advances on royalties, although advances for scholarly books are relatively rare and, when they are given, relatively small. At most, they will be a few thousand dollars, and even that is high for scholarly books. In general, unless you are a well-known author or have multiple competitive offers, you should not expect an advance on royalties.

17.3.3 Payment of Royalties

Check when royalties are paid. Most publishers pay once a year. However, it is to your advantage if the royalties are paid twice a year, because you receive them more quickly after books are sold. The month or months in which royalties are paid varies, although a typical schedule would be that royalties are paid once a year in May for sales of the preceding calendar year. Publishers are generally not flexible on royalty payment schedules, as they tend to do all their accounting for all their books at the same time.

17.3.4 Publication Lag

Publication lag is the time between the submission of the final draft of your book and the publication of that book. Publishers vary widely in how long it takes them to produce a book. Typically, the publication lag should be no longer than one year. We have worked with a publisher that has taken close to two years to publish a book, and for certain this will be the last time we work with that publisher. You can ask the publisher to write into the contract a "reasonable" amount of time, although the publisher will usually write the language to exclude delays due to unforeseen causes. Remember, to minimize publication lag, you should submit the book in a form that maximizes efficiency for the publisher. For example, having camera-ready figures that can be readily reproduced helps cut the time to publication. Submitting manuscripts electronically also can help.

17.3.5 Marketing and Promotional Efforts

Publishers will rarely write into a contract the specific marketing and promotional efforts that they will do for your book, but you may be able to get them to write a separate letter. Such a letter generally has no legal force, and thus it represents a moral rather than a legal commitment. In publishing, as in most endeavors, oral agreements mean little, if anything: If you do not have it in writing, you do not have it. You should get a clear sense of what the publisher plans to do to promote the book. Will the book appear at professional conventions? Will it be advertised in journals? Will there be direct-mail promotions? If so, to whom will the mail be sent? Books do not sell themselves. They need efforts not only on your part in writing but also on the publisher's part in marketing, and you should find out as much about the intended marketing as possible.

17.3.6 Physical Appearance of the Book

As we mentioned earlier, publishers differ widely in how attractive the books they produce are. Publishers also differ widely in the quality of their books' materials. The best indication of the quality of the production of your book is the quality of production of other books published by the same house. Therefore, review copies of other books that the publisher has produced and check the quality of the binding, the paper, the printing, and the like. Are the publisher's books attractive? A book should last for many years, and so it pays for you to know how well produced the book will be.

17.3.7 Out-of-Print Policy

Some publishers keep almost all of their books in print for many, many years; others put them out of print if the book stops selling some minimum number of copies. For some publishers, this minimum may be quite high. Therefore, it is to your advantage to inquire of the publisher as to its out-of-print policy, because it can have a major effect on the life of your book. And it is something that authors often forget to consider in choosing a publisher. Some houses will put a book out of print after only a couple of years, and you will want to know in advance if that is a possibility for your book. If it is, make sure that your book contract states that the rights to the book will revert to you in case the book does go out of print.

17.3.8 In-House Assistance

You need to make clear in negotiating a contract exactly who is going to do what. Sometimes publishers compile indexes; other times they expect authors to do them. Many scholarly books separate author indexes from subject indexes, and some publishers will do one (e.g., the author index) but not the other. Usually, authors are expected to obtain permissions for long quotations or figures taken from other volumes, but some publishers take on this responsibility. Some publishers have in-house copy-editors; others send their manuscripts to freelance copy-editors. Moreover, publishers differ in the care with which they copy-edit the manuscripts they receive. Copy-editing is important because it involves the correction of various errors, as well as the clarification of the text. Therefore, having a good copy-editor is important.

17.3.9 Communication

We have found that the quality and quantity of communication with publishers differ widely across publishers, and they depend on more than just how chatty we happen to feel about a particular book. Some publishers' representatives (acquisitions editors) seem to disappear the moment you sign the contract; others are there to support you throughout the entire book-writing process. Obviously, it is to your advantage to work with the kind of editor who is willing to communicate more rather than less. Having a good editor to work with can make the entire publishing process remarkably smooth, whereas having no one to work with or having someone who is unhelpful or unpleasant can turn a simple process into a nightmare. Therefore, know in advance with whom you are going to work and convince yourself that it is someone with whom you are going to enjoy working and from whom you will be able to profit.

17.3.10 Hidden Aspects of the Contract

Although we do not take our contracts for scholarly books to a contracts lawyer, we do take those for textbooks and trade books to such a lawyer. And it probably is not a bad idea to show even a contract for a scholarly book to a lawyer. There are often hidden features of the contract that you will not be able to see, but that a lawyer will see. Every contract that we have brought to a lawyer has contained passages that are unduly unfavorable to the author that we never would have recognized as such. Therefore, you should read the contract carefully; do not just assume that the contract will be written in a way that is favorable to you. On the contrary, it is generally written to be maximally favorable to the publisher. Business being business, publishers look out for themselves. Therefore, check your contract very carefully, and if you have any doubts about it, take it to a lawyer. We recommend that you consult a lawyer who specializes in contracts, because such attorneys, in our experience, are much more knowledgeable than general practice lawyers, who may have handled very few publishing contracts.

17.3.11 Reputation of the Publisher

The most important consideration of all we have saved for last, and that is the reputation of the publisher. Publishers, like organizations of any kind, differ widely in quality. Some of them are completely reputable, and others less so. Some of them are world renowned, and others are fly-by-night organizations that may disappear before your book is ever published. Investigate the reputation of the publisher with which you are considering signing by checking with others who have published there and by asking for a catalog of published titles. One of the best signs of a good publisher is the stable of authors who have published with it and who continue to do so. If possible, speak with authors who have worked with the press. Do not assume that a publisher must be good because you have heard of it or because it writes on impressive stationery or has fancy headquarters.

We especially warn readers about so-called subsidy publishers or vanity presses. These "publishers" require that you pay a large amount of money up front to have your book published. They will publish almost anything, provided that you are willing to pay the publication costs. Their royalties are much higher than those of other houses, but don't be seduced by this fact; such publishers can afford to pay higher royalties because they take essentially no risk. In our opinion, such publishers are houses of last resort, because authors rarely receive back in royalties what they have paid to have the books published. Moreover, vanity presses know this fact and may even state it in their literature. Such presses make little effort to promote the books because their real receipts are in the payments made by authors to get their books published. Even worse, publishing with such a press probably will not enhance your professional credentials. Psychologists and others know who these publishers are and may devalue rather than value a book published by one of these houses.

Let us make one last observation in closing. Between us, we have written or edited more than 100 books, and the writing and editing of books has been one of the most enjoyable experiences we have had as psychologists. Our experiences with publishers have ranged from excellent to poor, but we have learned from our mistakes, as will you. Going through the steps of publishing a book can be one of the most rewarding experiences of a career as a psychologist, and after all is said and done, many of the greatest contributions that have been made in psychology have been made through books. Therefore, although you may experience anxieties, enjoy yourself. If you write a book, you are in for an experience that is always challenging, often rewarding, and many times, great fun.

Give It Some More Thought

Just as you are concerned about a publisher's reputation, so is a publisher concerned about your reputation.

What are some of the factors that a publisher may look for in terms of your reputation when deciding whether to offer you a contract? For example, the publisher would want to know your scholarly reputation, your reputation for getting your work in on time, and your reputation with regard to collaborative skills – that is, will you be easy to work with, or a pain in the neck?

CHECKLIST FOR BOOK PROPOSALS

Content

☐ Have you stated what makes your book interesting and why it is important for your message to be published?

☐ Are your chapters supported empirically and theoretically?

☐ Are the facts in your proposal accurate?

☐ Did you define basic terms?

☐ Have you reviewed the relevant literature?

☐ Does your proposed book have the best possible organization?

☐ Do you have an outline of all the chapters with chapter names and summaries?

Market

☐ Have you shown that there is a need for the book?
☐ Have you shown that there is a market for the book?
☐ Have you shown that your book makes a unique contribution to the market?

Audience

☐ Have you described the target audience of your book?
☐ Have you specified at which level the book will be written?

Details

☐ Have you specified the suggested length of your manuscript, as well as the number of tables and figures you intend to use?
☐ Have you specified the expected completion date?
☐ Does your summary once more point out the special features of your book?

Credentials

☐ Have you presented your qualifications as an author?

18 | Writing a Lecture

Lecturing is one of the most important parts of being a psychologist. All of us have attended countless lectures and know what a difference it makes to listen to someone exciting versus someone dull. Sometimes you may not have any choice in terms of the material you present. But there are 20 keys that everyone can follow to write and deliver better lectures:

1. Do not read your lecture from a script.

2. Start off on an exciting note.

3. Organize and emphasize.

4. Say what you are going to say, say it, and say what you have said.

5. Use concrete examples.

6. Do not cram.

7. Be enthusiastic.

8. Make it relevant.

9. Know your audience.

10. Vary your pace and the kinds of content you present during the course of the lecture.

11. Pace yourself.

12. Do not be condescending.

13. Do not be defensive.

14. Do not wing it.

15. Be confident.

16. Tell a story.

17. Realize your purpose is to persuade as well as to inform.

18. Be careful with jokes, especially inside jokes.

19. End with a bang, not a whimper.

20. Keep audience participation under control.

1. Do not read your lecture from a script.

Listening to a lecture that is read directly from text is one of the more boring experiences known to humankind. Written language does not sound like oral language. If you ever read the transcript of a good talk, you will find it hard to comprehend. It should be! People just do not talk the way they read. When you hear a talk that is read word for word, the talk sounds unnatural. It is also boring to hear. Therefore, when you write a lecture, you are best off doing it in outline form or in some other form that will enable you to talk directly to the audience rather than reading the lecture.

Experience Is the Best Teacher

If you read an exact transcript of what you say in a conversation, or in a lecture, for that matter, you will find that the text is hard to understand and sometimes is incomprehensible in written form. Yet it may have been fully understandable in oral form. Unfortunately, the reverse also holds. Written text often sounds stilted and can be hard to understand when presented orally. As a result, it always is better, if you can, to speak in a lecture from notes (or from memory) rather than from fully written-out text.

---

2. Start off on an exciting note.

Listeners often decide in the first minute or two whether they will continue to listen to a lecture or tune out. Starting with an exciting opening can make the difference between capturing an audience and losing them from the start. Try to start off with an anecdote, a joke that is relevant to the lecture, a concrete example of something you'll be talking about, or some other topic that will catch the interest of listeners. Jokes can be good in an opening, but only if they are related to the rest of the talk. In fact, many people find it annoying to hear a joke that is obviously canned and that is used by either the same person or others as an opening for almost any speech they give. A creative opening can make the difference, but you have to be willing to put in the effort to make sure that it is creative.

3. Organize and emphasize.

A person who is knowledgeable about a field may be able to follow a poorly organized lecture, but someone who is new to a field is much less likely to be able to do so. Therefore, organize your lecture clearly and tightly. A logical sequence of points will help listeners understand. Moreover, organize hierarchically. Emphasize main points and deemphasize subordinate ones. Listeners who are new to an area cannot be expected to know what your main points are. You need to tell them, and to give them a sense of what is more important to remember and what is less so.

4. Say what you are going to say, say it, and say what you have said.

In giving a lecture, even more than in writing, it is important to start by foreshadowing your main points in the organization of your talk, then to give the main body of the talk, and finally to summarize the main points of what you have said. Such an organization helps listeners both to be prepared for the main body of the lecture and to understand what they have learned after the lecture is done. This organization may seem redundant, but some redundancy helps listeners better understand the content. Obviously, you do not want to say the same things again and again, but you do want to emphasize and reemphasize your main points to be sure that your listeners understand them.

5. Use concrete examples.

In speaking, as in writing, concrete examples help listeners understand fairly abstract points or points that may be slightly beyond their initial comprehension. A talk that never leaves the abstract plane is likely to be incomprehensible to many listeners. Whether or not people are willing to admit it, they learn best from general points that are illustrated by examples. Do not expect members of the audience to be able to fill in their own examples – you provide them.

6. Do not cram.

Don't you just hate it when someone tries to give 2 hours of material in 40 minutes? So do the people who are going to listen to you. Some lecturers try to show how erudite they are or how quickly they can think by cramming in too much material for the time that they are given to lecture. Most people in the audience will be unimpressed and, to the contrary, will come to the conclusion that you do not know how to lecture. The idea is not to present as much material as possible but to make the material you present as clear and as comprehensible as possible. Therefore, make sure that the amount of material fits the time you have to present it. It is better to present less and clearly convey main points than it is to overpresent and have your audience understand next to nothing.

7. Be enthusiastic.

Do not expect your audience to be enthusiastic if you are not. If you are enthusiastic, you may or may not transmit your enthusiasm to your audience. But if you are unenthusiastic, you certainly will not transmit any enthusiasm at all. Enthusiasm is contagious, and by showing yours, you may win converts to your way of seeing things that you otherwise would not win. You have most likely always hated to hear people who are bored with what they present; so will your audience.

8. Make it relevant.

One of the best things you can do to increase comprehension of a lecture is to make the lecture relevant to the people to whom you present it. The more you can adjust your lecture to the interests and prior knowledge of your audience, and the more you can make it relevant to their own concerns, the more likely the audience will be to listen and comprehend. You probably find that you listen more if you feel that you are learning something useful in a class. Your audience will do the same. Moreover, even if you cannot make the lecture completely relevant to your audience, show why it may be interesting anyway. Do not expect them to know. The more you can show why your audience should find something interesting, the more likely they are to respond to what you have to say.

9. Know your audience.

A corollary of making your talk relevant to your audience is knowing who your audience is in the first place. When we give a talk or a lecture, we always try to find out as much as we can about the people to whom we are talking. How much knowledge do they have about the topic? What are their interests? What are they looking for in your talk? The more you know your audience, and the more you can adjust your remarks to fit your audience, the better you are likely to be received.

What's Wrong Here?

Excerpt from a lecture to an undergraduate course in social psychology: "The investigators used stepwise multiple regression to assess the independent effects of the various variables. The advantage of this procedure, of course, is that it utilizes part correlations rather than correlations uncorrected for the full interrelations of the independent variables. The beta weights tell a compelling story..."

Answer: The lecture might be appropriate for an audience of advanced graduate students, but this excerpt is unlikely to be suitable for most undergraduates.

---

10. **Vary your pace and the kinds of content you present during the course of the lecture.**

   Varying pace and kinds of content helps maintain audience interest. Too much of anything can become too much of a good thing. Therefore, it helps to vary level of abstractions with concrete examples, generalities with specifics, and lighter topics with heavier ones. Variety is the spice of life, and it is also the spice of a good talk.

11. **Pace yourself.**

   Many people have a tendency to talk too fast. For listeners, the result is often that they are lost before they even begin to understand what the lecture is about. Therefore, you do not want to talk too fast, or labor so slowly over your words that people lose track of where they are. The best procedure is to vary your pace somewhat but to stay within a range of speed that enables you to remain comprehensible.

12. **Do not be condescending.**

   No one likes to hear a condescending lecturer or one who obviously has no respect for the audience. If people are turned off to you, they are likely to be turned off to your material as well. Being condescending or arrogant, or treating people as though they lacked even the most basic mental abilities, is a great way to turn people off completely to everything you have to say. It is generally better to err on the side of modesty than on the side of being a know-it-all, if only because your talk should speak for itself. If you give a good talk, people will respect you for doing it, without your acting as if you are the world's greatest expert on the topic of your talk.

13. Do not be defensive.

Accept questions, comments, and even criticisms openly. If you want people to learn, then it helps to give them a chance to interact with you. If you react defensively to what they say, the chances are that they will not want to say anything. Therefore, belittling the contributions of your audience or immediately defending yourself against anything you perceive as an attack hurts the audience's ability to learn from you and your ability to learn from the audience. Accept comments openly and profit from them.

14. Do not wing it.

People quickly recognize if you have come into a lecture unprepared. You have always recognized it in others, and people recognize it in you. Therefore, be prepared.

15. Be confident.

Perhaps most important, be confident and self-assured. No one is expected to be perfect, and no one is expected to know everything. If you have prepared for your lecture and have a reasonable command of your material, give it your best shot and have the confidence in yourself to do well. And then go and enjoy yourself. If you do, your audience probably will as well.

16. Tell a story.

Often, we think of fictional writing as about story-telling and non-fiction writing as about factual presentation. But a good lecture tells a story. It draws the audience in, the way a story does, and it has the elements of a story. It has a plot: What is the lecture about? It has themes: What are the main lessons to be learned? It has drama: If there is no drama in what you are talking about, how do you expect to hold your audience's attention? It has characters: Who were the people who contributed to the drama of whatever you are talking about? And it has a beginning, middle, and end. So try as much as possible to turn your lecture into a story – one that will capture and maintain interest and that will be memorable, because people remember stories much better than they remember disconnected prose.

17. Realize your purpose is to persuade as well as to inform.

Throughout this book, we have emphasized that the purpose of scientific writing is not merely to inform but also to persuade. This lesson applies especially to lectures. There are always competitors vying for an audience's attention or loyalties. Show the audience why your take on whatever you are talking about is especially compelling. Do not just assume that, because *you* are lecturing, your audience will accept what you say.

18. Be careful with jokes, especially inside jokes.

Jokes help enliven a talk. They often make a talk more memorable. And they typically make it more fun. They are also prone to backfiring. Jokes can backfire for any of a number of reasons. First, some in the audience may not get the joke. They may hear what you say and think it is nonsense, not a joke. Second, if audience members see others in the audience laugh when they find nothing funny, it makes those audience members uncomfortable and possibly resentful. Third, people have very different senses of humor. What's funny to one person may be unappreciated or even resented by another. Fourth, jokes usually require background knowledge, sometimes extensive background knowledge, to understand. You cannot assume that all audience members have the background knowledge. Fifth, sometimes jokes you find funny may be incredibly offensive to others. Any number of people have found themselves in serious trouble when they told jokes to spark laughs, and instead they sparked indignation or worse.

What's Wrong Here?

"A priest, a rabbi, and an imam enter a restaurant. The waitress asks them what they want to order..."

Answer: However funny the rest of the joke may be to some people, you should avoid religious jokes in talks, no matter how funny you think they may be. Almost certainly, some members of your audience will be offended.

---

19. End with a bang, not a whimper.

There are few endings worse in papers or in talks than "Future research is needed." Of course, future research is always needed. Endings are your chance to hit a homerun – or to punt. You definitely do not want to punt. You might end with a story, or with a personal experience, or with a strong statement about how views need to change. However you end your lecture, end it so that people will keep thinking about the talk, not file it under "Boring!"

20. Keep audience participation under control.

Whenever possible, you should encourage questions from your audience. Sometimes audiences – whether students or professionals – learn more from the back-and-forth of a question-and-answer session than they do just from listening to a lecture. But you need to keep audience participation under control. First, if someone keeps trying to ask questions, make sure others get a chance too. Second, if someone uses a question-and-answer period to give a lecture, feel free to cut them off. Simply explain that the purpose of the session is question-and-answer, not lecture. Third, if someone keeps interrupting you, ask him or her to stop; if the person does not, you are within your rights to ask the person to leave. (Just make sure that the person you are asking to leave is not someone who, for one reason or another, you really want to stay, such as the chair of a search committee considering you for a job!) Fourth, if someone's question just goes on and on, or the person compresses question after question into a single statement, stop the person, answer what questions you can or want to, and move on. Finally, don't allow yourself to get angry or flustered – ever. If you lose control, much of the force of your lecture will be gone. Audience members will remember how you got out of control, not what you said.

CHECKLIST FOR LECTURES

- [ ] Are you starting off in an exciting way?
- [ ] Is your lecture organized?
- [ ] Are you emphasizing your main points?
- [ ] Are you using concrete examples?
- [ ] Is your lecture relevant to your audience?
- [ ] Have you adapted your lecture to your audience?

19 | Doing a Job Interview

Job interviews generally follow a fairly standard pattern. First comes the invitation, usually in the form of an e-mail or a phone call. A date is set – a typical interview lasts one or two days. The candidate usually makes arrangements for travel, and hopefully, travel costs will be reimbursed (although they aren't always). The day comes, and the candidate takes off for the interview.

The interview usually consists of four main parts. The first part is individual or small group meetings with faculty members. These meetings are important because they are major way in which the candidate is evaluated. The second part is meetings with undergraduate and, where appropriate, graduate students. These meetings may be in small groups or may be over a meal or coffee. The third part is the job talk, which usually is extremely important. The fourth part comprises one or more meals with faculty members and possibly graduate students. Do not think for a moment that the meal is just for enjoyment. Your possible employers will evaluate your behavior and answers to questions carefully. If you drink, drink modestly. A dinner during a job interview is no time to look like a lush!

The job talk typically has two aspects, the presentation and questions and answers. Both are important. Be sure to leave time for questions. A good strategy is to accept questions of clarification during the talk and then questions about larger issues after the talk is over. Leave at least 15 minutes at the end for questions. Never go

This chapter is based on articles published in the *Chronicle of Higher Education*: R. J. Sternberg (2013). Twelve bloopers to avoid in job interviews. *Chronicle of Higher Education*, 59 (25), A31–A32. R. J. Sternberg (2013). How not to blow an interview. *Chronicle of Higher Education*, October 25, A27–A28.

over time. And don't try to present too much material. Remember that most people in your audience are not specialists in your field, so you will need to present in a way that is suitable for the level of the audience.

Beware of the possibility of technological glitches. Go into your job talk with a backup so that if the technology you plan to use fails, you have another option. For example, you might have PowerPoint slides on sheets of paper to which you can refer if the PowerPoint breaks down. Or if you are using traditional slides, have the content available in another format in case the slide projector fails.

In some institutions, especially small colleges, you will be expected to give two talks. One talk will emphasize your research accomplishments and the other talk will be a lecture, much as you might give to a class you might teach. When there are two talks, assume that both are equally important. In some colleges, the teaching talk may actually be more important than the research-based talk.

It's easy to blow a job interview. Sometimes, job candidates do it in a matter of minutes or even seconds. Here are some tips we offer to make the most of job interviews rather than blowing them. Our list includes both things to do and things *not* to do.

THINGS TO SAY AND DO

1. Tell me your concerns and let me try to address them.

No matter where you apply for a job, the search committee of the hiring institution is likely to have at least some doubts about you or about your credentials. It is useful to know ahead of time what the doubts are and why the search committee has them. When you interview, people will process what they hear you say through the filter of their prior expectations. One sensible strategy is to review your record and anticipate the kinds of concerns a hiring institution might have. What are the weaknesses in your record? How can you convince a search committee that they are not serious, or even that they are only apparent and not real? It is usually better to anticipate problems than to have them hit you in the face while you are unprepared.

For example, suppose you have spent much or even all of your career at elite institutions. Now you are a job candidate at a less elite or non-elite college. You reasonably can expect individuals on a search committee to question your ability – and your desire – to make the transition from one type of institution to another. Are you prepared for a job at a small college? How are you going to dispel any notion that you are not only from an elite institution but also an elitist; you need to think about this issue in advance, not, for the first time, at the job interview. Or suppose you spent your time in academia at large universities.

Do not wait to dispel a potential misconception until someone asks a question. Be proactive in addressing what you think might be people's concerns. When people at the hiring institution have concerns about you, they may not explicitly tell you what they are. You have to get inside information, usually from someone you know on the campus – or else figure out their possible concerns on your own.

2. **This worked for me before, but I just don't know if it will work here.**

We all underestimate how hard it is to sell people on new ideas. And we often believe that, if we have one or more great ideas, other people, except for total fools, will see how great our ideas are. In reality, the more creative an idea, the less others will immediately grasp its value.

You may want to assure members of the search committee that your great ideas will be as well received in their institution as they have been in your current institution. Resist that urge. Different institutions value different kinds of teaching and research, and what is viewed as terrific in one place may be viewed as sketchy in another. In our field of psychology, for example, one department may value individual-differences research highly. Another department may wonder why anyone would bother looking at individual differences rather than looking for how people are alike. Some departments may like behavioral economics, others feel that it is misguided. Some departments may value metaphysics, but others believe it is hokey. You get the idea: There is no one set of ideas that works for every department.

3. **What are the hot-button issues around here?**

Most campuses have one or more such issues. Often they are ones that have been decided but whose solution, or process of reaching that solution, left a bad taste in some people's mouths. You need to know about those issues and how they were resolved.

Why? Because someone on the campus is likely to ask you a question about such an issue, and a wrong answer will get your name crossed off the shortlist for the job.

For example, if the institution used to be almost exclusively oriented toward teaching but now has a push on toward faculty members' getting grants, you will want to know that so you indicate your willingness (if indeed you are willing) to compete for grants. Or if the campus has started placing a great emphasis on the use of modern technology in teaching, you will want to show that you understand such technology and view it as important (if indeed you do). It always helps, in getting a job, to know what the hot-button issues are that can make the difference between your getting hired and your being put into the rejects' bin.

Experience Is the Best Teacher

If you don't like the priorities of the college or university, consider withdrawing from the search, or not applying in the first place. You don't want to end up in an institution whose values are inconsistent with your own. Bob spent some time at an institution that had priorities radically different from his. He was miserable, and so were many people at the institution. He got out. Better not to land yourself in that situation in the first place.

---

4. I would like to solve all your problems, but let me tell you the problems I really can solve!

Yes, the department needs someone to do this and do that and do the other thing too. Be careful about what you commit to in an interview; the hiring department is likely to remember. And if you commit to too many things, you may find that you do not have the time to do what you were hired to do in the first place. It's fine to commit to teaching a particular course. But if you find they want you to commit to a whole bunch of courses and committees and other extra activities, beware!

5. Assume that anything you say to anyone in the interview could end up in the local news or somewhere on the Web.

During the job interview, you will be under stress. You may find yourself wanting to confide in someone, especially regarding concerns about the interview or the institution. You may even meet someone who invites you to confide in him or her.

Don't. Not even if it is someone you know. For one thing, that person's first loyalty is likely to be to the institution, not to you. For another thing, you have little way of knowing whether he or she can keep a confidence. Academe is a small world where secrets are rarely kept. But they are almost impossible to keep during a job interview. Don't lose out on the position because you mistakenly believe they will be. If you make a negative comment about the institution, or even your home institution, you never know where it may end up. Do not assume it will remain confidential.

6. Let me tell you the truth.

If there is one kind of headline that makes the higher-education news with unrelenting frequency, it is about people who have lied on their CVs and résumés, or in their comments during an interview. A lie may help you get the job, but when you are found out, it will very likely lead to your dismissal.

If you have something unpleasant in your record, bring it up yourself during the interview and be prepared to discuss it. Go ahead and put it in the best possible light, but don't lie. People almost always get into more trouble for their attempt at a cover up than for their initial mistakes.

7. How can I fit into the vision for the future here?

You need to find out where the hiring department, school, college, or university wants to go. And if you don't want to go there, then you don't want to go to that campus. If the institution wants to become a top research institution and your thing is teaching, the job is probably not for you. If the institution expects to move more and more toward online courses and you prefer teaching in person, it's not for you. Find out not only where the institution is, but also, where it wants to go.

If you do like the institution's vision, then try to show in the interview how you might fit into that vision. Don't waste time offering alternative visions.

8. Tell me the story of the institution.

What are its points of pride? Its points of shame?

If, for example, the institution takes pride in how research at the university has been applied to benefit the state's citizens, you probably don't want to stress the importance of basic research. If the department takes special pride in the quality of its teaching, you don't want to keep bringing up your research.

9. Who calls the shots around here?

The power structure of a hiring institution, in general, and even of a department, in particular is often opaque and, at worst, invisible to a job candidate.

You may assume that the chair of a search committee has a major say in who is hired. But the chair may or may not be an important voice in the final hiring decision. Even the person who picks you up at the airport may be a decision maker.

How, then, should you proceed? Just assume that everyone you speak with is important.

10. I really want this job!

Playing hard to get may or may not work in romantic relationships. But it's a bad strategy in job interviews. And candidates can give that impression all too easily in an off-the-cuff comment (like breezily mentioning that you have another offer before you've even been offered this job).

Hiring institutions want to hire someone who wants the job, likes the place, and is going to stick around – and willingly so. If you really want the job, make sure your responses convey your interest. And if you don't, consider withdrawing.

Experience Is the Best Teacher

On the one hand, institutions want people who are desired as well by other institutions. The fact that other institutions value the candidates validates the judgment that they are worth being hired. On the other hand, institutions hate to be turned down for job offers. It is embarrassing and makes people feel like they are being dissed. Often, the conclusion people draw is that you never were interested in their institution in the first place. So your best way of getting a job offer is to let it be known (preferably through others) that you are desirable to other institutions but emphasizing in the job interview that you are seriously interested in the institution at which you are interviewing. If it is your first choice, say so.

Those are 10 things to do. Now consider what *not* to do!

1. **Good question, but now let me answer the question I wish you had asked.**

   When you receive media training, you learn a technique called "bridging." The idea is that, in a media interview, when asked a question, you briefly, perhaps super-briefly, address the question that was asked and then bridge to the point you really want to make. In this way, you appear to have heard and paid attention to the question but get the opportunity to say what you really want to say. However useful this technique is in media interviews, it is a bummer in job interviews. Chances are the questioner is asking the same question of every candidate: If you do not answer it properly, the questioner will assume that either you can't answer it or, just as bad, you don't want to. The questioner thought the question was a good one, and if you don't answer it, he or she is not likely to think more of you for it.

2. **I have no clue but I'll be damned if I'm going to let you know that.**

   It's hard to say "I don't know" in a job interview, but interviewers will think more of you if you say it than they will if you give a poor or irrelevant answer. Sometimes, they will be impressed that you were willing to admit your ignorance on the matter. There is nothing wrong with saying you don't know, but if you are saying it too often during the interview, you might think about other job opportunities. And do due diligence: You don't want to show ignorance about the place where you want to work.

3. **I'm so glad you asked. I've got an excellent colloquium on just that question.**

   Occasionally you get just the question that you have been prepping for and can't wait to answer it – and answer it and answer it. Question periods usually are short. Questioners are looking for relatively short answers. If you find yourself going on and on, stop yourself before someone else does. Long answers suggest a lack of self-control, uncertainty about how to answer, or, sometimes, an outsized ego.

> ### Experience Is the Best Teacher
>
> If you have a great answer to a question, you may want to answer and keep answering and answering. The problem is that you then are cutting off the opportunity to answer other questions that may interest your audience. If you feel you have much more to say, offer to send an answer via e-mail or to provide further information in informal meetings during your time at the institution.

4. I'm going to keep that face smiling and that head nodding.

When you are talking to a search committee, there sometimes will be one or perhaps even two people in the group who consistently smile or nod their heads when you answer. Because they are rewarding you for your answers, your tendency more and more may be to talk directly to them and to say whatever it takes to get them to smile and nod more. The trouble is they are probably not the people you need to convince. You also need to pay attention to the stone faces and the frowners. They are the ones you need to persuade that you are viable for the job.

5. A little embellishment never hurt anybody.

It is so tempting to embellish your record just a little here and there. After all, you are facing stiff competition for the job and every little bit helps. There are two problems with embellishing your record. First, especially with the availability of the Internet for fact checking, it's just too easy for potential employers to figure out you're stretching the truth. Second, once you have shown you are not trustworthy, you can kiss the job good-bye. If the potential employer catches you stretching the truth with one thing, they are likely to assume you have done the same with other things and feel they cannot trust you, which is a recipe for disaster. Stick to the truth. You'll be better off.

6. You can count on me to make everybody happy.

Academic institutions look for people who are compatible with their values. The problem is that different groups within the institution are likely to have somewhat different values and sometimes the differences cause conflicts. One approach an interviewee can take is to show how he or she can get along with absolutely everyone. The problem with this approach is that you may give the impression of being wishy-washy or unwilling to stand up for any principles, if indeed you are perceived as having any. No one expects you to be best friends with everyone. Show who you are. If they don't like who you are, you don't want to go there and should thank them if they reject you.

7. Weaknesses? Me?

Bob once interviewed a candidate and asked what Bob considered to be a thoroughly standard question: What do you see as your major weaknesses? The candidate replied that no one had ever asked him that and he had not really thought about it. Bob knew he would not hire him – and he didn't. Someone who is unaware of his or her weaknesses is not going to be effective at any job. Know what your weaknesses (and strengths) are and be prepared to talk about them. Just make sure that, whatever they are, your weaknesses are not fatal for the job for which you are applying. For example, if you do not particularly like teaching, an interview for a faculty position is probably not the place to mention it; and if you don't like to teach, you might want to reconsider whether you want to be a faculty member in the first place. Similarly, if you can never stand to suffer fools with a smile, you may find an administrative position very challenging.

8. I've got this great new technology for my talk.

One job candidate for an academic position was unable to make her technology work; she was unwilling to start her job talk until she could make it work. She was not hired. Another job candidate boasted in his job talk that he was using a new technology that he had never tried out before. The technology did not work for him. (It did not help that his field was engineering.) He was not hired either. Try to ensure the technology will work and always have a backup in case it doesn't.

Experience Is the Best Teacher

There have been times in his career when Bob has thought that the best test to give to a job candidate is to have the

> technology fail and see whether the candidate still can give his or her talk. If someone cannot adapt flexibly to the loss of technology, the candidate is most likely rigid and probably a bad hire. Go into any talk with a backup plan in case the technology fails.

9. We really know how to handle that problem at my university.

Everyone wants to hear about your experiences and how you have handled them. But if you show yourself to think your current university or your graduate institution has the answer to every problem, some people may wonder why you don't just stay there. We had a job candidate who seemed to be totally in love with his current institution. He received little support because no one could figure why he wanted to leave where he was.

10. Here's what I need to make this job work.

OK. Bob made this mistake once. Bob was asked what he needed to make the job work. He made the mistake of going into too much detail. The problem was he didn't yet have an offer. He didn't get one. You have to be careful about specifying conditions of employment before you are offered the job. You will be in a bargaining position after you're offered the job, but not really before. And remember never to accept or turn down a job you have not been offered. If you don't have an offer in writing, you really don't have the offer, as he learned painfully many years ago when what he thought was an oral offer evaporated into thin air.

11. I'll teach you never to ask such a stupid question again.

It was Bob's first job interview ever. He was 25 years old and naive. A scruffy looking guy in the audience who looked like a first-year graduate student asked what Bob thought was a really dumb question. Bob gave a response that was too clever by half – sort of a put-down. How was Bob supposed to know the questioner was the chair of the search committee? He has never given a put-down answer again, no matter how weak he thought the question to be.

12. That will never work.

When someone on the search committee offers a solution to a problem the college or university faces and you don't think it will work, the job interview is not the time to tell him or her that it will never work. You are better off saying you would have to think about it, or saying that there might be ways to make it work. Who knows? If you think about it more, you just might be able to think of ways in which it actually could work.

Ultimately, what works best in a job interview is for you to be yourself. Speak honestly, and if the institution does not hire you, be glad you avoided landing at a place where you will not fit. In the end, jobs are about fit, and your best bet is always to be yourself to ensure that when you do take a job, it is at a place that is a match for you. Bad romances are painful not only in one's choice of partners, but also in one's choice of jobs.

20 | Doing Media Interviews

At some time in the careers of many psychologists, an opportunity arises to do an interview with the media. Virtually none of us are taught in graduate school how to do media interviews. The rules are very different from those of job interviews. Here is what you need to know:

■ **Only accept an interview if you are comfortable doing so.**
You may be asked to speak on a topic closely related to your research and teaching interests. In this case, congratulations: You may have an excellent opportunity to showcase your work. Sometimes, however, you may be asked to speak on a topic about which you know very little. In that case, decline the opportunity. Media interviews pretty quickly reveal, at least to those in the know, who is really an expert and who is pretending to be one. You don't want to get a reputation as a windbag. It won't do the radio show any good – or you either.

■ **Give brief answers.**
As academics, we often learn to go on at great length to show how much we know, or at least to convey all the complexities and fine points of a topic that sometimes comes across as oversimplified. Avoid the temptation to go on and on. Media interviews lend themselves well to short answers but poorly to long ones. If you go on too long, the interviewer may cut you off, so that you never get to finish what you wanted to say in the first place. Be brief and get quickly to the point.

■ **Use simple, nontechnical language.**

As psychologists or even aspiring psychologists, we get used quickly to complex technical language. We often stop even seeing it as complex or technical. In the media, complex technical language and jargon are the kiss of death. Your listeners won't understand what you are saying and will quickly tune you out. At worst, the interviewer will cut off the interview prematurely if he or she sees you cannot connect with the audience.

■ **Be direct – don't beat around the bush.**

In academia, we can acquire the bad habit of talking around an issue. Don't. In a media interview, you need to be very direct and get to the point. If you digress or otherwise beat around the bush, listeners will lose interest and you will lose your audience.

■ **Don't exaggerate.**

It is tempting in media interviews to exaggerate. Most findings in psychological research are of weak to moderate effect, and we realize that people don't want to hear lots of qualifiers: "maybe," "sometimes," "likely," "often," "to some extent," and so on. While you do not want to use a lot of qualifiers, you also do not want to exaggerate to the point that what you are saying simply is no longer true. Interviewers like strong statements but you have your professional integrity to guard. Don't give it up.

What's Wrong Here?

Excerpt from a media interview:
  "We found that people just are unwilling to criticize superiors if their job may be at risk."

Answer: The finding is probably generally true. But the way it has been stated, it sounds like no one is willing to criticize a superior at the risk of a job. This conclusion is almost certainly false. Some people do take the risk and criticize the superior. Most of the time, the criticism costs them; but sometimes the superior actually appreciates the different point of view and respects the subordinate for being willing to say what he or she thinks.

■ Don't keep saying "I think."

You can assume that the interviewer and audience will know that what you say is what you think. You do not need to keep reminding them.

■ Be careful of what you say.

Anything you say in a media interview is available potentially forever to interested persons. If you say something you later will regret, you may hear about it for your entire life. It thus behooves you to speak carefully so you do not find yourself in a situation in which you spoke in haste and, as the saying goes, get to repent at leisure.

■ If you need to think before answering, think before answering.

There is a lot of pressure in a media interview to answer questions quickly. Obviously, no one wants to listen to a radio or television show with long pauses; you can afford longer waits for print-media interviews. But even if you are on radio or television, think about what you are going to say before you say it, even if there is a "pregnant pause." You don't want to end up saying something that, upon reflection, you never would have said.

■ Don't allow yourself to be led to say things you don't believe.

Often, interviewers want to hear certain things from you. Indeed, they may have selected you for an interview because they expected you to take a particular stance. Do not let yourself be led on. Interviewers often are very skilled in leading people to say things that the interviewers want them to say but that the interviewees do not mean. Don't be the gullible interviewee: You guide your own comments; don't let the interviewer put words in your mouth.

■ Smile or at least don't frown.

No one wants to see a grump. If you look like a grump, you may end up making a bad impression, regardless of what you say.

■ Avoid emotional outbursts.

Interviewers (or panel members) sometimes bait their interviewees so that they will lose their self-control. Don't be the interviewee who loses his or her cool. Keep your emotions under control. If you lose your temper, all of what you said may be dismissed as unreliable.

■ **If you misspeak, correct your misstatement as soon as possible.**
In the course of an interview, especially a long one, it is frighteningly easy to misspeak. If you find yourself misspeaking, correct the error as soon as possible. Don't wait for the interviewer or anyone else to pick up on it. People will respect you for correcting your mistake. You don't want to be stuck on record for the rest of your life with a statement you did not mean.

■ **Don't say "No comment."**
When you say "no comment," it often comes across as though you have something to hide. You don't want to go there. If you don't want to comment on something, politely explain that you are unable to answer the question, and if relevant, explain why.

■ **Dress appropriately.**
You don't want people to remember you for the odd way you dress. Indeed, you don't really want people much to remember at all how you dressed. People should pay attention to what you have to say, not to how you dressed.

■ **Watch your body language.**
Body language gives off cues. You don't want to be giving off cues that create an unfavorable impression, such as always looking off into outer space, or gesticulating wildly, or staring fixedly at your feet. It is totally fine to use gestures and body language but make sure that you are sending the message through your nonverbal cues that you want to send.

■ **Ask where to look and then look there.**
Before you start the interview, ask the interviewer where you should be looking. Should you be looking at the interviewer, at the camera, at other panelists? Find out in advance where to look and then stick with it.

■ **Beware of tricks and be ready for surprises.**
Most interviewers will not try to trick you. But then, some will. Don't let yourself be forced into topics about which you cannot adequately speak or into positions that do not reflect what you think.

Experience Is the Best Teacher

Many years ago, Bob was interviewed on a major television show. The interview was on the topic of love. He had published some books on the topic and felt prepared to talk about it. The interview was going fine until, all of a sudden, the interviewer asked: "How is your marriage going?" At that point, the marriage (which later ended in divorce) was not going well. Bob had not expected any personal questions. He should have been prepared for such questions, especially when talking about a topic such as love. He blurted out a childish answer: "That's for me to know and you to find out." The interview might as well have ended right there. He was not ready for the surprise question, and he handled it poorly. A better answer, given his situation, would have been "My relationship, like all relationships, no matter how good they are, can be still better." This noncommittal answer would have spared him the embarrassment he felt during and after the interview.

■ **Assume the interviewer and your listeners know relatively little or nothing about your work.**

Most of the time, interviewers are not nearly so well prepared as interviewees expect them to be. Often, they are relying for the interview on notes created by someone else. So always assume as little as possible of your interviewer and your audience. The less you expect them to know, the better off you probably will be.

■ **Don't be condescending.**

Although you should assume that interviewers and audiences know very little, you never want to speak to them in a condescending tone, as though what kind of fool would be unfamiliar with my work? Treat the interviewer and the audience with respect, not with condescension. It sometimes helps to practice before an actual interview to ensure you are striking the right tone.

■ **Be concrete.**

Give concrete, colorful real-world examples. People often have trouble understanding abstract concepts. Help them by illustrating any abstract concepts with everyday concrete examples.

■ **Use appropriate language.**

You need to get the "register" right. To whom are you speaking? You want to speak their language. Don't swear. It almost never comes off well in the media. Don't use highfalutin' jargon. You are the expert: You need to sound like one.

■ **If you don't know an answer, admit it.**

Don't be sucked into giving an answer when you don't know what the correct answer is. If you don't know an answer, say so. You don't want to give a wrong answer that forever comes back to haunt you.

■ **When appropriate, bridge between what you were asked and what you want to say.**

Sometimes an interviewer does not get to ask what you really would like to tell him or her. What you should do in that case is take an opportunity to answer a question, and "bridge," or relate your answer to another point that gets across what you really want to say.

There never is any guarantee that an interview will go the way you hope it will. But following these suggestions at least will help you maximize your chances that the way you come off is the way you hoped to.

Epilogue

Many factors will affect your career success. Some of them are out of your control. You generally can't control, for example, who will review your work, or what the fads will be in psychology at a given point of your career. But there are so many things you can control – how you choose to teach, the research you choose to do, the service you decide to perform.

When Bob was in graduate school, he often wondered which of his colleagues would succeed and which would not. He wondered too whether he would succeed. During the early years after graduate school, he heard a lot about his various graduate-school colleagues. As the years went by, however, he heard about more and more of them, less and less. The ones who started to disappear into the woodwork were not the ones who seemed to be less intelligent, or less creative, or less willing to work hard. Rather, the ones who disappeared, he thought, had a different challenge.

Over the course of a lifetime, many things unexpectedly go wrong. One may become ill; family members may become ill; family members may unexpectedly die; one may end up getting divorced; one may lose a child; one may lose one's job; one may get into financial difficulties. The list is endless. It is hard to get through a life without some really major things going wrong. In the end, the graduate-school colleagues that stayed visible were the ones who had high levels of resilience, or grit. They could get through the tough times without just giving up. They plowed ahead, looking forward to better days, and those days came, sooner or later. So our best advice to you is to remember that the courses of a professional life and a personal life are almost never smooth. Things go wrong, often in quick succession. The people who succeed are the people who forge ahead – who continue to perform while looking ahead to a better future. As you wend your way through your career and your life, keep in mind that, no matter what happens, there is always the possibility of a better future. Put your mind to making that better future, and you will make the most of your career.

References

American Psychological Association (2009). *Publication manual of the American Psychological Association* (6th edn.). Washington, DC: American Psychological Association.

Aron, A., Aron, E. N., & Coups, E. (2012). *Statistics for the behavioral and social sciences* (6th edn.). Upper Saddle River, NJ: Prentice Hall.

Bem, D. J. (2000). Writing an empirical article. In R. J. Sternberg (ed.), *Guide to publishing in psychology journals* (pp. 3–16). New York: Cambridge University Press.

Calfee, R. (2000). What does it all mean: The discussion. In R. J. Sternberg (ed.), *Guide to publishing in psychology journals* (pp. 133–145). New York: Cambridge University Press.

Cleveland, W. S. (1994). *The elements of graphing data*. Summit, NJ: Hobart Press.

Dietz-Uhler, B. (2002). The effectiveness of an exercise to critically examine information on the World Wide Web. Unpublished manuscript, Miami University.

Dowling, D. (2008). *The wrong word dictionary*. Victoria, BC, Canada: Castle Books.

Ehrenberg, A. S. C. (2007). *A primer in data reduction: An introductory statistics textbook*. New York: Wiley.

Eisenberg, N. (2000). Writing a literature review. In R. J. Sternberg (ed.), *Guide to publishing in psychology journals* (pp. 17–34). New York: Cambridge University Press.

Federal Bureau of Investigation (2005). *Crime in the United States* [Electronic Version] from www.fbi.gov/ucr/05cius/data/table 05.html.

Federal Bureau of Investigation (2006). *Crime in the United States* [Electronic Version] from www.fbi.gov/ucr/cius2006/data/table 05.html.

Federal Bureau of Investigation (2007). *Crime in the United States* [Electronic Version] from www.fbi.gov/ucr/cius2007/data/table 05.html.

Garner, B. A. (2009). *Garner's modern American usage* (3rd edn.). New York: Oxford University Press.

Gravetter, F. J., & Wallnau, L. B. (2012). *Statistics for the behavioral sciences* (9th edn.). Belmont, CA: Wadsworth.

Grigorenko, E. L. (2000). Doing data analyses and writing up their results: Selected tricks and artifices. In R. J. Sternberg (ed.), *Guide to publishing in psychology journals* (pp. 98–120). New York: Cambridge University Press.

Hair, J. F., Black, W. C., Babin, B. J., & Anderson, R. E. (2009). *Multivariate data analysis* (7th edn.). Upper Saddle River, NJ: Prentice Hall.

Harris, J. S., & Blake, R. H. (1976). *Technical writing for social scientists*. Chicago: Nelson-Hall.

Kahneman, D., & Tversky, A. (1971). Subjective probability: A judgment of representativeness. *Cognitive Psychology, 3,* 430–454.

Kahneman, D., & Tversky, A. (1979). Intuitive prediction: Biases and corrective procedures. *Management Science, 12,* 313–327.

Kendall, P. C., Silk, J. S., & Chu, B. C. (2000). Introducing your research report: Writing the introduction. In R. J. Sternberg (ed.), *Guide to publishing in psychology journals* (pp. 41–57). New York: Cambridge University Press.

Krantz, J. H., & Dalal, R. (2000). Validity of web-based psychological research. In M. H. Birnbaum (ed.), *Psychological experiments on the Internet* (pp. 35–60). San Diego, CA: Academic Press.

McGuire, W. J. (1997). Creative hypothesis generating in psychology. *Annual Review of Psychology, 48,* 1–30.

Merriam-Webster's collegiate dictionary (2005) (11th edn.). Springfield, MA: Merriam-Webster.

Milgram, S. (1974). *Obedience to authority: An experimental view.* New York: Harper & Row.

Piaget, J. (1952). *The origins of intelligence in children* (M. Cook, trans.). New York: International Universities Press.

Pinker, S. (2014). *The sense of style: The thinking person's guide to writing in the 21st century.* New York: Viking.

Radford, M. L., & Barnes, S. B. (2005). *Web research: Selecting, evaluating, and citing* (2nd edn.). Upper Saddle River, NJ: Pearson.

Reips, U.-D. (2000). The Web experiment method: Advantages, disadvantages, and solutions. In M. H. Birnbaum (ed.), *Psychological experiments on the Internet* (pp. 89–120). San Diego, CA: Academic Press.

Reis, H. T. (2000). Writing effectively about design. In R. J. Sternberg (ed.), *Guide to publishing in psychology journals* (pp. 81–97). New York: Cambridge University Press.

Salovey, P. (2000). Results that get results: Telling a good story. In R. J. Sternberg (ed.), *Guide to publishing in psychology journals* (pp. 121–132). New York: Cambridge University Press.

Smith, R. A. (2000). Documenting your scholarship: Citations and references. In R. J. Sternberg (ed.), *Guide to publishing in psychology journals* (pp. 146–160). New York: Cambridge University Press.

Sternberg, R. J. (1997). *Thinking styles*. New York: Cambridge University Press.

Sternberg, R. J. (1998). *Love is a story*. New York: Oxford University Press.

Sternberg, R. J. (ed.). (2000). *Guide to publishing in psychology journals*. New York: Cambridge University Press.

Sternberg, R. J. (2002). Smart people are not stupid, but they sure can be foolish: The imbalance theory of foolishness. In R. J. Sternberg (ed.), *Why smart people can be so stupid* (pp. 232–242). New Haven, CT: Yale University Press.

Sternberg, R. J. (2003). *Wisdom, intelligence, and creativity, synthesized*. New York: Cambridge University Press.

Sternberg, R. J. (2004). Why smart people can be so foolish. *European Psychologist, 9*(3), 145–150.

Sternberg, R. J. (2005a). Foolishness. In R. J. Sternberg & J. Jordan (eds.), *Handbook of wisdom: Psychological perspectives* (pp. 331–352). New York: Cambridge University Press.

Sternberg, R. J. (2005b). The theory of successful intelligence. *Interamerican Journal of Psychology, 39*(2), 189–202.

Sternberg, R. J. (2006a). The nature of creativity. *Creativity Research Journal, 18*(1), 87–98.

Sternberg, R. J. (ed.). (2006b). *Reviewing scientific works in psychology*. Washington, DC: American Psychological Association.

Sternberg, R. J. (2007). A systems model of leadership: WICS. *American Psychologist, 62*(1), 34–42.

Sternberg, R. J. (2008). The WICS approach to leadership: Stories of leadership and the structures and processes that support them. *Leadership Quarterly, 19*(3), 360–371.

Sternberg, R. J. (2010). *College admissions for the 21st century*. Cambridge, MA: Harvard University Press.

Sternberg, R. J., & Bower, G. H. (1974). Transfer in part–whole and whole–part free recall: A comparative evaluation of theories. *Journal of Verbal Learning and Verbal Behavior, 13*, 1–26.

Sternberg, R. J., & Dobson, D. M. (1987). Resolving interpersonal conflicts: An analysis of stylistic consistency. *Journal of Personality and Social Psychology, 52*, 794–812.

Sternberg, R. J., & Lubart, T. I. (1992). Buy low and sell high: An investment approach to creativity. *Current Directions in Psychological Science, 1*(1), 1–5.

Sternberg, R. J., & Soriano, L. J. (1984). Styles of conflict resolution. *Journal of Personality and Social Psychology, 47,* 115–126.

Sternberg, R. J., & Sternberg, K. (2008). *The nature of hate.* New York: Cambridge University Press.

Sternberg, R. J., & Tulving, E. (1977). The measurement of subjective organization in free recall. *Psychological Bulletin, 84*(3), 539–556.

Tabachnik, G. B., & Fidell, L. S. (2012). *Using multivariate statistics* (6th edn.). Upper Saddle River, NJ: Pearson.

Tesser, A. (2000). Theories and hypotheses. In R. J. Sternberg (ed.), *Guide to publishing in psychology journals* (pp. 58–80). New York: Cambridge University Press.

Tufte, E. R. (2001). *The visual display of quantitative information.* Cheshire, CT: Graphics Press.

Tukey, J. W. (1977). *Exploratory data analysis.* Reading, MA: Addison-Wesley.

Tulving, E. (1966). Subjective organization and effects of repetition in multitrial free recall learning. *Journal of Verbal Learning and Verbal Behavior, 5,* 193–197.

Wagner, R. K. (2000). Rewriting the psychology paper. In R. J. Sternberg (ed.), *Guide to publishing in psychology journals* (pp. 187–198). New York: Cambridge University Press.

Warren, M. G. (2000). Reading reviews, suffering rejection, and advocating for your paper. In R. J. Sternberg (ed.), *Guide to publishing in psychology journals* (pp. 169–186). New York: Cambridge University Press.

Webster's third new international dictionary, unabridged (2002). Springfield, MA: Merriam-Webster.

Index